JN411499

Sam-ae [三愛] Spirit Amid Planetary 'Spirits'

Essays Celebrating the Philosophy and Life of Reverend Pai Min-Soo

Edited By

Samuel Y. Pang

&

Chammah J. Kaunda

SAM-AE [三愛] SPIRIT AMID
PLANETARY 'SPIRITS'

ESSAYS CELEBRATING THE PHILOSOPHY AND LIFE OF REVEREND PAI MIN-SOO

Published and Printed in the Republic of Korea by **Yonsei University Press**.
50 Yonsei-ro, Seodemun-gu, Seoul, 03722, Republic of Korea
Tel: (+82-2) 2123-3380~2 **Fax:** (+82-2) 2123-8673 **E-mail:** ysup@yonsei.ac.kr
http://press.yonsei.ac.kr

ISBN 978-89-6850-763-2 (03230)

₩ 14,000

CONTENTS

17th Pai Min-Soo Memorial Lecture Opening Address

Suh Seoung-Hwan
President of Yonsei University

Greetings, I welcome everyone to the 17th Pai Min-Soo Memorial Lecture held to honor Rev. Pai's lifelong sacrifice and devotion to *Sam-ae* Spirit (三愛). This is the first time in three years we are holding this conference since the fall of 2019. I would like to thank Professor Wang-bae Kim for preparing today's special lecture, as well as all the other attendees who will be presenting at the conference. Above all, I would like to express my sincere gratitude to Professor Young-cheol Pai's family for travelling all the way from the United States to take part in this commemorative lecture. I am also grateful to the faculty and staff of United Graduate School of Theology for making preparations to celebrate Rev. Min-Soo Pai's life of dedication through this commemorative lecture and opening ceremony for the memorial hall.

The *Sam-ae* Memorial Lectures were begun in 1993 to safeguard and proliferate the philosophy and teachings of Rev. Pai. We have endeavored to diagnose the reality of rural areas in Korea, and through various academic research and discussions on rural movements and rural education, we seek to expand and advance the fertile ideas of Rev. Min-Soo Pai and his wife Sun-ok Choi. This year's lecture theme is, "The Legacy of Rev. Pai Min-Soo: A Global Perspective" – it is an opportunity to disseminate Pastor Min-Soo Pai's concept of *Sam-ae* Spirit to the wider world through academic discourse geared towards finding workable directions.

Rev. Min-Soo Pai put his country and citizens above himself – a calling he prioritized his entire life and led by example. Despite being imprisoned twice by the Japanese for being a resistance leader and participating in the March 1st Movement, he never lost his desire for independence or love for his nation. After Korea's independence, Rev. Pai came to realize that the peasants were "the poorest and most unfortunate" members of society and he actively campaigned for rural reconstruction. Rev. Min-Soo Pai was the architect of a rural movement centered on the theological idea that Christians should join together to build the kingdom of God on this land.

If the rural movement was the mission that Rev. Min-Soo Pai devoted his entire life to, one would be remiss not to recognize Mrs. Soon-ok Choi as the faithful partner who helped him bear this cross. Rev. Pai and his wife's life philosophy was based on – listening to the pleas of while living together with – those suffering and in need. In 1976, *Sam-ae* Agricultural Technology Academy was donated to Yonsei University, and we feel honored to be entrusted with the mission to pass down the principles of *Sam-ae S*pirit to future generations. Yonsei University took steps to organize the *Sam-ae* Memorial Project Committee and succeeded in opening a course on Rev. Pai's *Sam-ae* Spirit at United Graduate School of Theology. Additionally, the Global Institute of Theology (GIT) has been established at Yonsei in 2015 in a manner that reifies *Sam-ae* Spirit. Just as advanced nations and international churches helped Korea plow its fields in the past, Yonsei University has been working with churches and leaders in Asia, Africa, and South America to spread the principles of *Sam-ae* Spirit outwards into the international community.

The life and ministry of Rev. Min-Soo Pai and his wife Soon-ok Choi touch our hearts and move us to extend our hands and follow their example. With their lifelong sacrifice and commitment to serving the common good, their great legacy has tilled and laid the groundwork to help Korea reach its promise. Yonsei University will endeavor to ensure their work will continue to pulse beyond our borders and blossom throughout the world beyond.

Once again, I pray that the peace of the Lord will bless each of you who have joined us for today's commemorative lecture – it is my hope that the faith shown by the late Rev. Min-Soo Pai and his wife Soon-ok Choi will be multiplied through our endeavors and broaden the fields of Christian praxis. Thank you.

26 September 2022

Prayer for the Opening Ceremony of Rev. Pai Min-Soo & Choi Sun-Ok Memorial Room

Chammah J. Kaunda

What a privilege,
What an honor indeed,
To gather in the name of the Lord,
On the great day of inauguration of
Rev. Pai Min-Soo & Choi Sun-Ok Memorial Room.
We are gathered indeed for the sake of the vision and dream of great couple.
Whose lives continue to speak beyond the grave
As Jesus said, whoever believes, lives always, even in death.
We're here, therefore, to immortalize the legacy,
An intellectual legacy,
A legacy of unconditional love,
A legacy of love's victory over evil
A humane, compassionate and generous legacy
Of a couple that lived not for themselves but for the world
The couple that spent and was spent in search for a new story in the world,
The couple that left the world a better place than they found it,
The couple that translated what seemed to be merely spiritualized words
into a praxis of life.
Despite being in the beyond, the couple's actions of love continue to resist
forces of death on our behalf.
We're here, indeed, to reflect on Rev. Pai Min-Soo & Choi Sun-Ok
so that we too can learn to be human,
can learn to love the world,
to passionately love others as ourselves.
This is the truest, authentic and highest expression of our love for God.
That love for God is the power that efficaciously transforms words into action
May we, with open hearts, learn the power of this love that creates a new human
out of the ashes of those who struggle, a new earth out of the damaged earth.
So, help us, oh Lord!
In your Name, even your Son, Jesus Christ,
Amen

Yonsei University, Songdo International Campus,
Global Institute of Theology
29th September 2022

DEDICATION

This book is dedicated to the memory of
Rev. Pai Min-Soo and Mrs. Choi Sun-Ok

FOREWORD

John Pai

Ever since early childhood, I understood that my father – an educator, leader and activist who would become a Presbyterian pastor – was in a far away land serving in his own father's honor. My grandfather Changun Pai, was a martyred hero who was executed by the Japanese in his fight for Korea's independence as a commander of the resistance in Northern Chungju. He bravely gave his life for his country. Although my understanding of geo-politics was very limited, I felt a deep sense of duty left to me by the legacy of my father and grandfather.

In 1909, when my father Minsoo Pai was 12 years old, my grandfather was captured by the Japanese and was sentenced to be executed at Seo Dae Mun prison for his activities in the Korean Independence Movement. Allowing one family member to speak to my grandfather before his death, my grandmother chose my father, her son. In those final moments, my grandfather told my father of his impending execution and that he had three promises he wanted his son to keep. One was to take care of himself; the second to love and care for his family; and lastly to "Take care of your land. It is our duty to care for her and save her . . ." Days later my father would bury my grandfather in the mountainside. This final oath to his father would define him for the rest of his life and form the founding principles of *Sam-ae*.

All during the Japanese occupation, my father was constantly in and out of Japanese prisons for his activities in the Independence Movement. Overcoming impossible odds he would travel to America to spread the plight of his people and to "learn about the spirit of freedom and democracy." As the War ended, he returned to Korea with the U.S. Forces to help set up the provisional government. The Korean War followed soon after and my father and mother made a brief trip back to the US to establish his Good Samaritan Project to send much needed food and clothing from the US to Korea for the War refugees. They then returned to Korea to continue to serve the Korean people. We still meet grateful individuals who thank my father for helping them to survive those harsh winters during the War.

When I search my mind for images of my father, what I find are vivid memories told to me by others of the dramatic impact he had on their lives. In one case, he was remembered decades later by a distinguished looking gentleman who pulled me aside and said, "Do you know that your father saved my life? If he hadn't sent me that winter coat, I surely would have frozen to death."

It was during this period, when everything was broken, that my father saw the need to rebuild the country from the ground up, literally brick by brick. I remember how excited he was when someone introduced a way to make more durable bricks out of mud. Initially, he focused on the small farming villages which made up over 90% of Korea at the time. He set up schools, libraries and classes teaching modern methods of farming, nutrition, energy conservation (converting manure into methane for cooking and heating). He set up clinics to help amputees learn to adapt to prosthetics. Teaching and self-help were important components of their larger rural development program, which was centered around the critically important *Sam-ae* Spirit and Academic Program for continuing growth.

As a young, eager artist, I had no idea just how I might fulfill my father's legacy, but I entertained all sorts of ideas where my skills and commitment could be put to use. I was especially inspired by the story of Albert Schweitzer who was awarded the Nobel Peace Prize for his philosophy of "reverence for life" and tireless humanitarian work. Schweitzer thought of devoting the first 25 years of life to his art and the rest of his life to God and humanity. This for me was a model for how a young artist could live.

In the summer of 1964, my father asked me to come to Korea to design a new wing for his school in Daejeon. I hadn't returned to Korea in 17 years, and I felt a deep sense of allegiance and sympathy for the amputees and beggars. As one of them worked his way towards me, I felt strangely relieved that I had something to give to him. I opened my wallet, took some bills and gave them to the amputee. With blinding speed the money was snatched out of his hands and into another pocket.

It was my Father!

He didn't have to explain. He was letting me know that if whatever I gave him doesn't help this man to help himself, it's a form of empty charity. After a hearty lunch, we visited the classrooms at a leisurely pace, stopping at times to ask questions or observe demonstrations. It looked like a small farm run by students. In fact, that's exactly what it was. Students were learning to harvest crops they planted and take them to market, thereby earning enough to cover tuition. It seemed that research and invention were highly encouraged, and the enthusiasm of the students was palpable.

Within all the hustle and bustle of rows of students planting rice, I felt the beckoning of the cool, moist, flesh-like clay under my feet to join in the ritual that reaches into the beginning of time. It was a scene from my childhood, yet something that I had never done before. Before I realized it, I was knee deep in the rice fields, catching on to the rhythm with everyone else. I felt like I was contributing.

A young soldier, who had been observing all the goings-on approached me and asked, "What do you think you're doing?" I replied, "I am just trying to help." "We can do this better than you can," he said, "but you can do something we can't do, and you can't do it here. You should go back to where you can do your work best."

I am still far from answering the question: "How can I best serve God and humanity?" But my journey became a little clearer when that young soldier gave me permission to be me.

My father believed that the most critical need to successfully rebuild his country lay in helping individuals find their way spiritually, socially, intellectually and economically within the aftermath

of war and the chaotic changes that challenged everyone. For this reason, he established the "*Sam-ae* Spirit and Agricultural Program." His method was to educate at the grassroots level to provide individuals with the tools they needed to survive and progress in their journey to emerge as productive citizens. Many of the courses the program offered were helpful to those who needed to improve or to go to the next level. By using flexible scheduling, he was able to introduce a wide variety of subjects that were innovative and visionary. His primary goal was always to help individuals learn to help themselves. Providing accessible, affordable education was the chief means by which he hoped to achieve this goal. And this self-sustaining model of education is foundational to the school's duty of care.

As I reflect on the enormity of the dedication of my father, mother and grandfather towards the rebuilding of Korea and the sacrifices they made for the love of their country and its people, I am overcome with emotion and gratitude. I imagine my father as a young man as he boarded a ship to America to spread the word of the oppression and injustices Koreans faced. The tremendous courage and commitment of my parents to the rebuilding of the country they loved. Dedicating their lives to protect and uphold the very principles of freedom and democracy.

My father could not have imagined that his profound commitment to the *Sam-ae* Spirit would have inspired so many students, theologians and activists from the farthest reaches of Africa, Asia and his homeland of Korea. Yet by living his life in true service to others, the impact of his teachings have reached far and wide, across geography and generations. Today, I deeply believe in the need to redouble our efforts to spread the *Sam-ae* Spirit to imbue our citizenry with the fundamental strength and fortitude that comes from not just economic but also spiritual empowerment for the benefit of all humanity. I hope for my own children and grandchildren that this spark of *Sam-ae* Spirit becomes a beacon of light that will guide generations to come.

NOTES ON CONTRIBUTORS

Cyril Emeka Ejike is of the Department of Philosophy, Faculty of Arts, Nnamdi Azikiwe University, Awka. His research interests straddle metaphysics, development studies, social and political philosophy, ethics, African philosophy, and intersection of philosophy, religion, socio- economic and cultural phenomena.

Felix Kang Esoh is a lecturer at the Presbyterian Theological Seminary Kumba, affiliated to the Protestant University of Central Africa, Cameroon. He holds a Doctor of Theology Degree from the Global Institute of Theology at the United Graduate School of Theology in Yonsei University, South Korea. Over the years, he has developed interest in a number of academic and theological fields, including: History, Indigenous Studies, Inter-Cultural and Mission Studies.

Chammah J. Kaunda is a Zambian scholar currently working at the United Graduate School of Theology, Yonsei University, Korean Republic. He has authored over 100 and still counting peer-reviewed journal articles and book chapters in internationally renowned journals and book publishers. In the last nine years, he has authored over 100 and still counting peer-reviewed journal articles and book chapters in internationally renowned journals and book publishers. He also co/edited eight volumes, authored two books and co-authored one book. He has been a guest editor for various academic journals.

Wang-Bae Kim is a professor of Sociology at the College of Social Science, Yonsei University. His fields of specialty and interests are: Work and Industry, Stratification, Urban Sociology, and the Sociology of Emotion.

Izak Y. M. Lattu is an associate professor of Interreligious Studies and Sociology of Religion at the Faculty of Theology, Satya Wacana Christian University, Salatiga, Indonesia. He earned a Ph.D. in the Interdisciplinary Study of Religion from the Graduate Theological Union, Berkeley, California, under the Fulbright Scholarship and a Dissertation Writing Grant from Harvard University. Izak is also a regular visiting professor at the Center for Religious and Cross-cultural Studies, Universitas Gadjah Mada. He published books, book chapters, and journal articles in Brill, Routledge, Bloomsbury, Kompas Press, Satya Wacana University Press, Gadjah Mada University Press, and Baylor University Press.

Atola Longumer is a Baptist from Nagaland, India and teaches at the United Theological College, Bangalore. Her recent writings include, *Christianity and COVID-19: Pathways for Faith*, co-edited with Chammah J. Kaunda, Atola Longkumer, Kenneth R. Ross, Esther Mombo (Routledge, 2021); and "Christian Mission and Religious Studies: The Case of Indigenous Religions," in *The Oxford Handbook of Mission Studies*, edited by Kirsteen Kim and Alison Fitchett Climenhaga (Oxford, 2022).

Irene Ludji is an assistant professor of Religious Ethics at the Faculty of Theology, Satya Wacana Christian University, Salatiga, Indonesia. She earned a Ph.D. in Philosophy of Religion and Theology from the Claremont Graduate University, Claremont, California, under a scholarship from the Indonesia Endowment Funds for Education provided by the Ministry of Education. She published articles and book chapters with The Ecumenical Review, BPK Gunung Mulia Publishing House and offset, and Satya Wacana University Press.

Frans Best Soma Marpaung is an ordained minister in the Batak Christian Protestant Church (HKBP). He is currently working as a lecturer at the HKBP Theological Seminary, in Pematang Siantar, North Sumatra, Indonesia. He is also the chief of the education department and a counselor at Rihand Kreatif Indonesia.

Oxana Mechsherskaya is an independent researcher with a focus on the relationship between church and state in the Russian Federation. She obtained a Ph.D. degree in church history from Yonsei University. Oxana was actively involved in full-time ministry at a local Presbyterian church in Kazakhstan. She also gained experience working at the Moscow Bible College, where she interpreted international conferences and seminars, as well as translated lectures and books.

Buhle Mpofu is a senior lecturer with the Department of Practical Theology and Mission studies with the Faculty of Theology and Region at the University of Pretoria, South Africa. Mpofu has an interest in the interface of mission studies with socio-economic trajectories such as poverty, homelessness and migration. He is also an ordained and active minister with the Uniting Presbyterian Church in Southern Africa (UPCSA).

Nelly Mwale is a senior lecturer in the department of Religious Studies at the University of Zambia. Her research interests are religion in the public sphere, religion and education, religion and development, religion and environment, church history and African Indigenous Religions.

Samuel Y. Pang is a professor of Intercultural Theologies and World Christianities at Yonsei University, where he is currently the dean of the College of Theology & the United Graduate School of Theology.

Nitoli Sheqi is a lecturer at Living Bible College, Dimapur, Nagaland, India. She received her Ph.D. from Global Institute of Theology, Yonsei University, South Korea. Her research interests lie in Biblical Studies, feminist theory, and postcolonial studies.

Shakespeare Sigamoney is an ordained minister of the Church of South India. He received his Ph.D. from Yonsei University. He is now teaching as a lecturer at Yonsei University, South Korea. He is also the coordinator of the SEST Masters program at Hanshin Graduate School of Theology, South Korea.

INTRODUCTION

SAM-AE SPIRIT AMID PLANETARY 'SPIRITS'

CHAMMAH J. KAUNDA & SAMUEL Y. PANG

Contemporary modes in the study of religions have taken epistemological preference for the voices of the marginalized peoples (the *minjung*, the Dalit, the black-ish, the indigenous, the aborigines, women, various minorities, and nature/creation). This project seeks to engage the Korean concept of *Sam-ae* Spirit in dialogue with various planetary epistemologies in the search to innovatively, creatively, and imaginatively rearticulate alternative epistemologies of love in the search for the planetary flourishing in the postcolonial era. The idea of the "spirit" is utilized in a metaphorical sense to refer to the intrinsic energy of all thought systems and the effective inner driving force by which those philosophies are validated, critiqued, deconstructed, or rejected altogether. The effectiveness of the spirit of the concepts helps them to plasticize into multiple transformations and circulations without losing their primal essence. In this way, a concept can interact and shape and be shaped by foreign concepts without colonizing or being colonized. This planetary approach to the *Sam-ae* Spirit anchors all epistemologies between plurality and cosmic interconnectivity in mutual recognition and respect that posits that no one way of life or thinking is more valid than another. This approach is about seeking ways in which differences in cultural ways of life could be mutually mobilized to the fight against a common enemy, ideological dominion, and search for the possible recovery of the damaged home – earth. It is about critical dialogue, constructing, deconstructing, and reconstructing mutually shaped languages of various forms of resistance and transgressive movement from the margins to multiplicities of centers of mutual recognition in the search for post-indigenous ways of "thinking freedom"[1] or thinking anew a politics of planetary emancipation. It is about searching for ways of liberating the language of struggle from colonial mimicries and holding each other's hands and standing in "struggle side by side a gesture of defiance that heals, that

[1] Michael Neocosmos. *Thinking Freedom in Africa: Toward a Theory of Emancipatory Politics* (Johannesburg: Wits University Press, 2016).

makes new life and new growth possible."[2] It is that act of post-indigenous dialogic imagination among global south scholars that "is no mere gesture of empty dialogue, that is the expression of our movement from object to subject – the liberated voice."[3] This is a kind of post-comparative dialogical mutuality that subverts simple comparisons. This is the theoretical practice of creating imaginary neutral spaces of trans-plural interactions of ideas from various cultural contexts to give rise to other ways of thinking and becoming. In this way, planetary is a site of consenting pluralism and its efforts for all cultural conceptions of reality to speak for themselves.[4]

The concept of the *Sam-ae* Spirit is significant in this sense because of its roots in the Korean Struggle against Japanese occupation. The concept was coined by Rev. Pai Min-Soo, a Korean Presbyterian minister, as a 'mobilizing discourse'[5] for rural emancipation and transformation during the Japanese colonization of Korea.[6] It is a language that points not only to nonviolent forms of resistance, but also pragmatic political struggle against colonization which was embedded in reconstructing the Korean mind for social reconstruction and economic development. The mind reconstruction as decolonization for economic development was articulated in the concept of *Sam-ae* Spirit which refers to threefold love- the love for God, the love for humanity, and the love for work. It can be described as 'love's multiplicity.'[7]

This threefold conceptual framework of love engages love, neighbor love, and love as meaningful social action in an uneven world. Love is a human condition. Where there is no love, there is no human. Everything human beings do is summarized in a word – love. As Martin Luther King in a speech in 1967 put it, "Power without love is reckless and abusive, and

[2] Bell Hooks, *Talking Back: Thinking Feminist, Thinking Black* (London: South End Press, 1989), 9.

[3] Hooks, *Talking Back,* 9.

[4] Hans-Georg Moeller and Andrew K. Whitehead, eds., *Imagination: Cross-Cultural Philosophical Analyses* (London: Bloomsbury, 2018), 3.

[5] Gayatri Spivak, *A Critique of Postcolonial Reason* (Cambridge, MA: Harvard University Press, 1999).

[6] Chammah J. Kaunda and Sang-man Kim, "'*Samae* Spirit' Assist toward 'Ubuntu Spirit' Model for Rural Adult Christian Education in Zambia," *Religious Education* 117, no. 1 (2022): 33-49.

[7] One such multiplicity is the Korean concept of *Jeong*, see Wonhee Anne Joh, *Heart of The Cross: A Postcolonial Christology* (Louisville, KY: Westminster John Knox, 2006); and Wonhee Anne Joh, "Loves' Multiplicity: Jeong and Spivak's Notes Toward Planetary Love," *Planetary Loves: Gayatri Spivak, Postcoloniality, and Theology,* eds. Stephen Moore and Mayra Rivera (New York: Fordham University Press, 2010), 169-190.

love without power is sentimental and anaemic."[8] *Sam-ae* Spirit is not a love for idealized existence. It is concrete love that translates into concrete social action. As Slavoj Žižek argues, "It is easy to love the idealized figure of a poor, helpless neighbor, the starving African or Indian, for example; in other words, it is easy to love one's neighbor as long as he stays far enough from us, as long as there is a proper distance separating us. The problem arises at the moment when he comes too near us, when we start to feel his suffocating proximity – at this moment when the neighbor exposes himself to us too much, love can suddenly turn into hatred."[9] *Sam-ae* Spirit, like ubuntu spirit, is both a conceptual framework and social praxis for decolonizing minds and setting nations on a radical path of social transformation. *Sam-ae* Spirit is both theory and a method of love. *Sam-ae* Spirit "promoted the creation of new spaces of stability in the countryside."[10] *Sam-ae* Spirit is an otherworldly, political, neighbor, ecological love that underpins singular of love's multiplicity as planetary praxis of all forms of emancipation, decolonization, and transformation. Love is the condition of flourishing becoming.

Given the interdisciplinary, dynamic, and malleable nature of the concept of the *Sam-ae* Spirit, this volume takes multiple approaches such as philosophical, theological, religious, sociological, anthropological, political, gender, sexuality, ethics, etc. All contributions to this volume methodologically and theoretically deployed the idea of 'love' – the spirit of *Sam-ae* – as the overarching conceptual framework within their specific contexts. They engaged and theorized love within a particular context of lived realities, cultures, social locations, and religious, political, and economic challenges. *How can* Sam-ae *Spirit in dialogue with other planetary epistemologies from the margins critique dominant (secular or religious) loves and contribute to the imaginative articulation of alternative loves that can contribute to the search for planetary flourishing and the construction of love-entrenched futures?* In what ways can a dialogue between the praxis of *Sam-ae* Spirit and planetary epistemologies assist in

---

[8] Martin Luther King, Jr., "Where Do We Go from Here?" (16 August 1967), https://kinginstitute.stanford.edu/where-do-we-go-here.

[9] Slavoj Žižek, *Enjoy Your Symptom! Jacques Lacan in Hollywood and Out* (New York: Routledge, 2013), 8.

[10] Albert L. Park, *Visions of the Nation: Religion and Ideology in 1920s and 1930s Rural Korea* (Ph.D. Dissertation, Univ. of Chicago, 2007), 13.

both interrogating contextual issues, and critically and constructively reclaiming 'planetary loves' in the postcolonial era.[11]

All contributors to this volume initially presented their manuscripts at the Seventeenth International Conference on the *Legacy of Rev. Pai Min-Soo: A Global Perspective*. The aim was to roughly engage the idea of the *Sam-ae* Spirit in contemporary dialogue with other contextual concepts. In addition, to make sense of how employing familiar cultural terms is imperative for advancing "public, political, ecological and prophetic love" for thinking freedom that could lead to mind reconstruction and promote social reconstructive decolonization for socio-political, ecological religio-cultural, and economic transformation in contemporary in the global south contexts.

This volume consists of eleven chapters, ordered to show the connecting threads. Different contextualized approaches are used to engage the *Sam-ae* Spirit in relation to the particular context. The first chapter, written by **Wang-Bae Kim** takes an introspection into the question and validity of the *Sam-ae* Spirit in the post-human era. He argues that in this age of complex and insurmountable challenges, humanity cannot help but look back on the life trajectories of the pioneers who struggled with similar hardship, adversity, helplessness, and despair through their capacities to take on challenges and maintain hopefulness. He argues, Rev. Pai Min-Soo's philosophy of the *Sam-ae* Spirit, advocated and practiced, can serve as a theoretical framework for addressing the problems facing society and for reflecting on the future of humanity. In this way, Kim lies the philosophical foundation for **Cyril Emeka Ejike**'s chapter on Rev. Pai Min-Soo's *Sam-ae* Spirit as a panacea for religious intolerance in Nigeria. Ejike demonstrates how the *Sam-ae* Spirit focuses on rebuilding people's love for God which presupposes tolerance of the religions of others. He concludes that love for God that is founded upon the *Sam-ae* Spirit has the potential to foster religious tolerance and make Divine-love a force immanent in Nigeria which is indispensable for building God's kingdom in the country. The third chapter by **Atola Longumer** focuses on how *Sam-ae* Spirit can strengthen the indigenous attitude towards wealth and self-preservation. She argues that the *Sam-ae* Spirit in conversation with the practice of Mithun sacrifice underscores the imperative principle of mutuality in justice movements. Recognition of the sacred is often intertwined with respect and care for the neighbors and a flourish of the creation includes mutual accountability.

---

[11] Stephen Moore and Mayra Rivera, eds., *Planetary Loves: Gayatri Spivak, Postcoloniality, and Theology* (New York: Fordham University Press, 2010).

Chapter four focuses on farming initiatives in Cameroon. **Felix Kang Esoh**'s chapter is a search for the solidarity of economic and social empowerment through farming initiatives among women groups in Cameroon. He draws from *Sam-ae* Spirit and ubuntu to demonstrate the emancipation and transformation taking place through the various Christian women groups. Chapter five is a critique of particularism in Igbo communities in Nigeria. **Cyril Emeka Ejike** and **Chammah J. Kaunda** propose African Ubuntu and *Sam-ae* Spirit as frameworks and social praxis for dealing with particularistic strains of traditional Igbo religious and communal philosophies, ethics, and practices. They demonstrate how such humanistic frameworks could help address particularism in traditional Igbo communities. Ejike and Kaunda conclude that framing indigenous Igbo structures, religious ideologies, and practices around philosophies of Ubuntu and *Sam-ae* Spirit is a path to the attainment of universal humanhood bound by agapeic love in Igbo society.

Chapter six constructs local theology in Indonesia. **Izak Y. M. Lattu** and **Irene Ludji** explore the possibilities of engaging the *Sam-ae* concept with folklore to develop a theology from the margin. They employ ethnography research to argue that the *Sam-ae* Spirit has the potential to create space for engaging voices from the margin and rural living texts to construct a life-giving theological discourse in Indonesia. **Nelly Mwale**'s seventh chapter demonstrates a dialogue between *Sam-ae* Spirit and indigenous knowledge in Zambia can contribute to ecological well-being and a sustainable future from a gendered perspective. She argues that Annie's creation of the learning hub was a way of problematizing the dominant self-love and providing an alternative love centered on empowering communities through offering natural wellness education services and growing organic food. She concludes that indigenous knowledge systems do not only offer an alternative to addressing contextual realities but also provide an avenue for a gendered dialogue with the threefold loves.

Shakespeare Sigamoney and **Frans Best Soma Marpaung** in chapter eight analyze *Sam-ae* Spirit in the context of global migration. They argue that the concept of the *Sam-ae* Spirit embodies the principle of the Good Samaritan which makes it a global resource for constructing a missional praxis of life in the context of global migration. Chapter nine by **Oxana Mechsherskaya** takes the *Sam-ae* Spirit into the postmodern political love in Russian Orthodox society. *Sam-ae* Spirit and the Russian Orthodox notion of love are engaged from a hermeneutical axis (object-referent) to make sense epistemology of love as popularized in historical documents, mass media, literature, and social surveys, in order to uncover the critical elements suitable for the formulation of a postmodern epistemological version of love that is characterized by peace, harmony, and freedom for Russian political context. It will demonstrate that the Orthodox understanding of love for Self through the phenomenon of acceptance (of the hatred for Self-love), can benefit from the *Sam-ae* Spirit's pluralistic love in the reformation of its political theological love.

In chapter ten, **Nitoli Sheqi** takes the postcolonial feminist reading of Mari's colonial story. She employs the *Sam-ae* Spirit as a hermeneutical point of departure to reconceptualize postcolonial feminist love in the context of war/eros love. She emphasizes that the polyvalent concept of the *Sam-ae S*pirit reflected in Mari's story can serve as the locus of freedom, dignity, and liberation. The final chapter by **Buhle Mpofu** also draws on the concept of '*Sam-ae* Spirit' to reflect on the challenges of youth unemployment in South Africa. He maintains that the concept of the *Sam-ae* Spirit reinvents vulnerability and highlights how human relations need to be reconstructed to show that God is empathetic and stands on the side of the weak and vulnerable in the face of unemployment and contends that vulnerability experienced by economically marginalized youth deconstructs the concept of supremacy, superiority, and individualism and opens up new alternatives for human relations in the context of competition and limited resources.

The editors would like to thank all of those who have helped make this volume a reality. In particular, we would like to thank professor Seoung Hwan Suh, the President of Yonsei University for his ongoing struggle to transform Yonsei University into a global academic space and for the financial support for both the conference and the book project. Finally, Chammah J. Kaunda gratefully acknowledges the National Research Foundation of Korea (NRF) for providing financial support for research on Rev. Pai Min-Soo [Grant # **2021S1A5A806276313**].

CHAPTER 1

SAM-AE SPIRIT IN THE POST-HUMAN ERA: AN INTROSPECTION

WANG-BAE KIM

INTROSPECTION IN THE POST-HUMAN ERA: WHERE ARE WE HEADED?

Through the strong belief that development can occur rationally, humans have achieved unprecedented scientific technology and industrialization. As a result, many realities that merely existed within the realm of imagination in the past are being realized today. Today, people around the world are closely connected by the Internet, which enables nearly unlimited flows of information, showing that space has been destroyed by time. In this separate digital space that we have created, people engage in numerous activities. Indeed, this space is not simply a network but a hyper-connected global society.[1]

Humanity, which claims to be the supreme ruler of all things, constantly reflects upon and challenges both itself and the existence of all things in the universe. Science and technology, as well as knowledge itself, are the products and driving forces of such efforts. From classical mechanics to the theory of relativity to quantum theory and complex systems theory along with the concept of uncertainty, humanity has continuously studied the physical laws of nature and refused to give up on its desire to explore space. In addition, the human genome project, which aimed to uncover the secrets of DNA, the human body's biochemical knowledge system, has been completed. Meanwhile, neuroscience, which attempts to understand consciousness, has been developing at a rapid pace. Humans are regulating and creating life through in vitro fertilization, stem cell therapies, gene synthesis technologies, and animal cloning. By combining knowledge of the brain and information technology, humans have also produced AI technology that thinks and judges for itself. Scientific achievements and technological developments do not

[1] The distinction between on-line and off-line space has been erased to lead to a 'hybridized' world between the two. For more about the Network or Ultra–Network Society, see Manuel Castells, *The Rise of the Network Society* (Oxford: Wiley-Blackwell, 2009); and Mary Chayko, *Superconnected: The Internet, Digital Media, and Techno-Social Life* (Thousand Oaks, CA: Sage, 2016).

simply allow people to live better lives. Rather, it would be no exaggeration to say that the palm-sized smartphone, which stores and distributes much more information than the supercomputers that surprised the world just a few decades ago, is already an inseparable component of our lives to the point that they have become a part of our bodies.

Humans are also witnessing the birth of cyborg-like androids equipped with AI as well as other "living with" technologies, such as AI. Indeed, the era in which people transcend and surpass their own human limitations, the so-called post-human era, has arrived. Some intellectual circles assert that humans "created" new forms of life and describe this process as a challenge to God. The emergence of a hyper-connected, post-human society due to scientific and technological development further bolsters the belief that we are living in an era of progress. However, the answers to questions that humanity has long asked – such as, "What does it mean to be human?"; "Are we happier now than before?"; and "Is history really progressing?" – remain unanswered. Human history is filled with war and death. Since the Industrial Revolution, humanity has extinguished the lives of tens of millions of people through World War I and World War II. Following the proclamation of the Declaration of Human Rights at the end of World War II, human rights have, on the one hand, steadily improved. However, human rights violations and massacres still take place around the world.

Regional wars, civil wars, and terrorism are still a part of today's reality – as can be seen through the examples of the Korean and Vietnam Wars after World War II, the Rwandan civil war, the war in Afghanistan, the 9/11 attacks, and the Russian invasion of Ukraine. Despite the cries for peace and reconciliation for all humanity, the Cold War is still not over. The United States and China, which are competing for global political and economic supremacy, have established a new front in this conflict. Meanwhile, the world is still engulfed in tension, confrontation, and anxiety due to the emergence of nationalist right-wing governments around the world.

The new Cold War international regime has led to the emergence of far-right groups that are leaving their marks around the world. Hate crimes committed by racists as well as violence against women, minorities, immigrants, refugees, and religious groups continue to occur all over the world. The threat of fundamentalists who are totally dedicated to their factional ideologies is also increasing worldwide.[2] These right-wing political and religious groups demonize others and mobilize direct and indirect violence, ignited by feelings of hatred and hostility. There is still a long way to go in the struggle for peace and reconciliation between races, ethnic groups, and other types of communities.[3] With the development of science, technology, and people's productive capacities, humanity has opened the door to mass production and mass consumption. However, inequality between classes, social groups, and countries is worsening. While wealth and poverty coexist, hundreds of millions of people on Earth are still suffering from poverty. Despite the enormous overall increase in wealth, the world is becoming increasingly polarized with a rich minority enjoying nearly unlimited wealth and the majority living in poverty.[4] Inequality between regions, countries, and classes continues to grow. Unpredictable natural and social disasters are the product of such inequalities. In the process of responding to the COVID-19 pandemic that has recently affected the world, the visible inequalities between countries, classes, and groups was shown more clearly than ever, such as vaccine inequality between rich and poor countries and the fact that those living in poverty died at higher rates than those who did not.

However, above all else, the most alarming phenomenon facing society today is global warming caused by climate change. Life as we know it is not possible without society and society is founded on nature. After all, we obtain life-sustaining food and resources from nature. When nature disappears, human society is bound to disappear as well. Today, the earth is in crisis as a result of global warming. This global crisis does not only affect humans but all living things. Some argue that the current era should be called the Anthropocene to reflect how humans have changed Earth's destiny due to their merciless destruction and oppression of nature.[5] There is even an apocalyptic narrative becoming popular which states that the planet will be thrown into catastrophe due to its indiscriminate destruction by humans,

---

[2] 'Trumpism' as a form of right–wing political activity – overtly declaring the discrimination of the social weakness such as refugees, immigrants, female, etc. – has spread throughout the world. Even in South Korea, right–wing political voices have adopted similar strategies.

[3] During the Covid19 pandemic era, it has been well-documented that hate crimes perpetrated by racists against Asians have increased.

[4] Korean society cannot be exceptional. Korean society has been given much of attention as an iconic model successfully achieving both industrialization and democratization among third-world nations after World War II. However, Korean society has been suffering from class polarization, ideological conflicts, and the fallout from the Cold War, etc.

[5] See Erle C. Ellis. *Anthropocene: A Very Short Introduction* (Oxford: Oxford University Press, 2018).

which is only one group of living things on Earth.

Humanity still largely believes in the neoliberal principle of infinite competition, which quantifies human life and talent and trades them at market prices. The field of education, in which people critically reflect on the meaning of life and pursue social justice, has become, to put it harshly, the handmaid of capital and state power, promoting neoliberal competition, including its emphasis on hierarchy and ranking. Reification by bureaucracy and commodification by the market are also worsening. The freedom, equality, solidarity, and social justice that humanity had once pursued have now become mere slogans, while anger, cynicism, hatred, nihilism, and depression have dominated people's lives today.

What should humanity do in moving forward? In this age of complex and difficult problems that cannot be easily solved, we cannot help but look back on the life trajectories of the pioneers who overcame similar hardship, adversity, helplessness, and despair through their capacities to take on challenges and maintain hopefulness. This paper highlights the life of Rev. Pai Min-Soo who shared the hope of the Christian gospel and led the revitalization movement in the rural regions of Korea, which was once the poorest country in the world under the oppression of imperialism. Rev. Pai's philosophy of 'three loves' (*Sam-ae*), which he advocated and practiced, can serve as the foundation for addressing the problems facing society and for reflecting on the future of humanity.

THE LIFE OF REV. PAI MIN-SOO

Rev. Pai Min-Soo (1896–1968) was born at the end of the Han Dynasty when imperialist powers were competing over East Asia and the country's fortune was looking increasingly bad. He was a pastor, social activist, and leader who played a pioneering role in spreading the Christian gospel and in the rural revitalization movement in Korea during its modernization, which followed liberation from Japanese colonial rule. Influenced by his father, who was arrested and killed after founding a movement against the Japanese annexation of Korea, Rev. Pai carried on the spirit and activities of national independence from an early age. He was arrested and imprisoned during such activities along with other patriotic youth. While attending the Soongsil school in Pyongyang (Union Christian College), he organized the Christian Rural Research Association with Cho Man-sik and others. He continued his activities with them until he studied abroad in the United States in 1931, later graduating from McCormick Seminary in Chicago. After returning to Korea, he reconstructed the Christian Rural Research Society with Cho and the other activists. While under the surveillance of the Japanese police for a series of events, such as his refusal to partake in Shinto shrine worship, he returned to the United States and toured the country, giving sermons and lectures.[6] After returning to Korea when it was under US military rule, he worked as an interpreter and worked to help build the Republic of Korea. After that, he moved to the United States with his family but returned to Korea in 1952 during the Korean War to promote the Christian gospel and rural revitalization projects. Rev. Pai established the *Sam-ae* Agricultural Technology Institute in Ilsan in 1967 and passed away in the following year.

Rev. Pai lived in an era characterized by imperial exploitation and oppression, but he did not submit to it. Rather, he tried to use the Christian spirit to build a new community of life in poor rural areas. His determination and efforts helped a great many rural people who were in despair and helpless due to their suffering under Japanese occupation. However, such hardships were not limited only to the Japanese colonial period. Even following liberation, the situation in rural Korea did not change much. At that time, 80% of the population were farmers living in rural areas, most of whom were poor peasants or self-employed farmers suffering from poverty. After the 1960s, as the population of rural areas rapidly decreased due to urbanization and industrialization, many rural areas are on the verge of disappearing.[7] Rev. Pai consistently shared the Christian gospel and love with the poor rural areas of Korea, many of which had nothing. Why did he choose these areas in particular? Pai explained as follows. At that time, rural Korea was one of the poorest and poverty-stricken places in the world. He believed that the mission of a pastor is to build the kingdom of God, so he should not go to serve the rich and those who had found peace, but rather the suffering, the poor, and the oppressed. The kingdom of God is built by overcoming the challenges and attempts of ministry in such places. In response to the question, "Why choose the Korean countryside as the place to build the Kingdom of God?" he said:

> Just as the gospel of God's kingdom was developed with a focus on rural, fishing, and mountain villages such as Galilee, Zebulun, Naphtali, and Samaria, Korean farmers are the poorest and unluckiest of all of the

---

[6] He built up a close relationship with Ahn, Chang-ho, one of the most esteemed leaders in Korea. He deeply mourned Ahn's death in 1938. See Minsoo Pai, *The Kingdom of God & Rural Korea*, ed. *Sam-ae* Memorial Association (Seoul: Yonsei University Press, 2017). The earliest Korean edition is Minsoo Pai, *Who Shall Enter the Kingdom of Heaven?*, 1st ed., trans. Nowon Park (Seoul: Yonsei University Press, 1952).

[7] For more about Pai's peasant movement (in Korean), see Kie-Chung Pang, *The Rural Movement and Christian Thought of Pai Min Soo* (Seoul: Yonsei University Press, 1999).

> farmers in the world. As such, the rural regions of Korea are the most suitable site for dealing with the issues of God's kingdom. . . . As a believer in God, the focus of this issue is that it is meaningful to save those who are faced with hardship through the practice of the love of Christ, which is why I have turned my attention to the Korean countryside.[8]

With this in mind, Rev. Pai traveled to the rural areas of Korea to personally fulfill the Christian mission of reaching out to the socially underprivileged and those who are faced with the greatest hardships, especially those who are suffering from oppression, exploitation, and helplessness. He aimed to save their lives through the love of Christ. Korea was one of the poorest countries at the time due Japanese colonial rule, war, and the division that followed the country's liberation from Japanese oppression. Within Korea, the rural areas suffered the pain of poverty and despair the most. As such, Rev. Pai visited those places to build them up with the spirit of the Christian kingdom. However, he was faced with the fact that the Korean countryside did not yet have the foundation for such a kingdom. Thus, his main mission was to lay that foundation. After all, a house without a solid foundation is like building a house on sand. The spirit of the kingdom is reflected in the quote, "Seek ye first his kingdom and its significance, and all these things will be given unto you" (Matt. 6:33). The concepts this quote encapsulates are love and sacrifice, humility and respect for others, as well as trust and honesty.

Love and sacrifice are shown through sacrificing oneself and saving others in order to love God and others. Humility and respect for others are shown through a democratic spirit that humbles oneself and respects the opinions of others. Trust and honesty are shown through a spirit of patience credibility and living honestly in word and deed. It was on the basis of these ideals that Rev. Pai preached his three loves philosophy. This text will reflect on this philosophy and consider its significance in modern times.

THE MODERN SIGNIFICANCE OF THE '3-LOVE' PHILOSOPHY

[1] *LOVE GOD*

Rev. Pai told believers to love their neighbors as they love God. Thus, their love should be directed not only toward God, but also toward people. According to Rev. Pai, to love God is to "exercise that principle and that very principle of God commands you to love your neighbor (other people)." He

---

[8] Pai, *The Kingdom of God & Rural Korea*, 118.

underlines, "Now let us love God, and let us love others as He taught us to. He who loves God must also love other people and he who does not love other people who can be seen cannot love God who cannot be seen. Therefore, to love God is to obey and put into practice the law that God has commanded. Loving others is at the center of God's principle and truth, which will open the path to your life."[9] To practice God's love means to deliver love, the universal spirit of Christianity, to our neighbors, especially those in need. Today, the Christian spirit of loving God is expressed in the values of respect, tolerance, service, and devotion to all humanity. It is embodied in the values of freedom, equality and solidarity. Also, to realize God's love is to create a world free from discrimination. However, in today's society, political oppression, economic inequality, and various forms of discrimination between races, religions, and other groups are occurring all around the world. As mentioned above, human society continues to face hatred and antagonism between races, regions, classes, and genders. Wars and massacres, large and small, never stop. Disregard and contempt for the socially disadvantaged, along with stigma and discrimination, continue. Hateful acts are committed toward particular races and religious groups in the form of hate crimes. Ignorance and contempt for others result in violence against the body, denial of ideas and beliefs, such as suppressing the freedom of thought or expression and the free exercise of religion, and reification of the self and others. Ultimately, such actions lead those things to lose their meaning.

Due to economic inequality and polarization, one side of the globe over-consumes while the other is trapped in poverty. Meanwhile, groups whose legitimate rights and dignity as human beings are not recognized are exposed to various types of violence. When Rev. Pai was conducting his work, the people of rural Korea were a typical example of the socially underprivileged. Today, the countryside where he wanted to build the kingdom of God symbolizes the poor and marginalized and the various minority groups around us today. Rev. Pai's love of God is a categorical command to take care of our neighbors all around the world. From this love grew aspirations for happiness and a fulfilling life for all people through freedom, equality, and solidarity. These worldly values must be achieved through the principles of the Gospel of God.

---

[9] Pai, *The Kingdom of God & Rural Korea,* 121. This view is defended below.

[2] LOVE RURAL AREAS

Rev. Pai's lifelong task was to care for the poor people living in rural areas through God's love and to improve their welfare. As mentioned above, the rural areas of Korea, which were among the poorest in the world, were the testing grounds where he took on the challenge of building the kingdom of God, who "preached the gospel of Heaven in Galilee." He focused on the voluntary participation and efforts of farmers who plowed the land in rural areas and fostered leaders among them to guide the others. The rural revival movement was a community-building movement that achieved success through self-interest, desire, temperance, humility, and devotion. He wanted to embody the Christian spirit of service, sharing, and devotion through this rural community movement. Eventually, Rev. Pai's community movement resulted in the formation of cooperatives. According to him, the spirit of cooperatives is "to lead a cooperative life of mutual aid apart from unlimited selfish privatization."[10] He was inspired by the successes of Rochdale in England and the cooperatives in Denmark, Norway, and Sweden, which were among the first cooperatives and founded in the 19th century. In Rev. Pai's view, those communities "secured the most precious values of morality and freedom, along with those of economic and political social living." Therefore, he determined that the secret to the success of cooperatives could be attributed to the cooperative spirit of love and mutual aid as advocated by Christ.

Rev. Pai stated that cooperatives should operate according to the following principles: the open-door policy, also known as the principle of union disclosure; democratic management in which each person gets one vote; the principle of refunding profits based on high utilization; not charging interest on loans; being politically and religiously neutral; cashism; and pursuing enlightenment projects. Rev. Pai especially emphasized the political neutrality of cooperatives, mainly because they had been used by special interest groups, political parties, and denominations to expand their own power. He also believed that cooperatives should make efforts to extend credit, increase consumption, improve farming efficiency, promote co-selling and co-purchasing, increase access to medical treatment, build sanitation facilities, help farmers find other sources of income, provide daycare for farmers' children, and build housing. His cooperative community movement was not only about increasing the income of the poor rural population and improving their material situation, but also about increasing their production,

---

[10] Pai attempted to distinguish the spirit of cooperation from the communism, by arguing that he is opposed to materialism and a totalitarian communist regime as well.

consumption, and welfare and cultivating a community spirit.

The spirit of Christian cooperatives is one of altruism, devotion, and service that grows out of the love of God. Various cooperative communities have emerged and disappeared throughout human history, including kibbutzim in Israel and producer and consumer cooperatives around the world. Spain's Mondragon has been recognized as one of the most successful cooperative communities. However, with the spread of capitalism, which is founded on selfishness, individualism, and exchanges between individuals, cooperatives are experiencing many difficulties.[11] The biggest trend in modern society is the rise in individualism that encourages people to be autonomous, free, and independent and to take responsibility for their actions.[12] As such, individualism is characterized by social fragmentation, isolation, materialism, egocentricity, self-interest, and indifference to public issues.

This spread of individualism is not independent of the capitalist drive to maximize ownership and profit. Today's global economic system that is centered on transnational giants demands unlimited competition between and the unlimited marketization of individuals. Public things are dismissed as ineffective, which is why neoliberalism promotes the marketization or privatization of public works, and the public spirit has gradually weakened. Rather than creating a foundation on which people can live together through altruistic cooperation, people are concerned about their own survival and are content to lead separate lives. Today, people are indifferent to public issues beyond their individual desires, such as protecting the human rights of minorities, sharing, consideration, dedication, participation, collective intelligence, distribution, and justice. For some, even human rights are seen as a way to secure their individual interests. The spirit of cooperatives that Rev. Pai founded based the utopian spirit of Christian community highlights and raises concerns about trends in contemporary society, which is dominated by selfishness and individualism.

---

[11] Recently the cooperative has grown through its embrace of market principles.

[12] Ulrich Beck, the well–known German Sociologist who introduced the concept of the Risk Society, argues that "individualization" is the unique feature of contemporary capitalism. The solidarity and 'glue' formerly provided by the group, nation, state, etc. has been weakened leading to an individualism that emphasizes individual autonomy, judgement, and responsibility. However, this individualistic tendency leads to 'ambivalence." He also points out that fragmentation and isolation are simultaneous by-products of "individualization." See Ulrich Beck, *Risk Society: Towards a New Modernity* (Thousand Oaks, CA: Sage, 1992).

[3] *LOVE LABOR*

One of Rev. Pai's three loves is the love for labor. Labor makes life possible by metabolically connecting people with nature as it is a performative process involving the brain and muscles. Labor is a historically creative act that combines concepts and execution. Throughout history, people have achieved material security through labor. Through labor, people can understand their own heritage and create society and history. However, Rev. Pai bitterly criticized the privileged class that takes the fruits of the labor of others while ignoring its essence. From time immemorial, Korea has had a Confucian culture in which there is a hierarchy of four classes. The ruling class, *yangban*, were immersed in study and did not know the hardships of labor. Thus, they were ignorant and only capable of reading and preparing for exams to advance their careers. They abused the working class, which is why Korean society has been plagued by poverty for a long time. Rev. Pai said the following:

> The reason we have become so miserable is because we have hated, feared, and humbled labor since ancient times. Our ancestors were physically weak, only concentrating on texts, and they looked down on labor and workers, believing that it was an honor to serve as a nobleman and take advantage of others. As a result, our people can't even live primitive lives in houses that are nothing more than dilapidated huts and find their lives in ruins. This evil outlook on labor still remains and workers envy those who do nothing but enjoy their free time and eat as they please, and those who are so privileged disrespect workers, shout at them, and harass them. This sense of superiority and a sense of desperation by being pampered and being looked down upon, respectively, is still prevalent.[13]

Rev. Pai emphasized the importance of manual labor. "Civilized countries, regardless of their status, find it a pleasure to work physically. We are aiming for an egalitarian society with no distinction between upper and lower classes." He insisted on loving labor that is characterized by effort and hard physical work:

> Now is the time for us to love work, respect those who work, and know that it is perfectly acceptable for us to be farmers and drive carts on the road so that discrimination between government officials, farmers, and workers is eradicated. We must pioneer our own path while leaning on others for help while, at the same time, helping others by working hard. If we live with the noble spirit of saving our nation by cultivating it with our own labor, our rural areas will be rebuilt and our nation will prosper much longer.[14]

---

13 Pai, *The Kingdom of God & Rural Korea*, 123.

14 Ibid., 123.

What significance does Rev. Pai's love for labor have in today's modern society? Today, capitalism is shifting into a financial mode in which money is not a means of material exchange or accumulation but has itself been commoditized and is exchanged in the market. Due to the speculative nature of capital, the global economy is always unstable. Societies around the world have been economically integrated. In London, New York, and Tokyo, trillions of dollars per day flow around financial markets. It is a well-known fact that most of these transactions are speculative in which money wins over money. Speculation is inherently risky. People's livelihoods, who are exposed to the incredible risk of speculation in transnational financial capital markets, are indefinitely in an unstable state. Transnational financial capital hunts for profits faster than the speed of light. Some call this style of capitalism 'casino capitalism.'[15]

Under this financial capitalist system in which money itself has been commoditized, many people find themselves wanting to engage in speculation as well from a desire to get rich quickly. Freeloaders who do not work on their own and ride on the coattails of others pursue consumption, leisure, and abundance without work. A society dominated by speculation and freeloaders is unjust and lacks trust and honesty. Rev. Pai's love for labor included distributional justice in which hard work is justly compensated. A society that respects labor, understands its cost, and gives fair compensation for it is a just society. Many social scientists today view trust as a form of social capital. Unlike economic capital, social capital is created by social institutions, networks of reciprocal relationships, and social values, such as trust. The more abundant trust and other forms of social capital are, the more mature and just civil society can become. Such societies do not have freeloaders or speculators and compensate labor fairly.[16]

PRAGMATISM AND SOCIAL INHERITANCE

Rev. Pai's *Sam-ae* philosophy can be used to solve many contemporary social problems. However, his philosophy does not end with a simple call for abstract values. He was a pragmatist who tried to link spiritual values with real life. He developed a detailed and specific strategy to put the three loves philosophy into practice. In other words, he developed practical ways to

---

[15] The term is borrowed from Susan Strange, *Casino Capitalism* (Manchester: Manchester University Press, 1997).

[16] Francis Fukuyama's argument – that trust is a form of social capital – has received tremendous attention from social scientists. See Francis Fukuyama, *Trust: The Social Virtues and the Creation of Prosperity* (New York: Free Press, 1996).

improve the lives of those living in rural regions. First, he recognized that leaders were needed to realize the rural communities that he envisioned. He met this requirement by creating an educational process that would foster both men and women as leaders. He planned to train 9,000 people, putting one male and one female leader in 4,500 villages across the country. He then established a rural training school in Daejeon where he taught agricultural techniques and nutritious recipes.[17] He also emphasized the importance of business success through growing fruit, pigs, chicken, and goats. He further proposed a blueprint for cultural houses that were superior to what most people in rural areas were living in at the time, including a dining room, living room, and a flushing toilet – even for houses without running water. He also addressed the poor sanitary conditions in rural regions with plans to improve the infrastructure in various ways, such as through better wells and reducing fly populations to prevent the spread of infectious diseases.

Rev. Pai also acted as a social activist, demanding that certain practices end. For example, he insisted on eradicating superstitions, rituals, alcohol consumption, and gambling – and he criticized not only arranged marriages but also ostentatious funerals and weddings. He also vehemently criticized discrimination against children and women, criticizing the patriarchal belief that men were in a higher social position than women and that women must absolutely obey men.[18] He said, "Let men do hard work and treat their sons and daughters equally, making rural regions a paradise for their wives and children"; he argued that women should be given educational opportunities and that organizations, such as women's associations, should be formed to help them lead social lives.[19] As such, Rev. Pai can be seen as a pioneer of the feminist movement in Korea today, which resists the long-established patriarchal order and strives to end gender discrimination. He emphasized the human rights of women and children, who are socially disadvantaged, and demanded that they receive the consideration they were due.

Rev. Pai's three loves philosophy does not stop there. His message about inheritance is still important today. "If you have an inheritance, you may donate it to a church, school, or social organization, but if you pass it on

---

[17] For more (in Korean), see Kyu-Moo Han, "The Establishment and Maintenance of Farmer's School by the Union Christian Service in the 1950s," *Christianity and History in Korea* 33 (2010): 109-131.

[18] He vehemently criticized the habitual attitude of degrading and discriminating females in Korean Society. For instance, despite the fact that most adulteries are instigated by men, the women end up bearing most of the blame.

[19] Pai, *The Kingdom of God & Rural Korea*, 194.

to your children, you are setting them up for failure," he said. "As long as parents put all of their energy into nurturing and educating their children, let them live independently and enable them to lead their own social lives. That is the parents' job. Children need to have a foundation for living an independent life on their own." As the French sociologist Emile Durkheim noted, inheritance reproduces social inequality. People's desire to possess more and more wealth to give it to their children when they die is a manifestation of selfishness. In this text, Rev. Pai's concept of inheritance, which is characterized by giving inheritance to the community instead of to children, as "social inheritance." His concept of social inheritance bears great significance in today's Korean society which lacks a culture of giving back to civil society and the community. For example, the practice of hereditary inheritance in some megachurches, which is a controversial topic in today's Korean society, differs significantly from Rev. Pai's teachings.

Rev. Pai's efforts were carried on by his family after his death. The possessions he left behind were donated to Yonsei University. His land and assets have been used by the university's Agricultural Development Center, reflecting Rev. Pai's spirit of interdenominational unity.[20] He gave not only material assets but also true Christian love and wisdom. Today, his interdenominational spirit is expressed through concern for church growth and serves as a strong warning against the exclusive and hostile attitudes of some Korean churches that are in conflict with each other. This spirit encourages a move away from closed, doctrinal fundamentalism and towards a cosmopolitan love for humanity, reconciliation and peace with other religions, and tolerance and hospitality.

LIFE TODAY, ECOLOGY, AND THE GLOBAL ENVIRONMENT

Lastly, I would like to examine the significance of Rev. Pai's love for rural regions in terms of the global environmental crisis, including the conditions of life today, ecology, and global warming. In nature wind and water mix with human sweat and labor to give birth to new life. Rural land is the source of primordial life that supports the existence of not only humans but also various non-human living and non-living things. Rev. Pai emphasized his

---

[20] See the following Korean articles: Chong-Hun Jeong, "The Situation and Vision of *Sam-ae* Church, and the Embodiment of *Sam-ae Spirit,*" *Theological Forum* 66 (2011): 109-124; Jae Keun Choi, "The Rev. Pai Minsoo's Life, Ideas, and Inheritance of His Legacy," *University of Christian and Mission* 39 (2019): 155-190; and Mee-Hyun Chung, "The Value of *Sam-ae* Campus and the *Sam-ae* Church of Yonsei University," *University of Christian and Mission* 43 (2020): 199-230.

love of rural soil, scenery, all kinds of natural life, livestock, houses, children, and people:

> Let us love the soil in the countryside, love the fields, love the mountains and hills and all the beautiful scenery, and love the climate of the countryside. Let us love babbling streams and clear springs, love trees and grass and flowers and beautiful birds. Let us love all livestock, love orchards, love gardens, and love houses. Let us love children and all people.
>
> If you do so, you will be rewarded several dozen times as much as you love. If you love the soil and fertilize it appropriately, the soil will give you all kinds of crops and fruits, thirty, sixty, and a hundredfold. If you love nature, it will delight people with its beautiful shapes, scents, and sounds. If you love livestock, it will give you abundant nutrients. If you love people, you will lead a peaceful and pleasant life of love. This love is only capable for those who have a heart, rather than material things. Anyone is capable of such love. Therefore, if you love the countryside, you will love the farmers in that village. When the farmers prosper, the whole country will prosper.[21]

Rural regions filled with various living things are places where the spiritual, the material, and life can grow. They are gifts that God has bestowed on humanity. "Rural regions are where ecological value; the aesthetic value of the natural landscape; the public value of food security; and the value of faith, hard work, gentleness, patience, hope, and spirituality are highest."[22] However, in today's society, these rural regions are victims of pollution. Rev. Pai warned about environmental pollution in rural regions early on:

> Soil quality is deteriorating due to the abuse of artificial chemical fertilizers used as part of modern agricultural production methods. Bacteria and earthworms that enrich the soil are disappearing due to acidification and, as a result, abundant natural nutrients are disappearing with them. Ultimately, humans who eat these crops become weak and suffer from all kinds of diseases.[23]

This perspective reflects Dr. Nichols's 1955 theory. Rev. Pai promoted the use of compost as an alternative to chemical fertilizers.

As mentioned in the introduction, the earth today is threatened by the destruction of nature by humans and their disturbance of the ecosystem. As early as the 1960s, Rachel Carson warned that natural ecology was in crisis in

---

[21] Minsoo Pai, *The Kingdom of God & Rural Korea,* 122.

[22] Yong-Hun Jo, "A Study on the Christian Rural Community Movement in the Korean Church," *Journal of Presbyterian College and Theological Seminary* 42, no. 2 (2015): 231. In Korean.

[23] Minsoo Pai, *The Kingdom of God & Rural Korea,* 122.

her book *Silent Spring*. She was becoming increasingly worried that birds, which produced the sound of spring, were disappearing as a result of humans' reckless use of herbicides, such as DDT (*Dichloro-diphenyl-trichloroethane*), to increase agricultural productivity. She regretted that she could not hear the sound of spring any longer. Concentrated on modernization and industrialization, humans have come to view rural areas only as a means to increase productivity. Land itself has been converted into the commodity of real estate. The concepts of ecosystems, their circulation and reproduction, and their ecological and aesthetic values have long been forgotten.

Today, pollution, disturbance of ecosystems, climate change, and global warming are not only problems limited to rural regions. The effects of these crises are being felt around the world, from rural areas to deserts cities. As mentioned earlier, many are raising their voices of concern that we are entering a new geological era called the Anthropocene that is characterized by environmental crises. A fear of catastrophe and the end of history as we know it is spreading not only in theological but also scientific discourse. Today's global crisis is the result of human self-righteousness and arrogance. Whether in the name of scientific and technological progress, capitalism, or socialism, humans have destroyed vast amounts of nature and continue to do so. For material abundance and profit, humanity regards nature not as something that must be coexisted with but as an object of conquest and thus has enacted heinous acts of violence against it. Obsessed with the idea that growth equals progress, humans are losing an ethical and aesthetic sense of coexistence with nature. The heat waves, heavy rains, droughts, floods, and wildfires that are appearing all over the world today can be seen as the planet's counterattack against humanity's unbearable acts of violence.

The universe is composed of a comprehensive, organic network of relationships between various living and non-living things. One part of this network is the earth, which is full of various forms of God's creation. When these creatures' lives are respected, the earth is healthy. Humans must be aware that they are just one of many creatures on the earth and so must engage in deep introspection about their relationship with non-human parts of creation, such as animals, plants, rivers, forests, and fields, and the rights of all things. All of creation has the right to survive and prosper. Rivers, forests, animals, and plants all have their own rights. The concept of earth law recognizes that the rights of all creation are ontologically equal is necessary and grants personal legal rights not only to human beings but also nature. Today, legal rights have already been granted to the Whanganui River in New Zealand and nature has rights guaranteed by constitutions or statutes in some South American countries, including Ecuador. For India's Ganges River and some rivers in the United States, various types of laws and ordinances have been enacted to protect them. Similarly, there are movements to legislate the rights of animals and prohibit animal cruelty. In Korea, Earth and People is leading the Earth Law movement and the Jeju Island Assembly has created an ecological corporation to protect the Indo-Pacific bottlenose dolphin.

Rev. Pai's love for rural regions and his message to others encouraging them to love the land, wind, animals, plants, landscapes, and people is connected to these efforts to promote earth law. Rev. Pai's three loves philosophy emphasizes the value of communion between God and humanity, people, and between humanity and nature. The love for the soil and land in the countryside is a show of gratitude and respect for the nature that God has provided.

CONCLUSION

Where is humanity headed? Humans – possessing reason, emotion, and rich imagination – have always sought to overcome challenges and try new things. Through scientific and technological development, humans are learning biological and medical knowledge about the body, exploring space, and uncovering countless artifacts from the past. We are living in a post-human era in which humans are moving beyond their natural limitations. However, in this world, the concurrency of asynchronization is also emerging. On the one hand, mass production has enabled mass consumption while, on the other hand, poverty and hunger persist. On one side of the planet, life is becoming increasingly dependent on artificial intelligence while on the other side, life seems to be moving backward. The end of racism, abuse of minorities, terrorism, and war is nowhere in sight. We have also not stopped violence against nature, so we are desperately experiencing a crisis of life and ecology due to global warming.

In these times of uncertainty and anxiety, we must consider the legacy of Rev. Pai who preached the Christian gospel in a land of suffering and spread hope. Witnessing to and serving the marginalized, poor, neglected, and socially disadvantaged who suffer from hardship and oppression are the two pillars of the Christian mission. Rev. Pai's three loves philosophy and the legacy of his cooperatives' experiments and challenges are relevant today in the face of various dangers and crises we are facing, including poverty, discrimination and neglect, conflict and antagonism, and violence and suffering. Rev. Pai's spirit that led to the foundation of cooperatives and his concept of social inheritance are relevant in light of today's social and legal system that allows for unlimited private ownership of wealth and is saturated with selfishness and greed. His cooperative spirit promotes values (of 'commons') that can be shared assets to communities. Rev. Pai's spirit of love for rural regions promotes life and seeks to save humans and nature, which are experiencing ecological crisis in the Anthropocene era due to global warming.[24]

Regarding human relationships, Rev. Pai emphasized understanding and empathy for others. Depression, anxiety, fear, hatred, and jealousy harm our bodies and minds.[25] In conflict, he said that people should, rather than questioning their opponent's wrongdoing, reflect on whether they did something to make the other person angry first, admit their own faults, and forgive the faults of others. He emphasized an attitude of empathy for others, responsibility, understanding, and tolerance. Rev. Pai said that Christian love relieves all worries, fears, and impatience; eliminates hatred and resentment for others; and enables tolerance and hospitality.[26] Rev. Pai's *Sam-ae* philosophy, which emphasizes introspection, empathy, tolerance, and hospitality, is still alive and breathing and can serve as a guide not only for Korean society but for human society as a whole.

---

[24] Today, the peasant society cannot be defined as the only indicating place. Pai's peasant society is required to symbolize the locus of realizing the love for the neighbor and of the peace. His idea of peasant community is still influencing not only the developing countries in which the agricultural industries are predominant but even the urbanized developing countries.

[25] He explained that the critical reason of short expectancy of life is due to the shortage of ingredient, illness, toxin etc., but at the same time, is caused by the physical suffering from the failure of emotion control.

[26] Pai, *The Kingdom of God & Rural Korea*, 145.

CHAPTER 2

SAM-AE SPIRIT AS LIVED RELIGION: A PANACEA FOR RELIGIOUS INTOLERANCE IN NIGERIA

CYRIL EMEKA EJIKE

Rev. Pai Min-Soo [also Pae Minsu; 1896-1968] is a Korean Presbyterian pastor who contributed immensely to the institution of religion-based modern life in South Korea. He was educated at Soongsil University (Union Christian College) in Pyŏngyang where he learnt about the meaning of Christianity and its nexus with society. At the university, he came in contact with Cho Man-Sik and worked with him to improve deplorable living conditions of peasants through the Presbyterian-based Christian Rural Research Institute from 1928 to 1931. Afterwards, he attended McCormick Theological Seminary in Chicago, U.S. from 1931 to 1933. During his studies at the seminary, he continued with Dr Syungman Rhee, who later became the first President of South Korea, the struggle for Korea's independence from Japan. After completing his studies, he returned to Korea and became the head of the official, rural construction movement of the Presbyterian Church, and committed himself to rebuilding rural Korean society.[1]

The introduction of the writings of the Japanese Christian socialist, Kagawa Toyohiko (a social reformer), centered on socialism of love that combined Marxism with the teachings and examples of Christ, motivated Pai and other Korean Christian leaders to fight economic inequality and social injustice in order to form a new society by which people could experience God's love.[2] The writings were buttressed by clarion call by Korean Christian socialists like Tong-hwi and Pak Hŭi-do who urged Christians to collaborate with socialists to build an ideal society by constructing a just world based on political, economic and social equality.[3] In response, Pai's

[1] Albert L. Park, *Building a Heaven on Earth: Religion, Activism and Protest in Japanese-Occupied Korea* (Honolulu: University of Hawaii Press, 2015), 106.

[2] Park, *Building a Heaven on Earth*, 57.

[3] Ibid., 97.

created *Sam-ae* Spirit and spread it throughout Korean society with a view to fighting social and economic injustice, protecting spiritual and material lives of Koreans, and negotiating the forces of capitalist modernity.

Pai left an enduring legacy of lived religion in South Korea in particular and in the globe in general through his philosophico-theological concept of *Sam-ae* Spirit. Lived religion is a religion that transcends merely personal belief and spirituality to encompass religious ideas and practices that gain meaning and value (*kachi*) in a matrix of social relationships, interactions and events.[4] In this sense, religion is not just only a medium for encountering the sacred and other spiritual experiences, but also a way of valuing things, forming and molding personality, and enhancing material conditions. *Sam-ae* Spirit is a tripartite philosophical theology of love, namely, 'Divine-love' (love for God), 'neighbor-love' (love for community/people/humanity) and 'work-love' (love for work/labor/occupation).[5]

I attempt in this paper to utilize Pai Min-Soo's idea of lived religion that is grounded in *Sam-ae* Spirit to address religious intolerance and conflicts in Nigeria. Since the incursion of Islam and Christianity (the two dominant religions) in Nigeria, there has been a string of religious intolerance that usually sparks violent conflicts and disturbances, with all their attendant killings and destruction of property. The reason usually adduced in justification of this despicable act of vandalism is that it is done in defense of a religion as a way of demonstrating love for God or *Allah.* I will argue in the spirit of *Sam-ae* that 'neighbor-love' is a precondition for loving God (*Allah*), and that it is made manifest in religious toleration, as God is foundational to both Islam and Christianity. I will posit the need for religious clerics, leaders and scholars to deemphasize subjecting the faithful to intense fanatical indoctrination, and implantation of idea of superiority of a religion over others in the faithful, and to focus more on preaching Pai's message of 'neighbor-love' and 'work-love' in words and deeds as an effective means of realizing 'Divine-love' and establishing God's kingdom in Nigeria.

---

[4] Ann Taves and Courtney Bender, eds., *What Matters? Ethnographics of Value in a not so Secular Age* (New York: Colombia University Press, 2012), 10.

[5] Chammah J. Kaunda and Kim Sang-man, "'*Samae* Spirit' Assist toward 'Ubuntu Spirit' Model for Rural Adult Christian Education in Zambia," *Religious Education* 117, no. 1 (2022): 40. https://doi.org/10.1080/00344087.2021.1990474

PAI'S LEGACY OF LIVED-RELIGION

Modernity marked by capitalism (*chabonjuŭi*) was viewed as a rupturing phenomenon during Japanese colonization of Korea (1910-1945), as it occasioned the disruption and disintegration of social and cultural fabric of Korean society by vast ideological, material and structural transformations.[6] This resulted in social exclusion, abject poverty and misery, and great hardship among rural Koreans. Modern Koreans were therefore faced with the challenge of establishing an ideal modern life that would enable them to cope with the demands of capitalist modernity. Religion was widely and heavily criticized as an anti-modern and archaic force that stifled the unfolding of an ideal modern life needed to negotiate the challenges of forces of modernity. The deprecation of religion stemmed from the widely held view that religious organizations focused mainly on spiritual matters and paid little or no attention to socio-economic and cultural problems that beset colonial Korea in the wake of capitalist modernity.[7]

Early development of a capitalist economy in Korea which began in the 18th century with internal development like technological innovations, which underwent industrialization during Japanese colonial rule in the 1920s,[8] was initially frowned upon by conservative Protestant church leaders like those of Presbyterian church who regarded the pursuit of profit and accumulation of wealth through capitalist economic and commercial activities as being destructive to society. A case in point that lent weight to the popular criticism of religion in colonial times was a hard-line posture of conservative Presbyterian leaders who initially remained aloof from the task of rebuilding rural Korean society ruptured by forces of capitalism. For them, what was required of followers in the face of Korean existential socio-cultural and economic problems was just to concentrate on prayers, Bible study, and other spiritual issues in the expectation of Christ's return to earth to liberate them from the shackles of colonialism.[9]

In response to the scathing attacks on religion and contrary to the orthodox views on religion by conservative Presbyterians, Pai developed lived

---

[6] Albert L. Park, "Reclaiming the Rural: Modern Danish Cooperative Living in Colonial Korea, 1925-37," *Journal of Korean Studies* 19, no.1 (2014): 116, https://doi.org/10.1353/jks.2014.0007. See also Park, *Building a Heaven on Earth,* 2.

[7] Park, *Building a Heaven on Earth,* 2-3.

[8] Michael D. Shin and Pang K. Chung, eds. *Landlords, Peasants, Intellectuals in Modern Korea* (Ithaca, NY: Cornell East Asia Program, 2005), 7.

[9] Park, *Building a Heaven on Earth*, 107.

religion which was grounded in his concept of *Sam-ae* Spirit as his point of departure by establishing a nexus of relationships between religion and society.[10] He demonstrated inextricable connections between religion/church (Christian life, spirituality and enterprise) and society/economy (everyday social thought, behavior, relations and practices, and economic activity) so as to adapt Christianity and Christian teachings to the Korean present day needs. Unlike conservative Presbyterian ministers who held the orthodox view that the role of the church is to teach the principle of love, not the method of love,[11] *Sam-ae* Spirit is both a theory and a method of love that portrays the mode of religious, socio-economic and political life to which humanity must adopt in this modern era for the realization of God's kingdom on earth.

'Neighbor-love' finds expression in being altruistic, beneficent and benevolent towards the other, especially the poor, the needy and others living on the margins of society. Pai stressed the need for 'neighbor-love' as a means of demonstrating and realizing 'Divine-love' on earth by making reference to the Christ's ministry that was used not only to teach spiritual truths, but also to provide people with their concrete needs like feeding the hungry, healing the sick and fighting all forms of injustice.[12] Under capitalism in colonial Korea, people became materialistic (*mulchiljuui*), pursuing material wealth at the expense of others. The law of the jungle was the order of the day. However, for Pai, wealth and profit should be accumulated justly and be utilized for doing good, helping the poor and the needy and supporting God's evangelical works so as to create a new space, a 'heaven on earth' (*chisang ch'ŏn'guk*).[13]

'Work-love' finds expression in being industrious, productive and dedicated to one's work (labor/occupation), and working in harmony with co-workers/laborers so as to not only enhance the economic power and material security of Koreans, especially peasants, but also produce copious commodities for Korean population in order to cushion the socio-economic impact of capitalism on Koreans' daily lives. Pai believed that 'work-love' is made manifest in cooperative agriculture modeled on the cooperative system (*hyŏptong chohap)* of Denmark as an effective means of fostering the moral

---

[10] Minsoo Pai, *Who Shall Enter the Kingdom of Heaven?*, 1st ed., trans. Nowon Park (Seoul: Yonsei University Press, 1952), 395.

[11] Ibid., 347.

[12] Park, *Building a Heaven on Earth*, 111.

[13] Pai, *The Kingdom of Heaven*, 347. See also Albert L. Park, "Encountering a Sacred Economy of Value and Production: Capitalism and Early Modern Korea (1885-1919)," in *Encountering Modernity: Christianity in East Asia and Asian America*, ed. Albert L. Park and David K. Yoo (Honolulu: University of Hawaii Press, 2014), 25.

principle of mutual cooperation (*sangho pujo*), improving the economic conditions of community of individuals and the quality of human life, and achieving self-sustaining (*chajak chagŭp*) life.[14] In 'work-love,' labor (or work) is re-conceptualized as a requirement for maintaining a good relationship with God, promoting God's work and leading a decent life.

Pai Min-Soo from the Presbyterian Church together with Pyŏngsŏn, a leading theologian from the Young Men's Christian Association (YMCA) and other religious figures from the Presbyterian Church, the YMCA and the Ch'ŏndogyo Church carried out large-scale agrarian reconstruction campaigns in the 1920s and 1930s "to build a new modern Korea centered on agriculture and rural culture."[15] All three of the organizations led by officials focused on reconstructing peasants' lives by placing agriculture at the center in spite of their differing religious beliefs. They regarded "agricultural production as the primary source of Korea wealth and the foundation for the national economy since manufacturing could not take place without the raw materials agriculture produced."[16] They "valued both peasants and agriculture because both constituted Korean ethnic identity."[17]

Motivated by Pai's agrarian-based reconstruction campaigns that were anchored in *Sam-ae* Spirit, Presbyterians and other Protestant Christian community in colonial Korea were urged by their conservative leaders, who were initially indifferent to the task of rebuilding Korean society, not to be lying idle, but rather to be industrious and productive laborers in economic and commercial activities such as farming, trading and industry, and to see practicing Christian faith as involving practical labor.[18] Economy became part of the sacred order, as the earning of money and accumulation of capital were viewed as having sacred purposes and not just for material gain: they were considered to be a legitimate way of advancing the mission of Protestant Christianity.[19] Through their economic activities and productivity, productive Christians could provide money and capital needed to promote God's work in

---

[14] Min-Soo Pai [Min-Su Pae], "The Rural Evangelistic Movement," *The Korean Mission Field* (1935): 150. See also Park, "Reclaiming the Rural," 127.

[15]Albert L. Park, Social Renewal through the Rural: Agricultural Cooperatives in South Korea as a form of Critiquing Capitalism," *Global Environment* 9 (2016): 92. https://doi.org/10.3197/ge.2016.090105

[16] Park, "Reclaiming the Rural," 121.

[17] Ibid., 122.

[18] Park, "Encountering a Sacred Economy of Value and Production," 26.

[19] Ibid. 26-27.

Korea. Thus, labor or work and the money or profit accruing from it became sacred acts and ceased to be regarded as mundane economic practices.[20]

Through *Sam-ae* Spirit, Pai contributed immensely to the growth and expansion of religion-based emerging native capitalist economy in modern Korea. By linking religion to societal conditions, he set a new standard for Christian living. Instead of retreating from the world and focusing only on spiritual matters, while waiting for God's deliverance in the future, Christians are spurred through *Sam-ae* Spirit to engage the world and build a just, peaceful and moral society for the realization of heavenly kingdom on earth. On the whole, Pai made religion a lived social phenomenon in that it creates values, ideas and mechanisms for making sense of, and negotiating, myriads of economic, social, political and cultural forces that present serious challenges to modern Korea in particular and humanity in general.

RELIGIOUS INTOLERANCE AND VIOLENCE IN NIGERIA

Nigeria has experienced a series of religious intolerance that usually provoked violent conflicts and disturbances, with all their attendant killings and vandalization of property since the incursion of Islam and Christianity in the country. The inter-religious intolerance and disturbances are usually between Muslim and Christian students or community who constitute the two dominant religious groups in the country. Some religious intolerance and violence include:

- Christian-Muslim disturbance in 1986 at Ilorin, Kwara State: Muslim youths attacked Christians who were marching in procession on Palm Sunday for following a Muslim part of the town and maimed many of them.[21]
- Conflicts between Muslim-Christian students at University of Ibadan (UI) in 1986: Muslim students staged a protest demonstration against the position of the cross of Jesus Christ in front of a church at the university, claiming that the cross was obstructing their view during prayers in the mosque.[22] The protest turned out to be a violent one, as they burnt the carved door of the chapel on which the statue of the Risen Christ was

---

[20] Park, "Encountering a Sacred Economy of Value and Production," 26.

[21] Emehie Ikenga-Metuh, "Two Decades of Religious Conflicts in Nigeria: A Recipe for Peace," *BETH* 6, no. 1 (1994): 69-70.

[22] Bala Takaya, "The Foundations of Religious Intolerance in Nigeria, Backgrounds for Understanding Maitatsine Phenomenon," *Bulletin of Ecumenical Theology*, 2, no. 2 (1990): 1989-3/1: 1. See also Ikenga-Metuh, "Two Decades of Religious Conflicts in Nigeria," 70.

erected.[23] It is worthy of note that the church (building) was in existence prior to the mosque.

- Inter-religious violence involving Christians and Muslims at the College of Education, Kafanchan, Kaduna State in March 1987 due to misunderstanding over religious matters:[24] the violence which erupted at the college later spiraled out of control and spread through a large part of northern Nigeria, thus leading to vandalization of churches and mosques by Muslims and Christians respectively.
- Urban religious riots in Kano, Kano State between Muslims and Christians on 16 October 1991: Muslims mounted protests against the visit of a German-American Pentecostal evangelist, Reinhard Bonnke who was invited by a Christian organization to conduct a week crusade in Kano. During the angry protests, thousands of Muslim youths thronged into the town and started tearing up all posters, banners and handbills advertising the crusade.[25] It later degenerated into brutal attacks and killing of Christians, and destruction of their property.[26]
- Muslim protests at UI in August 2010: a female Christian student disguised as a female Muslim by wearing a hijab and joining a *Jumat* service in the mosque at UI on 13 August 2010 during which she preached against Islam.[27] But for the swift intervention of the security personnel at the university, she could have been beaten up and lynched by angry Muslim students who gathered after the service. This was followed by angry protests by thousands of Muslim students. The protests paralyzed all academic and commercial activities in the institution and could have degenerated into killings and destruction of

---

[23] Takaya, "The Foundations of Religious Intolerance in Nigeria," 22. See also Ikenga-Metuh, "Two Decades of Religious Conflicts in Nigeria," 70; and Jonathan O. Chimakonam, and the Conversational School of Philosophy (CSP), "Indigenous African Religions (IARs) and the Relational Value of Tolerance: Addressing the Evil of Violent Conflicts in Africa," *Filosophia Theoretica: Journal of African Philosophy, Culture and Religions* 11, no. 1 (2022): 104.

[24] Ikenga-Metuh, "Two Decades of Religious Conflicts in Nigeria," 83. See also Chimakonam and the CSP, "Indigenous African Religions (IARs) and the Relational Value of Tolerance," 102.

[25] Ikenga-Metuh, "Two Decades of Religious Conflicts in Nigeria," 61.

[26] *The Guardian* 1991, as quoted in Ikenga-Metuh, "Two Decades of Religious Conflicts in Nigeria," 70.

[27] Ola Ajayi, "Muslim Students Paralyse Academic Activities in UI," *Vanguard Nigeria*, 16 Aug. 2010, https://www.vanguardngr.com/2010/08/muslim-students-paralyse-academic-activities-in-ui/.

property but for the efforts of the university management who nipped the matter in the bud by strongly and publicly condemning the student's act of religious intolerance and appealing to the Muslim community in the institution.

- The lynching of Miss Deborah Samuel, a home economics Christian student of Shehu Shagari College of Education, Sokoto, Nigeria on May 12, 2022 by a wild mob of Islamic extremists parading as students over alleged blasphemy against Prophet Muhammad and/or Islam:[28] the alleged blasphemous act the young Deborah committed was that she advised her Muslim classmates to desist from sending and discussing religious contents in the class *WhatsApp* group forum created for the sole purpose of disseminating information about course matters without mentioning any religion or religious figure in her posts.[29]

LIVED RELIGION IN *SAM-AE* SPIRIT AS A PATH TO RELIGIOUS TOLERATION

The instances of religious intolerance and the ensuing religious disturbances in the preceding section are the product of intense and fanatical religious indoctrination to which religious adherents are subjected, as well as the implantation of the idea of superiority of a religion over others in the faithful in schools, mosques and churches by religious clerics, scholars and leaders. Armed with this form and nature of religious teachings, adherents of either Islam or Christianity are brought up to treat adherents of other religions as out-groups (infidels and unbelievers in Muslim and Christian parlance respectively). Such teachings engender and reinforce religious extremism, bigotry and intolerance. Hence, religious adherents can maim and kill people and vandalize people's property at the slightest provocation.

The perception of religious extremists who destroy lives and property is that they do so in defense of their religions or *Allah* (God) as a demonstration of their love for *Allah* or God (Divine-love). However, such a despicable act of killing and vandalism in the name of love for God

---

[28]"Editorial: Justice Must Be Served in Deborah's Killing," *Premium Times*, 26 May 2022, https://www.premiumtimesng.com/news/headlines/532587-editorial-justice-must-be-served-in-deborahs-killing.html. See also Obi Nwankanma, "Killing Deborah, Killing Harira… When Does It End?," *Vanguard Nigeria*, 5 June 2022, https://vanguardngr.com/2022/06/killing-deborah-killing-harira-when-does-it-end/.

[29] Ikechukwu Amaechi, "Deborah Yakubu: Killing in the Name of God," *Vanguard Nigeria*, 19 May 2022, https://www.vanguardngr.com/2022/05/deborah-yakubu-killing-in-the-name-of-god/. See also "Editorial," *Premium Times*, 26 May 2022, https://www.premiumtimesng.com/news/headlines/532587-editorial-justice-must-be-served-in-deborahs-killing.html.

constitutes an affront to God and His attribute as Supreme and Omnipotent. God, if He wills, can defend Himself or a religion based on the life and beliefs of His son, Jesus Christ or those of Prophet Muhammad in the case of a truly blasphemous act or remark against Him, Islam or Christianity. Therefore, indulging in any act of killing and vandalism in the name of love for God or fighting for *Allah* is in direct contradiction to the claim to love God. In Pai's *Sam-ae* Spirit, 'neighbor-love' and 'work-love' which are made manifest in concrete inter-human relations in social and political institutions and other organizations are a true measure of 'Divine-love.' They are path to the experience of God and 'Divine-love.' 'Neighbor-love' and 'work-love' are the bedrock of 'Divine love.' They are preconditions for loving God. They are indices of 'Divine-love'; the yardsticks for measuring and determining the authenticity of one's claim to love God. This implies that one cannot genuinely love God without first of all loving the other (people/humanity) and one's work or occupation. 'Divine-love' therefore presupposes 'neighbor-love' and 'work-love.' Genuine love for God is manifested in human relationships that pave the way for one's religious experience of God. Everyday life (*ŭisikchu*) is therefore the ground for meeting God; the means to experience God. One's love for God should not be considered in isolation from one's love for adherents of other religions which presupposes tolerance of religions of others.

It is worth-stating here that Pai, Hong, and other Korean Christian leaders collectively embarked on largest agrarian reconstruction campaigns that were anchored in the Danish cooperative system, despite their differing religious ideologies and doctrines in order to negotiate the crisis of modernity and build God's kingdom in modern Korea. As a matter of urgency, Muslim and Christian clerics, scholars and leaders should in the spirit of *Sam-ae* take their cue from Korean religious figures by soft-pedaling, or placing less emphasis on, fanatical indoctrination of the faithful and focusing more on preaching Pai's message of 'neighbor-love' and 'work-love' as an effective means of demonstrating and actualizing 'Divine-love' on earth. Their commitment to preaching the message is a demonstration of their 'work-love' (love for their religious vocations/callings).

Beyond this, Pai affirmed that not only did Jesus Christ teach the life of love, He also lived such life as well;[30] and motivated by Christ's exemplary life, he declared that he "wanted to find out how to feed the hungry, clothe

---

30 Pai, *Who Shall Enter the Kingdom of Heaven?*, 315.

the naked, and help the needy ones as Jesus commanded."[31] He committed himself to rebuilding Korean society by spreading the spirit of *Sam-ae* in words and deeds across the length and breadth of his country. Muslim and Christian clerics, scholars and leaders in Nigeria must practice what they preach by being committed to 'neighbor-love' that entails being tolerant of another's religion as an expression of 'Divine-love,' as God is foundational to both Muslim and Christian religions. It also necessarily involves helping the poor and the needy and others living on the margins of society, irrespective of underprivileged religious affiliations. Such religious practices will shift the focus of religion from intense and fanatical religious indoctrination to 'neighbor-love' and 'work-love' that are basic to 'Divine-love,' and encourage other adherents to do likewise to pull the country out of intense religious fanaticism and intolerance, and all the attendant violence, that have eaten deep into the country's social fabric.

CONCLUSION

In this paper, I have demonstrated that Pai left an enduring legacy of lived religion in modern South Korea in particular and the world in general through his framework of *Sam-ae* Spirit. I have attempted to propose his construction of lived religion that is rooted in *Sam-ae* Spirit as a remedy for intractable religious intolerance and its concomitant violence that has disintegrated the social fabric of Nigeria and ruptured harmonious relationships and peaceful coexistence of Nigerians. The trichotomic love in *Sam-ae* philosophy represented in a triangular diagram indicates that 'neighbor-love' and 'work-love' are at the base, while 'Divine-love' is at the top of the triangle. 'Neighbor-love' and 'work-love' are preconditions for 'Divine-love.' One's love for God presupposes love for one's neighbor and one's work that is made manifest in concrete social actions, relations, institutions and practices. 'Neighbor-love' and 'work-love' are the yardsticks for measuring and determining one's claim to love God. To remedy the problem of religious intolerance in Nigeria and form a heavenly paradise in the country, all adherents (both the leaders and the led) of Islam and Christianity must imbibe and cultivate the spirit of *Sam-ae* by deemphasizing fanatical indoctrination and giving primacy to lived religion which entails practicing and living out 'neighbor-love' and 'work-love' as a genuine expression of 'Divine-love' on earth.

---

[31] Pai, *Who Shall Enter the Kingdom of Heaven?*, 347.

CHAPTER 3

SAM-AE SPIRIT AND *ATSÜ TSÜ*: TOWARD A NAGA INDIGENOUS RADICAL ATTITUDE TO WEALTH AND SELF-PRESERVATION

ATOLA LONGUMER

INTRODUCTION

In January 2022, Oxfam published a report titled "Inequality Kills" that reported the global reality of inequality that is "contributing to the death of at least 21,000 people, or one person every four seconds."[1] Lack of access to healthcare, hunger, gender-based violence and impact of climate change are causing loss of lives. Another despairing summary of the global situation of stark inequality is captured in the following words, "the coronavirus has itself destroyed the myth that the pandemic is 'the great equalizer.' It has not only exposed the criminal inequalities in health care. It has exposed all the entrenched structural, institutional, and systemic economic, social and political inequalities, and the incessant, comprehensive war against the poor and the vulnerable, globally and nationally."[2] These reports of devastating poverty and brutal inequalities make it even more poignant because humanity has surely made progress in many levels as Kim Wang-Bae highlighted in the keynote address in the international conference on the Legacy of Rev. Pai Min-Soo, September 2022. Today the world is indeed, a hyper-connected global society, where technology has seemingly broken barriers and even biases.[3] Yet, in many ways, the social, economic, environmental and political challenges share similarities with the context of Korea when Rev. Pai Min-Soo began his movement of three loves (*Sam-ae*) – love of God, love of humanity, and love of work.

---

[1] "Inequality Kills," *Oxfam International*, 18 Jan. 2022, https://www.oxfam.org/en/research/inequality-kills.

[2] *ZacTax Toolkit* (Geneva: World Council of Churches, 2021), 31. https://www.oikoumene.org/sites/default/files/2021-11/ZacTax_Toolkit_Web.pdf.

[3] Kim Wang-Bae, "Introspection in the Post-human Era and Reverend Pai Min-Soo's 'Sam-ae' Spirit," Paper presented at the *17th International Conference on The Legacy of Rev. Pai Min-Soo: A Global Perspective*, Yonsei University, September 2022, 27-42.

While the world has seemingly made tremendous progress aided by technology and subsequently bringing economic progress with unprecedented wealth, humanity continues to inhabit a highly fractious world with inequalities of many layers. It is therefore, important to engage the thoughts and practices that Pai Min-Soo developed guided by a vision of a just and sustainable humanity. The fact that the wealthy got richer while the world endured the corona pandemic illustrates that the systems and structures are skewed and calls for alternative reality that is more just. What explains the fact that human life is threatened with poverty amidst tremendous wealth of the rich? What could be the alternative practices and attitude? Part of the answer could be found in the economic practices that are undergirded by inherent human nature of self-preservation as exemplified in the tremendous wealth accumulation by the few. Pai Min-Soo's three principles provide resourceful direction to explore the antidote to greed. Pai Min-Soo's movement of three loves can be constructively supplemented with the Ao Naga ritual of *atsü tsü*. A radical attitude to wealth and self-preservation is demonstrated in the *atsü tsü*. Beginning with description of the *atsü tsü* ritual, the essay will demonstrate alternative practices that may counter prevalent dominant and selfish way of life.

Ethnographic description of mithun (*bos frontalis*/gayal) sacrifice of the Ao Naga Indigenous people will be followed by comparative dialogue with the *Sam-ae* Spirit as expounded by Pai Min-Soo. In the comparative dialogue, three perspective of wealth management in relation to neighbors will be addressed: wealth that acknowledges the sacred, wealth measured in sharing, and wealth for stewardship not accumulation. The essay will conclude emphasizing *Sam-ae* Spirit as a witness to creation flourish that is responsible, sustainable, and inclusive.

INDIGENOUS PEOPLES' LIFEWAYS

Indigenous Peoples (IP) are the inhabitants of diverse environments in different regions of the world. IP are the people that have a long history of being colonized, discriminated, exploited and dismissed. However, beginning the late twentieth century, global organizations have recognized the distinct history and rich traditions of the IP to be embraced as resources for the challenges of the times. IP is described as the following:

> Indigenous communities, peoples, and nations are those which, having a historical continuity with pre-invasion and pre-colonial societies that developed on their territories, consider themselves distinct from other sections of the societies now prevailing on those territories, or parts of

> them. They form at present non-dominant sectors of society and are determined to preserve, develop, and transmit to future generations their ancestral territories, and their ethnic identity, as the basis of their continued existence as peoples, in accordance with their own cultural patterns, social institutions, and legal system.[4]

In Asia, the Federation of Asian Bishops' Conference (FABC) was one of the earliest organizations to affirm the religio-cultural traditions of the IP. The FABC prepared a document titled, *The Spirit at Work in Asia Today* (1997), which highlighted the value of the religio-cultural traditions of the IP, as valuable traditions to learn from them "new insights in areas such as ecology, community life and the celebration of life's joys and tragedies."[5] The openness to learn from the lifeways of the IP was a radical paradigm shift from the earlier condescending attitude held towards the IP as encapsulated in the following assessment: "The primal religions were often accused of propagating idolatrous and satanic practices. Their members were called people living in "darkness and far from God," because they were considered to believe in a world full of evil spirits and powers and to depend on the intercession of dubious magicians, witch-doctors, healers and exorcists."[6] While paternalizing attitudes and cultural biases exhibited historically towards Indigenous peoples are acknowledged, radical inclusion of IP in society still remain a challenge. Furthermore, despite the affirmations for the traditions of IP exists, it must be recognized that in many parts of the world IP continue to face discriminations and comprises one of the most vulnerable section of the society.[7] IP have diverse historical experiences and cultural practices, yet, they share a commonality of proximity to the environment and inherent knowledge of the natural world. In other words, IP around the world share a common lens of being sensitive to their natural rhythm of life and social relationships. A marked feature of IP community is the sense of solidarity and mutuality contra greed and self-centeredness. Although, risking romanticization, yet, the nature and the organization of the

---

[4] "Workshop on Data Collection and Disaggregation for Indigenous Peoples," *United Nations*, New York, 19-21 Jan. 2004, https://digitallibrary.un.org/record/517063.

[5] "The Spirit at Work in Asia Today," FABC Papers 81(Hong Kong: Federation of Asian Bishops' Conferences, 1998), 21.

[6] Ibid., 21.

[7] For instance, the coronavirus pandemic devastated IP communities with lack of medical care and negligence from the state. See Atola Longkumer, "Christianity and Covid-19: A Reflection from Indigenous Lifeways" in *Christianity and Covid-19: Pathways for Faith,* eds. Chammah J. Kaunda, Atola Longkumer, Kenneth R. Ross, and Esther Mombo (London: Routledge, 2021).

communities of IP makes it easier to practice mutuality and solidarity. A community outlook is fundamental to many IP communities. It is, therefore within this social and cultural worldview, the essay develops the proposition of alternative love that is marked by love for God, love for humanity and love for work.

NAGA INDIGENOUS PEOPLE OF INDO-MYANMAR

Naga are one of the IP communities from about 260 million Indigenous Peoples in Asia. Naga is an umbrella term given by the neighbors to minority communities described as 'tribe' nestled on mountain tops of the Indo-Myanmar mountain range in east Asia. Each tribe have their distinct name for their group, such as Ao, Angami, Chang, Lotha, Konyak, Khiamungan, Mon, Sangtem, Tangkhul, Moyon, Sumi, Mao etc. While the demarcation of modern nation states placed most Naga tribes with modern India, there are also Naga tribes in Myanmar. The encounter with the imperial power of Britain resulted in tremendous shift and momentum of their identity.

The transmission of tradition and history for the Naga is through oral stories and cultural practices. Beginning late nineteenth century, the Naga responded to Christianity favorably in response to evangelistic mission of American Baptists. Before the embrace of Christianity, the Naga had a religious landscape that was characteristically shamanic, wherein individuals with distinct abilities to traverse the layers of cosmic realities, and shamanic practices were central to the religiosity of the people. Today, most of the Naga people are members of churches, with Christianity's rites and practices very central in the lives of individuals and the larger society. Devout prayer life, Baptism, church attendance, and participation in mission activities are significant marks of Naga Indigenous people.

The oral traditions pertaining to many socio-cultural practices of the fore-parents are strictly adhered to despite the adaptations made as a consequent to the modernization that was initiated with the encounter with the colonial and the Christian mission. In that, Naga communities continue to be organized along clan lineage and cohesion. Their encounter with the modernizing forces of colonial administration and Christianization began in the nineteenth century. Much changed in their ways of living, such as shift from agrarian economy to monetary economy. Significant transformations took place with the conversion to Christianity as a result of the evangelization of American Baptist missions. Oral base knowledge and traditions transitioned to modern forms such as education and written history. Today the Naga rank among the highest adherents of Christianity in the country. The church therefore plays a social important role in the larger society.

According to oral traditions and records of observations of the earliest ethnographers of the West, the Naga religious sphere was predominated by shamanic practices. Significant practices illustrated the keen consciousness of the idea of sacred which were expressed in rituals and sacrifices. The expert in the community, who exhibited abilities to transcend the levels of mundane to access the "sacred realm" directed the ritual and sacrifices performed by the community. The expert was identified by certain abilities, such as, dreaming, enter into trance, communicate between the realms of reality, and exhibit knowledge of herbs and tree barks with healing power. The expert could be both male and female, there were no gendered religious role and function in the pre-Christian period. These characteristic are akin to shamanism of other IP and Asian communities, which counters the earlier classification of the Naga religious practices as animist.[8]

ATSÜ TSÜ / MITHUN SACRIFICE

Atsü tsü is a ritual performed within this shamanic religious sphere of the Ao Naga. In ethnographies of the Ao Naga by British administrators, the term Feast of Merit is use to described the mithun sacrifice/*atsü tsü*. *Atsü tsü* means 'mithun slaughter' in the Ao Naga dialect._As the term indicates, *atsü tsü* is a ritual when a family that has been recognized by the community as wealthy, slaughtered a mithun for different reasons, such as religious and social. *Atsü tsü* is not perform today but descendants of the family that performed *atsü tsü* carry the memorialized names such as Tsüpong (mithun slayer) even in the new reality of a Christianized society. Most probably, *atsü tsü* was translated as Feast of Merit because performance of the mithun slaughter bestowed status upon the performers and their descendants, such as a revered name and exclusive patterns in costumes. It was told that to perform *atsü tsü* was also to be assured of well-being of life after death. Above all, *atsü tsü* was an act of merit, a goodwill gesture to the community by the wealthy family, a sharing of their abundance with the neighbors.

As mentioned above, prior to the transition to modern life and Christianity, the Naga people were an agrarian people inhabiting the verdant

---

[8] Ethnographic and historical documenting of the Naga is a growing project with a variety of publications available, from among these growing resources, for a helpful reference that situates the ethnography on Naga within the colonial period, see Julian Jacobs, *The Nagas: Hill Peoples of Northeast India, Society, Culture and the Colonial Encounter* (London: Thames and Hudson, 1998).

mountains subsisting on annual rice cultivation, foraging herbs and hunting for meat. Even today, a substantial population of the Naga is engaged in agriculture, growing rice and other staples, along with meat that is predominantly pork and poultry. Within the shamanic religious sphere, according to oral traditions, the Ao Naga performed a number of rituals to maintain the relationship with the sacred, who was known as Lijaba Tsüngrem. The Ao Naga believed that Lijaba was the sacred supreme who had the key to all good and evil in the life of the community and the individual. In other words, the Ao Naga held a teleological notion of living. Within this shamanic culture with a pronounced sense of sacred and the right relationship required for flourish, the *atsü tsü* was performed among the Ao Naga. *Atsü tsü* was sacrifice of a mithun by wealthy families. Ethnographers of the West have used the term Feast of Merit to describe this sacrifice. While the term Feast of Merit does not encapsulate the comprehensive performance and the rationale of the ritual, it does express a partial description. The one who performed *atsü tsü* had merits to gain, such as social recognition and status, as well as religious assurance of pleasing Lijaba Tsungrem. However, the term used by the ethnographers limits the profound purpose for the ritual. Therefore, this essay uses the local term *atsü tsü* to describe the sacrifice of mithun by wealthy families among the Ao Naga.

A word of clarification is required to note that after espousing Christianity, performance of *atsü tsü* ceased for obvious reasons – local practices were prohibited as they were deemed incompatible with the new faith. Interestingly, the spirit of *atsü tsü* still remains finding expression in families with means hosting community meals during Christian festivals such as Christmas. More will be discussed on this practice in the later section of the paper. *Atsü tsü* was performed by the wealthy families. When a family in village had bountiful harvest for consecutive years, their rice barns overflowed. This was an indication that a family was wealthy. The pre-modern Ao Naga community was primarily an agrarian society where rice was the staple supplemented by root vegetables such as yams, taro, and tapioca. Grains like millet and Job's tears were grown but only as a supplement. Pigs and chicken completed the husbandry of the Ao Naga.

The family that received a good harvest were nudged by the community to host the villagers to a sumptuous feast. Mithun sacrifice was then performed by the family. The family that had a bountiful harvest and had sufficient rice to feed the whole village and friends from neighbouring villages decides to perform the *atsü tsü*. Under the direction of the shamanic figure in the village, the family selected the time to sacrifice the mithun. An unmarried man could not perform *atsü tsü.* Within a patriarchal social structure, it is interesting to note that a married husband and wife performed the *atsü tsü. Atsü tsü* was a ritual that lasted for days. After buying a mithun for the sacrifice, the family began the preparation for the sacrifice. Collection of firewood from forest took days. Preparation of rice, from sunning to pounding with mortar and pestle, and making *azu* (fermented rice drink). According to oral traditions, the ritual of *atsü tsü* stipulated meticulous code of norms to be followed in the performance of the ritual. These included: stringent clan purity of the couple performing the sacrifice, accurate proportion of the mithun, precise process of feeding the mithun before it is sacrifice, and the exact number of days for the festivities. On the first day of *atsü tsü*, the mithun was sacrificed and the meat apportioned to the relative and friends according to the custom of meat sharing as stipulated by the oral traditions. The feasting began with sufficient *azu* and meat for the whole villagers and friends from the neighboring villages. The celebration took place for days. It is said that some families emptied their barn and went into difficulties in order to complete the commitment to host the feast.

Why was *atsü tsü* performed? According to oral tradition, the primary reason for performing the ritual was to recognize the bountiful harvest that Lijaba had provided and therefore a thanksgiving ritual. Secondly, the family that performed *atsü tsü* earned social status and religious affirmation. The family that performed *atsü tsü* had distinct symbols in their costumes that set them apart from the common patterns. The descendants of the *atsü tsü -er* (one who performed mithun sacrifice) also bore names that signified their ancestors' feats. Thirdly, *atsü tsü* provided social cohesion not only within the village but also beyond. In a culture based on raiding other villages, social bonding was important because it ensured loyalty. These were the reasons that undergirded the vigorous ritual of *atsü tsü* of the Ao Naga.

It must be mentioned that the *atsü tsü* ritual was not performed following the embrace of Christianity and the cultural changes it entailed. However, to a keen observer, the residue of the ancestors' ways can still be deduced in forms such as names given to descendants. Most importantly, the practice of hosting a feast for the whole village often finds expression in the Christian practice. For instance, families with means often host meals during Christmas and New Year after the regular church services. A common practice of Ao Naga Christians is sharing community meals on Christmas day and the first day of the New Year.

ATSÜ TSÜ AND AN ALTERNATIVE ECONOMY

The interpretative meaning of the ritual of *atsü tsü* can be seen in the rationale that undergirds the performance of the ritual. Acknowledgement of sacred and human relationships is central to the performance of *atsü tsü*. If, ritual is an expression of human desire "to create and renew community, transform human identity, and remake our most existential sense of being in the cosmos"[9] – *atsü tsü* enables the renewal to the commitment of individual to the collective. The IP Ao Naga held the worldview that bountiful harvest is not only for the family but for the whole community. As it was described above, when a family had a bountiful harvest, they shared their abundance by slaughtering a mithun for two primary reasons. Firstly, to give thanks to the sacred one (Lijaba) for the bountiful harvest because a good harvest was believed to be God's favor upon one's effort of tending the earth. Secondly, to share with the community members, this included friends from the neighboring villages as well. *Atsü tsü* was therefore a religio-cultural rite of sacrifice to give thanks and provide social cohesion or flourish of the community. Once, a family has committed to perform an *atsü tsü* they were obliged to complete the ritual even when the harvest was not sufficient.

Atsü tsü of the Ao Naga Indigenous people clearly expresses the relational aspects of human living – which can be restated as: what is good for an individual or particular family is only good if it benefits the community. A bountiful harvest had meaning when it was shared, contra accumulation. Sharing their plenty brought new identity to the performer and solidified social relationships, ensuring friendship. As Bell summarizes, the value of ritual is in its transcultural method of "promot[ing] a sense of common humanity";[10] *atsü tsü* among the Ao Naga nurtured a shared social cohesion that was critically important for collective survival. The practice of sharing one's good fortune with neighbors has the potential to help those with a lesser harvest – those threatened with hunger until the next sowing and harvest season.

COMPARATIVE DIALOGUE BETWEEN *SAM-AE* SPIRIT & ATSÜ *TSÜ*

The challenges of poverty and the deep levels of inequality that continue to plague humanity clearly calls for an alternative mechanism and practice to replace existing structures and attitudes marked by self-gain and

[9] Catherine Bell, *Ritual: Perspectives and Dimensions* (Oxford: Oxford University Press, 1997), 264.

[10] Bell, *Ritual*, 266.

accumulation at the expense of neighbors and the natural world. The concept of *Sam-ae* Spirit formulated and practiced by Pai Min-Soo is worthwhile to explore in relation to the *atsü tsü* ritual of Ao Naga of the Indo-Myanmar mountainous region. As observed earlier, the realities of poverty and its debilitating conditions exist across the global communities, while the wealth of the rich doubled during the pandemic.[11] The realities of present times might be different compared to the conditions of exploitation imposed by imperial powers, yet the struggles of the poor and the destruction of the eco-system is not very different. Pai Min-Soo developed the *Sam-ae* Spirit to counter the oppression of colonial structures and emancipate the poor. *Sam-ae* Spirit finds expression in three approaches to counter the conditions that produced debilitating poverty during Korea's transition to a modern-industrial nation: love for God, love for humanity, and love for work. Pai Min-Soo saw in the local tradition of *Sam-ae* Spirit the resources to undergird the movement to flourish as a community. As Chammah J. Kaunda and Sang-man Kim aptly summarize, the "hermeneutical point of departure was to engage and transform the mindset that shaped the imaginations of rural people in order to empower them to understand their struggles and move to issues of rural development through embracing the *Samae* spirit."[12]

LOVE FOR GOD AND ACKNOWLEDGMENT OF WEALTH

In the concept of *Sam-ae* Spirit, according to Pai Min-Soo, love for God was central to the life of the faithful. Love for God becomes the fulcrum for any movement seeking emancipation and prosperity for humanity. Loving God enables love for the common good:

> Now let us love God, and let us love others as He taught us to. He who loves God must also love other people and he who does not love other people who can be seen cannot love God who cannot be seen. Therefore, to love God is to obey and put into practice the law that God has commanded. Loving others is at the center of God's principle and truth, which will open the path to your life.[13]

---

[11] "Wealth of World's 10 Richest Men Doubled in Pandemic, Oxfam Says," *BBC News*, 17 Jan. 2022, https://www.bbc.com/news/business-60015294.

[12] Chammah J. Kaunda and Kim Sang-man, "'Samae Spirit' Assist toward 'Ubuntu Spirit' Model for Rural Adult Christian Education in Zambia," *Religious Education* 117, no. 1 (2022): 40.

[13] Qtd. in Kim Wang-Bae, "Introspection in the Post-human Era and Reverend Pai Min-Soo's 'Sam-ae' Spirit," 32.

Pai Min-Soo's source of inspiration for the movement for rural emancipation was a conscious awareness of God and the response it entailed. Love for God affirms a faith that recognizes that humanity begins in God and the final accountability rests in God. When there is love for God, there is recognition that all goodness and well-being such as bountiful harvest is from God. Human's flourish is not isolated, neither is it accounted as independent, but rather, the good enjoyed by humanity is considered as God's blessing. In the ritual of *atsü tsü* of Ao Naga, the primary rationale for the performance of the ritual is acknowledgement of God's provision to human efforts. An awareness of sacred/God/power transcending human level of existence is a marked characteristic shared across different IP groups across the globe. Therefore, the acknowledgement of God's blessing is natural to them, and find expression in forms of sacrifice and worship. A pre-Christian ritual of the Ao Naga IP therefore supplements the *Sam-ae* Spirit that positions love for God as the point of departure for movement of emancipation and economic justice. A movement for human flourish can be sustained when there is an inspiration fed by recognition of a creator and sustainer. A conversation between *Sam-ae* Spirit and *atsü tsü*, therefore complements the vision of a shared humanity, made possible by loving God.

LOVE FOR HUMANITY AND WEALTH SHARING

Love for God manifests in love for humanity. And to love is to share. Pai Min-Soo's movement of *Sam-ae* Spirit understood this fact. That humanity is an inter-related, inter-dependent web of existence is central to *Sam-ae* Spirit's love for humanity. The rural revitalization movement initiated by Pai Min-Soo was driven by his love for humanity, especially the poor and marginalized in post-war Korean society undergoing modernization. The rural movement of revitalization was supported by collaborations in the community and formation of cooperatives. By their nature, cooperatives entail mutual trust and care among the members. Inspired by other global movements of cooperatives, the spirit of cooperatives that Pai Min-Soo was purposed "to lead a cooperative life of mutual aid apart from unlimited selfish privatization."[14] The centrality of community wherein love for one another finds expression and is put into practice has a rich history in Christianity. Dietrich Bonhoeffer and the underground seminary of Finkenwalde during the brutal regime of the National Socialists is one such example. Influenced and inspired by his travels in the USA, Bonhoeffer

---

[14] Kim, "Introspection in the Post-human Era," 33.

started Finkenwalde Seminary to provide a model of a community that survives through cooperation among its members.[15]

A community that loves God loves one another – this might sound simplistic, yet, where there is love for God, a love for humanity is a natural consequence. As in the ritual of *atsü tsü*, the recognition of God's blessings engenders the sharing of a bountiful harvest with one's neighbors. Love for God motivates love for humanity, and where there is love, there is radical care for the welfare of one's neighbors. Pai Min-Soo's movement of rural cooperative was rooted in a deep love for humanity, which fostered collective efforts leading to a holistic improvement of the community. To envision the common good is to believe in a shared humanity as it is also encapsulated by the concept of Ubuntu. Writing on *Ubuntu*, Michael Onyebuchi Eze, contends that a person is a person through other people.[16] The notion of a shared humanity is best expressed in relationships of care, as Eze expounds on this awareness of a shared humanity in relationships:

> A person is person through other people strikes an affirmation of one's humanity through recognition of an "other" in his or her uniqueness and difference.... This idealism suggests to us that humanity is not embedded in my person solely as an individual; my humanity s co-substantively bestowed upon the other and me. Humanity is a quality we owe to each other. We create each other and need to sustain this otherness creation. And if we belong to each other, we participate in our creations: we are because you are, and since you are, definitely I am.[17]

LOVE FOR WORK AND SELF-SUSTENANCE

Pai Min-Soo developed the *Sam-ae* movement to revitalize rural lives within the context of Confucian culture, wherein a rigid hierarchy of social status was operative. This entrenched hierarchy influenced people's attitudes towards labor and the poor workers of the land as being lower in status, while the members of the higher ruling social class were exempt from labor. Pai Min-Soo understood the destructive consequences of social hierarchies and the detriment to the individual and society wrought by social privilege. The following quote from Pai Min-Soo spells out the conditions that called for reforming attitudes regarding labor:

---

[15] For more details, see Dietrich Bonhoeffer, *Dietrich Bonhoeffer Works, Volume 14: Theological Education at Finkenwalde, 1935-1937*, trans. Douglas W. Stott (Minneapolis, MN: Fortress Press, 2013).

[16] Michael Onyebuchi Eze, *Intellectual History in Contemporary South Africa* (New York Palgrave Macmillan, 2010), 155.

[17] Eze, *Intellectual History*, 190-191.

> The reason we have become so miserable is because we have hated, feared, and humbled (sic) labor since ancient times.... This evil outlook on labor still remains and workers envy those who do nothing but enjoy their free time and eat as they please, and those who are so privileged disrespect workers, shout at them, and harass them. This sense of superiority and a sense of desperation by being pampered and being looked down upon, respectively, is still prevalent.[18]

One of the distinguishing aspects of IP communities is the relative egalitarian relationship existing between different categories such as men, women, young and old, rich and poor. All the members of the community perform duties and labor as required to meet the needs of the family. IP communities in many contexts also exhibit shared labor for the community, such as clearing the common path, cleaning the village water source, and building the community house. Labor was not a mark of distinction, labor was an essential part of sustenance. Every household grew their own food and collected their own firewood. In many IP communities, to work, to labor was a matter of pride. Therefore, the direction of *Sam-ae* Spirit to appreciate labor in a context of rigid hierarchy is one aspect that differs significantly. However, the ritual of *atsü tsü* affirms labor for the sake of self-sustenance and community cooperative in a similar manner to Pai Min-Soo's call. Respect for labor and collective labor for the good of the community, an inclusive practice in the community is engendered. Furthermore, labor for the purposes of providing for the community can be understood as antidote to personal greed. To labor each season for a sufficient harvest, instead of exploitative labor seeking profit and accumulation helps fulfill a crucial need: care of the environment. Toiling as needed for one season and rituals of sharing a plentiful harvest express a respect for the natural rhythm: sowing and harvest. The worldview undergirding *atsü tsü* – that wealth is for stewardship not accumulation – indicates an openness to labor at the right time for the right purpose. When one's goal is not accumulation nor merely individual benefit, then the *Sam-ae* Spirit of love for labor is established as an attitude for the common good. A balance of consumption and labor is needed today to counter the depletion of natural resources with the greed and accumulation of resources by the few. In her book, *The Mercy of God for a Planet in Peril,* the feminist theologian Elizabeth Johnson, calls for eco-

---

[18] Qtd. in Kim Wang-Bae, "Introspection in the Post-human Era and Reverent Pai Min-Soo's '*Sam-ae*' Spirit," 35. Work, labor and productivity need, however, be self-regulated and balanced, to avoid making work as an instrument of accumulation. For more discussion, see Michael Barram, *Biblical Justice and Christian Formation*. (Grand Rapids, MI: William B. Eerdmans Publishing, 2018), 13-14.

justice by making "[t]he profound step of conversion to the earth as God's beloved creation."[19] She continues,

> This is the turning that will impact our whole lives. It will expand our understanding of the God we are called to love with all our heart and soul, mind and strength, making clear that the Creator is also the Redeemer who accompanies the whole natural world with saving compassion. It will also expand the neighbor we are called to love as ourselves, since the beaten-up traveller left by the side of the road whose wounds we must tend to includes needy and poor human beings along with natural ecosystems and all their creatures.[20]

It is important to heed her criticism of selfish anthropocentrism that has put the planet in peril and embrace an attitude that affirms God's love for all creation.

CONCLUSION

Joseph Stiglitz, writing in the beginning of this century on evaluating globalization stated optimistically that globalization can be a force of good, if reformed and regulated. At the same time, Stiglitz, cautioned with realism, that "making globalization work will not be easy" because "those who benefit from the current system [globalization] will resist change, and they are very powerful."[21] Humanity indeed has made tremendous progress in every aspect of life, generating humungous wealth and drawing diverse cultures together. However, such progress and wealth has not benefitted all creation. In fact, environmentally, humanity faces unprecedented climate change that threatens existence. Therefore, the challenge posed by the nobel laureate in economics, Stiglitz, "how to make globalization work?" remains a pressing question. In exploring urgent answer to make the tremendous wealth and technological advancement work to fight poverty and injustice, the resources of *Sam-ae* Spirit supplemented by *atsü tsü* are viable alternatives.

---

[19] Elizabeth A. Johnson, *Creation and the Cross: The Mercy of God for a Planet in Peril* (Maryknoll, NY: Orbis Books, 2018), 195-196.

[20] Johnson, *Creation and the Cross*, 222.

[21] Joseph Stiglitz, *Making Globalization Work* (New Delhi: Penguin Books, 2007), 13.

CHAPTER 4

SAM-AE SPIRIT AND *AZOUK A MOH* SPIRIT: A SEARCH FOR SOLIDARITY OF ECONOMIC AND SOCIAL EMPOWERMENT THROUGH FARMING INITIATIVES AMONG WOMEN GROUPS IN OBANG OF CAMEROON

FELIX KANG ESOH

INTRODUCTION

Different economic strategies have been attempted to bail out the Cameroonian economy by substituting a Social Solidarity Economy (SSE) as a viable alternative. SSE increasingly plays an important role in sustainable and inclusive development.[1] With the recent trends of extended poverty and dwindling state involvement in local development, small group networks are being seen as vectors of local development and social transformation in the North West Region of Cameroon.[2] Over the years, there have been several cooperative movements with similar objectives.[3]

This article employs the possibility of *azouk a moh* (one spirit)[4] farming initiatives among the women of Obang from the prism of Pai Min-Soo's *Sam-ae* Spirit as a concrete way of translating SSE for rural social

---

[1] See Susan Steinman, "*Public Policies for the Social and Solidarity Economy: Towards an Enabling Environment: The Case of South Africa,*" (Turin, ITC-ILO, 2017). UNRISD, *Policy Innovations for Transformative Change: Implementing the 2030 Agenda for Sustainable Development* (UNRISD,2016).

[2] Charles C. Fochingong, "The Mechanics of Communitarianism and Social Capital in North -West Cameroon," *International Development Planning Review* 27, no. 4 (2005): 427-449; Charles C. Fochingong and Canute A. Ngwa, "Grassroots Participation for Infrastructural Provisioning in North-West Cameroon: Are Village Development Associations the Panacea," *Canadian Journal of Development Studies* 26, no. 3 (2005): 443-460.

[3] Noelle Lechat, "Organizing for the Solidarity Economy in South Brazil," in *The Social Economy: International Perspectives on Economic Solidarity*, ed. A. Amin (London: Zed Books, 2009): 159-175.

[4] *Azouk a moh* (one spirit) is an Obang cultural concept which refers to the idea of group solidarity. It expresses the fact that group solidarity remains an important capital for societal emancipation and development. The notion that "together we stand, divided we fall" encapsulates the essence of *azouk a moh* for the Obang people.

transformation in Cameroon. The *Sam-ae* Spirit model refers to a trinitarian spirit of love: love for God; love for people/community, and love for work. Pai used this theory to emphasize the role solidarity among people plays in social emancipation and the benefits of group solidarity in community development. Seen as a new way of mobilizing to reverse the dissipations of capitalism towards citizens' emancipation, this study discovers the motivation of *azouk a moh* solidarity from the perspective of citizens organizing from below. Solidarity is situated within the sphere of people propelled development with religio-cultural identity and social capital as a strong orientation. The following questions are vital for this study: What lessons can *azouk a moh* learn from the *Sam-ae* Spirit model to create a social solidarity based economic model for rural women in Obang, Cameroon? Can small village-group solidarity contribute to freeing women from their position as non-economic entities, and then re-situate them into agents of socio-economic transformation of society?

This paper suggests the importance of *azouk a moh* in the light of the indigenous Korean *Sam-ae* Spirit as both a contextual theory for inculturating the Christian faith and a practical approach to rural social change.[5] The momentum of this approach draws from the bottom-up features of solidarity drawn from empirical data among the Obang women groups,[6] unrivalled in local development discourses. Hence, how the *Sam-ae* Spirit galvanizes local capital to promote emancipation and development through group solidarity forms a good conceptual framework for how *azouk a moh* might assist in proffering the social and economic transformation of the rural masses in Obang. Let us briefly look at *azouk a moh* within the general notion of Social Solidarity Economy.

AZOUK A MOH AS SOCIAL SOLIDARITY ECONOMY: A THEORETICAL PERSPECTIVE

> Solidarity economics embraces a plural and cultural view of economy as a complex space of social relationship in which individuals, communities, and organizations generate livelihoods through many

---

[5] Chammah J. Kaunda and Sang-man Kim, "'Samae Spirit' Assist toward 'Ubuntu Spirit' Model for Rural Adult Christian Education in Zambia," in *Religious Education* 117, no. 1 (2022): 33-49.

[6] Although this study constantly refers to these groups as "Women Groups," they are increasingly becoming mixed groups of men and women. In the Obang cosmology, farming in general carries a feminine connotation.

different means, with different motivations and aspirations – not just maximization of individual gain.[7]

Unlike the profiteering agenda of capitalist propelled elites/state organizations, SSE is an alternative informed by ethical and social goals. This new configuration subordinate's profits and market relationships under the ideals of community emancipation.[8] Small groups, religious and non-religious are championing the course of community development due to lessening state intervention. Bolstered by a strong feeling of love, social justice, mutual help, social/economic empowerment, ecological consciousness, and a common destiny, *azouk a moh* (one spirit) farming groups among women (Christians and non-Christians) in Obang, Cameroon, have been contributing to their socio-economic and community transformation.[9]

The seemingly incapacity or unwillingness of post-colonial states in Africa to guarantee basic life jackets and livelihoods for its citizens, is evidenced in the continuous subjugation of the masses by a few elites. In protest, forms of identity, affiliations, and access to resources are being reconceptualized in terms of one's place within a social order established on family, kinship, and community relationships.[10] One of the things that distinguishes the Obang people is their strong bond with one another and their community. Group solidarity is an essential element in their religion and culture, expressed through ritual activities, ceremonies, and festivals that bring the people together.[11]

Within the Obang cosmology, *azouk e moh* embodies the idea of group solidarity from the very prism of love deeply engrained in the relationship between the supreme being, humanity, and creation. It combines elements of social responsibility with those of environmental accountability. In the Obang world, *azouk a moh* sees creation as an integrated dynamic connection of love for humanity rooted in the supreme being. *Azouk a moh* combines to words,

---

[7] See Ethan Miller, "Other Economies Are Possible!" *Dollars & Sense* 266, no. 11 (2006); and Charles Che Fonchingong, "Citizen Strategizing Amid a Solidarity Economy in Cameroon: Are Village Development Associations (VDAs) Resilient?" Draft paper prepared for the *UNRISD Conference*: Potential and Limits of Social and Solidarity Economy, 6–8 May 2013 (Geneva, Switzerland, 2013).

[8] Democratic Left Front (DLF), "South Africa: Building the Solidarity Economy from Below," *Pambazuka News* 513 (2011).

[9] Through such solidarities, women who used to till a single farm are now able of have more than two, three or even five farms depending on the number of groups they belong to.

[10] Fonchingong, "Citizen Strategizing Amid a Solidarity Economy in Cameroon."

[11] Felix Kang Esoh, "Christianity and *Sarh/Ezul* (Libation) in Obang, Cameroon: A Cultural Historical Reconstruction," *Unpublished PhD Dissertation* (South Korea: Yonsei University, 2019).

azouk (breath, spirit, power, force) and *moh* (one) to express the idea of oneness, relationship and relatedness. Like the generality of African societies, *azouk a moh* sees existence as an integrated reality. For most African societies, life is a continuum of social, cosmic, personal and communal event, from which they develop their ideas of group solidarity.[12] Jean Marc Ela refers to the notion of group solidarity among Africans as a 'sacramental act,' during which the people are called to live out the values of the Kingdom.[13] *Azouk a moh* reflects the concept of *ubuntu* (community-driven) as part of the generalities of the African heritage.[14] It follows Mbiti's summation of African solidarity in his famous Kamba prism, "I am because we are; and since we are, therefore I am."[15] *Azouk a moh* is a system that deprioritizes sovereignty as an individualistic notion and prioritizes the sense of community, as opposed to the Western individualization of theology (ideology).[16]

Like *ubuntu*, *azouk a moh* subtly rules out the Western concept as espoused by Rene Descartes' philosophical approach: *cogito ergo sum* (I am therefore I exist). *Azouk a moh* articulates the ubuntu spirit of interdependency and expresses the fact that no one is born fully formed, for, everyone is born into a community with each person always needing others. For the Obang people, a child belongs to the mother only when it is in the womb. As soon as one is born, one automatically belongs a member of the community. Therefore, within the framework of 'community spirit,' *azouk a moh* has become a platform for women social solidarity endeavor through which they take charge of their lives and their future.

Social Solidarity Economy suggests an overturning of conventional approaches to both the processes and the meaning of development. Unlike the idea of development as defined by elite super structures, social solidarity networks suggest a turn towards the under-exploited agencies (women and the Marginalized) of village or base communities. The notions of social relations, based on supportive association, capable of guiding local development are

---

[12] John S. Mbiti, *Introduction to African Traditional Religion* (London: Heinemann, 1975), 164-165. See also Kwesi W. Dickson, *Theology in Africa* (Maryknoll, New York: Darton, Longman & Todd, 1984), 62.

[13] Jean Marc Ela, *My Faith as an African* (Eugene, Oregon: WIPF & STOCK publishers, 1988).

[14] Julius Gathogo, "John Mbiti's Ubuntu Theology: Was Rooted in his African heritage," *Studia Historiae Ecclesiasticae*, (2022): 1-22.

[15] John Samuel Mbiti, *African Religions and Philosophy* (London: Heinemann, 1969); 108.

[16] Gathogo, "John Mbiti's Ubuntu Theology: Was Rooted in his African heritage,"

fundamental functions of a social solidarity economy,[17] otherwise known as "the communalistic perspective in African theological discourses."[18]

Azouk a moh articulate Africa's ubuntu theology, what Gathogo refers to as 'relational theology':

> Which necessitates a deeper dialogue between people's experiences and indigenous resources of the African peoples, as the hallmark of authentic Christian faith in tropical Africa. It also points to the importance of celestial and human hospitality, which is an ideal goal and trajectory of being in Africa, as it acknowledges both the humanity of others and the theo-social diversity of others as God's plan for the world. Ubuntu theology… is dialogical, inclusive, community-driven, humane, just, and methodologically contextual and reconstructive in its motif.[19]

An important trajectory in understanding African religio-culture and worldview is the value of 'community-mindedness.' Most African cultures have serious affinity to their communities, where transactional and supportive initiatives are reached through bonding and forming meaningful relationships. Community consciousness is essential in social capital development. Social capital defines contexts in which transactional and supportive initiatives are reached through bonding and forming meaningful relationships. Social here is "concerned with human beings in their relations to each other, their living conditions, and living together in organized communities."[20] Castles suggests that social transformation usually takes place in respond to unstable economic and political environments usually characterized by upheavals and war.[21] In fact, social solidarity economy describes the change influence on local and national communities by global processes.

Applying this to the Cameroonian (Obang) context, social transformation refers to the ways in which different women groups respond by carving out a space for their social, political and economic inclusion following a long period of exclusion. As a fundamental technique in human development, family, social groups or village solidarity resides on the efforts of village groups to

---

[17] David Barkin & Blanca Lemus, "Rethinking the social and solidarity society in light of community practice," *Towards Sustainability* 6, no. 9 (2014): 6432–6445. Donghyun Kim and Up Lim, "Social enterprise as a Catalyst for Sustainable Local and Regional Development." *Towards Sustainability* 9, no. 8 (2017): 1427. Peter Utting, *Public Policies for the Social and Solidarity Economy: Assessing Progress in Seven Countries* (Geneva: International Labour Organization, 2017).

[18] Gathogo, "John Mbiti's Ubuntu Theology," *6.*

[19] Ibid., 4.

[20] Cornie Groenewald, "Social Transformation: Between Globalization and Localization," *Scriptura* 72 (2000): 15-19.

[21] Castles, "Development, Social Transformation and Globalization," 1.

improve local community access to scarce financing and essential services, all geared for livelihoods improvement. Guaranteeing these initiatives on a sustainable footing remains a daunting challenge for most developing economies. The following paragraphs present a brief description of the context of Obang that led to the great shift in gender considerations.

SETTING/ECONOMY OF OBANG & THE GROWING INFLUENCE OF WOMEN GROUPS

The Obang valley is located in the North West Region of the Republic of Cameroon. The land is largely arable, and endowed with unexploited numerous resources including timber and non-timber products. About 90 % of the territory is plain where rice, maize, groundnuts and other agrarian activities take place. It is a fertile alluvial valley with through which the river Mezam flows, and rich in fish, tadpoles, and sand. It is the main supplier of sand and river fish between Mezam and Menchum divisions of the North West region of Cameroon. The extensive undulating terrain is backed by a moderate climate congenial for cattle herding and market gardening.[22]

Before the late 1980s when the world economic crisis hit Cameroon, the rice sector and other economic activities in Obang were essentially male dominated activities with women only assisting. Women only went as far as tilling, planting and harvesting were concerned, while the selling was a preserve of the men. Precolonial and colonial economies created more opportunities for Obang men than women.[23] Men colonized the commercialization of crops like rice and coffee during this time. While the women were left to fend for the family through other means, the proceeds from the commercial products of the men were either used to invest in more lands, or to get marry to more women. The more the farm lands and more women, the more the men became influential in the society.[24]

In fact, Obang men dominated the women in almost all the sectors of their agrarian life: rice and maize production, palm oil production, cultivation and processing of coffee, timber exploitation, fishing, tapping, hunting and carving. Che argues that the main reason for male dominance in these sectors was the fact that women were mostly considered to be house

---

[22] Beicho Vivian Che, "The Origin and Evolution of Obang Village from Precolonial Period – 1996," unpublished *research project* (Buea: University of Buea, 1998).

[23] Henry Kam Kah, "Gender and Livestock Farming in Laimbweland, Cameroon, 1980s-2011," *Journal of Sustainable Development in Africa* 15, no. 1 (2013): 56-72.

[24] Men maintain their dignity by the number of wives they marrying and the number of farms they own. See Che, "The Origin and Evolution of Obang Village."

wives only limited to domestic affairs, like tending the children, cooking and keeping the home for the husband.[25]

By the early 1980s, agriculture was boosted by the introduction of the government's Five-Year Development Plans, aimed at promoting the production of other subsistence and economic crops.[26] Unfortunately, the plan could not work due to the general economic decline. With the rising cost of managing the growing families resting on the men, the scenario could not remain the same, and eventually, women would become the unmatched locomotive of rural economic development.[27] Today, Obang women are effectively playing the role of "bread winners" in the family and society. What the present Fon of Obang calls "the Obang agricultural miracle," has resulted from the manner in which through group solidarities, women have revolutionized the farming sector.[28] The question is why the sudden change in the fortunes of these women and the village? While the answer to this question is often provided to credit the men for opening up to women, the rise in women consciousness through the creation of small groups is very important.

This growing consciousness among women in Cameroon can be traced to the initiatives by the wives of the Basel missionaries who started introducing women to basic home crafts, sewing and hygiene way back in the 1930s.[29] By the 1960s, the women's work in the churches had been extended to include their social and economic emancipation. Keller notes that "work among women helped in an excellent way in building up the Christian Congregation."[30] Since then, the empowerment of women has been a regular feature in the programs of the Women Department of the Presbyterian Church in Cameroon. The Christian Women Fellowship (CWF) was officially created and registered as a Christian movement in 1961 with

---

[25] Che, "The Origin and Evolution of Obang Village from precolonial Period – 1996."

[26] Henry Kam Kah, "Local Government and Nation-Building in Wum Division, 1949-1972," *M.A. Thesis* (Buea: University of Buea, 1998), 122.

[27] Henry Kam Kah, "Women Resistance in Cameroon's Western Grassfields 1957-1961: Power of Symbols, Superb Organization and Leadership," *African Studies Quarterly* 12, no. 3 (2011a): 1-25; Henry Kam Kah, "'The Cutlass my Husband, the Hoe my Wife:' Women and Economic Development among the Laimbwe of the North West Cameroon in Contemporary Times," *Kaliao: Revue Pluridisiplinaire de L'ecole Normale Superieure Maroua (Cameroon)* 3, no. 5 (2011): 9-22.

[28] Fon Nanoh III is the present traditional ruler (Fon) of the Obang clan. It is during his reign that most of the transformations have taken place.

[29] Werner Keller and Jörg Schnellbach, *The History of the Presbyterian Church in West Cameroon: A Survey of the General Development of the Presbyterian Church in Cameroon Up to 1960* (PCC: Radio and Literature Department, 1968).

[30] Keller, *The History of the Presbyterian Church in West Cameroon,* 120.

an annual Study Book with a regular column on Gender and Development, focused on the mainstreaming of women in local and national development.[31] The projects started by employing strategies to alleviate the situation of vulnerable persons with particular attention to widows. Though it was initially limited to programs for the alleviation of the conditions of widows, it was extended to include women in general.

Through these initiatives, Christian women groups started constituting themselves into small self-help initiatives, and gradually extending their boundaries to help each other in economic sustainable activities within and out of the church. Otherwise known as "njangi" groups, these social solidarity initiatives which started through Christian women groups are being re-conceptualized in different ways, with women constituting themselves into small groups specifically for their empowerment and sustainability.[32] These initiatives which started among women of the Christian Women Fellowship of the PCC, like in other women groups of the Cameroon Baptist Convention and the Roman Catholic Mission, have been multiplied into other village groups like, *awuoh ka awuoh* (hand to hand); *Awuoh ka nyise* (putting hands); *item e moh* (one heart); *Awuoh ki ghran* (hands to till); generally conceptualized as *azouk moh* (one spirit).[33] Unlike the Christian women groups which include only women of their respective denominations, the other village women groups cut across denominational boundaries, and in some cases, they even include settler populations and men.

METHODOLOGY

The methodology used in this study is pluri-disciplinary and employed over a long period of time. We organized a series of face-to-face interviews with individuals (women and men) and focus group discussions in the area of study. This study benefited from our personal experience gathered over the years of observing women cope within a resource-constrained environment, with little or no government or limited state subvention in livelihoods, particularly in the rural areas. This phenomenal study uncovers the basis of solidarity economies

[31] For instance, in 2021, under the column on "Gender and Development," the book included the topic "Gender and Poverty: An Inclusive Approach in Eradicating extreme poverty." See "Cast All Your Burdens on to the Lord: For He Cares for You," *CWF/CMF Study Book*, Presbyterian Church in Cameroon, 2021.

[32] Vivian Bang, *Interview*, 14 Mar. 2020.

[33] Felicitas Iseh, Interviewed, 12 Jan. 2020. At this time, she was the Women's Work Helper of the CWF of the Presbyterian Church in Cameroon. Her task was to train and encourage women groups on sustainable activities.

through the *azouk a moh* philosophy. From these, we observed the changes that have taken place from what obtained in the past, from relegation, to women strategizing to resolve issues of their peripheral disadvantage.[34]

Our interviews (face-to-face and through phone calls) and observations probed the factors that contributed to the observable transformations and the ramifications on gender relations and sustainable development. As an exploratory case study, we utilized information obtained from varied sources. Exploratory case studies provide insights into and a core understanding of the phenomenon, enabling a deeper assembly of core opinions, motivations and reasons, taking into consideration the potential flaws in data generation and analysis which results from the researcher's subjectivity in observing and reporting.[35]

Through observations and interviews, the study revealed that though the women have greatly transformed the economy and livelihood of the Obang community, gender stereotypes still exist in the rice sector. Resistance to women entering this space is still very strong but it is gradually reducing today than it used to be. Today a good number of women, including widows are increasingly becoming bread-winners for the family.

TRANSFORMATION OF RICE FARMING IN OBANG

Through *azouk a moh* (one spirit) solidarity, Obang women are effectively playing the role of 'bread-winners' for their families and society today. The reason for this sudden transformation, what the traditional ruler of Obang refers to as the "Obang Economic Miracle" are diverse: political, social, economic, cultural and religious.[36] The background to the Obang economic transformation in the late 1980s and 1990s like the rest of Cameroon reflects a report on "Sustainable Agriculture and Rural Development in Cameroon":

> In 1986, a serious economic crisis struck the country as a result of changes in the world commodity market. The value of the export products such as cacao and coffee fell drastically and remained low. The consequences were felt throughout the countryside. Subsidies were completely removed and most agricultural development projects

[34] Charles Che Fonchingong, "Re-inventing Community Development: Utilising Relational Networking and Cultural Assets for Infrastructure Provision," *Societies* 8, no. 3 (2018); 84.

[35] Che and Mbah, "Social Solidarity Economy and Village-Centric Development in North-West Cameroon," 7; R.K. Yin, Qualitataive Research from start to finish (Guildford Press, 2011); Fonchingong, "Re-inventing Community Development," 7.

[36] Fon Nanoh III is the chief of Obang. As a Christian himself, he acknowledges the role the Church is playing in societal transformation through the emancipation and inclusion of women in community development. Interviewed in January 2021.

> collapsed. Poverty increased in the rural areas and thousands of people had to receive food aid.[37]

The statement above summarizes the economic meltdown that affected the country, especially those in the rural country-side to which Obang belongs. The challenges that followed the economic crisis almost compromised the Obang economy, if not of the changing gender roles leading to the accommodation of women into rice farming. Before now, women simply assisted their husbands in rice farming and had little or no say in the management of the results.[38] Women started occupying this space and contributing following the challenges of the economy and the devaluation of the franc CFA in the 1990s. Initially, the integration of women into this male arena was not taken lightly by a majority of men who saw that as a challenge, especially as it was going to economically empower the women and may eventually bring them to the same level as men. However, such opposition could not deter the women who were motivated by their economic conditions (especially the widows) and their solidarity in assisting one another.

Population changes equally posed great challenge to rice farming in Obang. These changes were multi-dimensional; growth of dependent population (women and children) in Obang resulting from early marriages and sexual promiscuity, declining mortality rate among men, increase in number of widows, the challenges of polygamous homes, and the increase phenomenon of single motherhood. Giving all these, a majority of women were left on their own to provide for their needs and that of their families, including the education of their children.[39] They could not manage all these from the meagre sums they make from groundnut, vegetables and cocoyam, beans, potatoes, okra, soyabeans, ginger, etc.[40] The proceeds from these could take care of some minor issues and not the major ones like education and the event of illness.

As stated earlier, the changing political climate in Cameroon which followed the liberalization laws saw the introduction of many political parties away from the single party that existed before 1990.[41] The participation of

---

[37] Henry Kam Kah, "Gender and Livestock Farming in Laimbweland, Cameroon, 1980s-2011," *Journal of Sustainable Development in Africa* 15, no. 1 (2013): 56 -72.

[38] Che, "The Origin and Evolution of Obang Village from precolonial Period – 1996,"

[39] Rebecca Bih, *Interview* (Obang, 2016).

[40] Some of the women we interviewed said the crops were produced in large quantities but could not give them profits like rice which was the main economic crop in the area.

[41] Robert Mbe Akoko, *"Ask and You Shall Be Given": Pentecostalism and the Economic Crisis in Cameroon* (Leiden, Netherlands: African Studies Centre, 2007).

more men in the initial movements for the introduction of multipartyism resulted in a decline in their farming activities. They became mobile moving from cities to cities abandoning the family to their wives, as a result, their wives were left behind to save the families from total collapse.[42]

Furthermore, cultural norms which previously prevented women from owning farm lands are greatly changing as a result of globalization. The society is being influenced by elites who have either lived in big cities like Bamenda, Douala, Yaounde, etc., or through education, they have come in contact with changing gender roles. Such men do not consider sharing their properties among their male and female children alike, as a way of empowering their children. These moves have encouraged them to keep their farms and eternalized in them the sense of independence in the future.

Above all, the Church has greatly contributed in the social, political, cultural and economic emancipation of the women in Obang. Since 1961, with the introduction of the Women's Department of the Presbyterian Church in Cameroon (PCC) and subsequently other Christian women groups of the Cameroon Baptist Convention and the Roman Catholic Church in Cameroon, a lot has been done in the area of women empowerment. For instance, the Christian Women Fellowship (CWF) of the PCC regularly organizes seminars and courses for the economic empowerment of women.[43] The activities of the CWF groups, especially those of the rural areas, include cooperative farming and 'njangi' to assist one another. These initiatives have been replicated in the village by forming farming groups that go beyond denominational boarders. Most of the women farming groups are made of majority Christian women. (Catholics, Baptist, Presbyterians, etc.).

TOWARDS A SOCIO-CULTURAL & RELIGIOUS ENTERPRISE MODEL

The above discussions highlight several connections between the Obang concept of *azouk a moh* and Pai's *Sam-ae* Spirit model from the perspective of social solidarity economy. Their connectedness is based on the fact that both are geared towards the rehabilitation of rural communities as a whole, but most especially, the emancipation of the despised in the society. Based on his passionate endeavors toward the holistic liberation of Koreans under Japanese colonialism, Pai's theological pursued led him to a shift from the

---

[42] A majority of such persons have not been able to return to the village, thereby leaving the women as custodians of their farm plots.

[43] At the end of the year, the groups are expected to exhibit the products learned from such seminars.

strict conservative Christian stands, to a more progressive and practical approach to Christianity. His ideas provide both a conceptual and practical paradigm for the framing of *azouk e moh* (one spirit) farming initiatives among women groups in Obang. Propelled by his passion for rural enlightenment and development: "Pai's work of love, mercy, and compassion for the rural and the people on the margins forced him to go against mainstream conservative Christianity to formulate Christian ideas that could help transform a fragmented and materially distressed rural society."[44]

Pai argued that the "dichotomy between the teaching of the Church and its practical life," is among the many problems inherited from early missionary approaches that did not effectively connect the gospel and the real life of the people.[45] According to him, the personal example of Jesus's life of love, should move every Christian toward relating the Christian life and community development, "the spiritual and practical life, the Kingdom of God on earth and the Kingdom of God in heaven, and the Church and society."[46]

Both Sam-ae Spirit and *azouk a moh* like the generalities of the African ubuntu worldview, sees religion and culture as essential elements in holistic development. Religion and culture permeate all aspects of life, including aesthetics, kinship, economics, ethics, and politics. In fact, social solidarity is intrinsic in religion and culture and entrenched in both concepts (*Sam-ae* Spirit and *azouk a moh)* and cannot be isolated from the numerous facets that form the pillars of African religio-cultural worldview.[47] Seen from the prism of ubuntu spirituality, *Sam-ae* Spirit and *azouk a moh* embrace the humanity of all and involve a belief system that is shared collectively. A belief system that is in tandem with the communal dimension of Christianity which seeks to give meaning to humanity and creation in an incarnational way. This was the perspective in which Pai pitched his dream and vision in translating the values of the kingdom of God in rural Korea. For him, the kingdom of God went beyond the salvation of soul to include that "A Christian way of bringing help to poverty-stricken people making life a little more comfortable and easier for them, sharing with them a technological

---

[44] Kaunda and Kim, "'Samae' Spirit Assist toward 'Ubuntu Spirit' Model for Rural Adult Christian Education in Zambia."

[45] Kaunda and Kim, "'Samae' Spirit Assist toward 'Ubuntu Spirit' Model." This idea resonates with the Cameroonian context which Jean Marc Ela describes and generalizes on the African continent; see Jean Marc Ela, *African Cry* (Maryknoll, New York: Orbis Books, 1986).

[46] Kaunda and Kim, "'Samae Spirit Assist toward 'Ubuntu Spirit' Model."

[47] Jesse N.K. Mungambi, *African Heritage and Contemporary Christianity* (Nairobi: Longman, 1989).

knowledge that has been discovered in other parts of the world . . . to elevating their physical conditions."[48]

In the context of the struggle for independence from Japanese colonization, Pai's *Sam-ae* Spirit model introduced a more sustainable paradigm of "reforming farmers' consciousness as imperative in the Korean search for independence."[49] In fact, in the situation of a 'transforming war,' Pai's approach could be referred to, as "beating their swords into plowshares, and their spears into pruning hooks" (*cf.* Isaiah 2:4), thus shifting the approach from an overt public revolution to a social solidarity revolution that transforms the mind and prepares a more sustainable future built on love and reconciliation. For Pai therefore, true independence starts with a conscientization of the most susceptible members of the society. In this process of emancipation, Che and Mbah note that, previous disadvantaged and excluded people in communities become conscious and stand as vanguards against oppressive structures and at the same time, constitute themselves as vectors of social transformation.[50]

The *Sam-ae* Spirit drives across Pai's rural development agenda as a galvanizing approach for rural Christian vitality. Like the *Sam-ae* Spirit, *azouk a moh* is characterized by group consciousness, hospitality, assistance, the promotion of human dignity and the sustainable management of creation. Pai took off from a hermeneutics that engages and transforms "the mindset that shaped the imaginations of rural people in order to empower them to understand their struggles and to move to issues of rural development through embracing the *Samae* spirit."[51] Like Jean Marc Ela puts it, "faith in the God of revelation cannot be lived and understood abstractly, in some temporal fashion. It can only be lived through the warp and woof of the events that make up history."[52] In most primal societies, religion plays a vital role toward positive change. Be it in the black struggles in the Americas or the struggles against Apartheid in South Africa, religion played a great role in the liberation of oppressed black people around the world. No matter the size of the group, religious groups are potential forces for social change.

In his conceptualization of the *Sam-ae* Spirit, Pai notes that, "the love for God provided a motive, a reason, and an obligation to love the farmers/

48 Adams qtd. in Kaunda and Kim, "'Samae' Spirit Assist Toward 'Ubuntu Spirit' Model," 40-41.

49 Kaunda and Kim, "'Samae' Spirit Assist toward 'Ubuntu Spirit' Model," 39.

50 Che & Mbah, "Social Solidarity Economy and Village-centric Development in North-West Cameroon."

51 Kaunda and Kim, "'Samae' Spirit Assist toward 'Ubuntu Spirit' Model," 39.

52 Ela, *My Faith as an African, 28.*

rural community (the *minjung*) and to love work/farming."[53] His motivation stemmed from his desire "to find out how to feed the hungry, clothe the naked, and help the needy ones as Jesus commanded."[54] Thus, by inspiring Christians toward their emancipation and economic sustainability, *Sam-ae* Spirit fits within God's plans of salvation, comparable to the divine 'preferential option for the poor.' Indeed, rural emancipation is a struggle against deprivation and at the same time, borrowing from *Fonchingong*,[55] a movement of populist forces yearning for alternatives, with citizens organizing from below.

According to Pai's trinity of "Love" – consisting of love for God; love for farm/work; love for community – the Church must be anchored upon the social, economic, cultural and political realities of humanity in general, and the rural people in particular. His 'Trinitarian Love' typology could be understood in the following ways: first, the love for God, seen from a perspective which shifts the narrative of development from an elite vintage point to a revitalized rural approach to development; second, the love for farm/work as new impetus to the whole idea of labor and the dignity of creation; third, the love for rural community as revitalizing their sense of community through social solidarity networking.

A socio-cultural and religious enterprise model that utilizes social solidarity economy gives citizens the chance to address excesses and shortfalls of capitalism and free markets. Social solidarity economy is based on rationality of common interests, and sets standards that help mitigate the exploitation of individuals by a few. A religio-cultural enterprise model's task is to reduce the burden on members through a business model that generates more resources for the single purpose of improving livelihoods for poverty-stricken citizens. As agriculture is backbone for most rural dwellers, creation of mutual agricultural cooperatives to better market goods and services is a proposition. Such schemes which hold both the potential of improving household cash income and reduce poverty, but at the same time may develop new oligarchies, should be guided by Samuels John's four ethical pillars of solidarity economy: ethical production, ethical investment, ethical market, and ethical consumption.[56] The core of solidarity is social

---

53 Kaunda and Kim, "'Samae' Spirit Assist toward 'Ubuntu Spirit' Model," 39.

54 Pai, quoted in Kaunda and Kim, "'Samae' Spirit Assist toward 'Ubuntu Spirit' Model," 40.

55 Foncingong, "Citizen Strategizing Amid a Solidarity Economy in Cameroon."

56 "Towards the Solidarity Economy," *Infochange*, Oct. 2008, http://base.socioeco.org/docs/doc-7832_en.pdf. Article based on John Samuel's keynote speech delivered at the Asian Meet on Solidarity Economy and Socially Responsible Business.

justice, impartiality, objectivity, fairness, and spreading of surplus while deemphasizing profit as driving force.

The following would constitute elements of a socio-cultural and religious enterprising model: first, the creation of Interdependent Supportive Networks (ISN like cooperatives and 'njangi' groups); second, needs mapping; third, Scaling-up incrementally; and fourth, Focus on the poor and marginalized. Poverty, soaring unemployment and inadequate access to essential services jeopardize and compromise efforts at community building.

CONCLUSION

Like the *Sam-ae* Spirit model, *azouk a moh* is a binding glue of Obang women strategizing, emblematic of a social solidarity economy for their social, economic, cultural and political emancipation. With focus on *azouk a moh* farming initiatives among the Obang women groups, this chapter has discussed some core elements of social solidarity economy buffered by social cohesive community and common good fostered by the spirit of mutual help. With lessons from Pai's *Sam-ae* Spirit, *azouk a moh* points to the proliferation of a wide variety of experiences involving women in Obang like other deprived persons all over the world. From a social perspective, the most important experience has been the resilience of the women folk and their gradual saturation of the previously held male-dominated agricultural spaces. Rather than crediting this to the willingness of men to incorporating women, we emphasize the unique character of Christian women groups and their importance in the emancipation and creating post capitalist communities, able to introduce ways to improve the well-being of the family and the development of the society.

Also, important is the revival of the structures of social relations, based on a cooperative organization capable of guiding the community's development and the lessons it lends to other communities and the developing state of which it is part. The two main fundamental features of social solidarity economy are: first, the ways in which different members and groups of the communities respond by carving out space for their social, political and economic inclusion, which was absent before now; and second, an overturning of conventional approaches to both the processes and meaning of development, one that turns away from super-structures in favor of marginalized agencies.

CHAPTER 5

SAM-AE SPIRIT AND UBUNTU SPIRIT AS PATHWAYS: A CRITIQUE OF PARTICULARISM IN INDIGENOUS AFRICAN (IGBO) COMMUNITIES

CYRIL EMEKA EJIKE & CHAMMAH J. KAUNDA

INTRODUCTION

In this study, we limit our exploration of particularism – exclusive attachment to, and interest in, one's own in-group (family, kinsfolk, kindred, community, or tribe) as well as exclusive dedication to one's self-interest – in traditional African society to particularism in indigenous Igbo communities. The Igbo community is concentrated in the Igbo homeland in Nigeria. The Igbo homeland mostly lies on the eastern side of the River Niger in south-eastern part of Nigeria, but a sizeable portion of it extends to the western side of the River Niger. A huge number of Igbo people reside in other parts of Nigeria, and abroad. Igbo traditional society bears the hallmark of communal life many contemporary African scholars have advanced and propagated as being essentially African. Igbo has a strong institution known as *ụmụnna* – literally 'father's children (kindred) but is usually employed to refer to a community of people bound by blood and religion. *Ụmụnna* is a repository of Igbo world-view (or philosophy) and its associated religious and socio-cultural practices. A good deal of Igbo religious philosophies (ideologies) and ethics and their associated religious and socio-cultural practices have been variously employed by many contemporary African scholars to frame African philosophy and religion that are grounded in communalism widely held to be the intrinsic and essential character of traditional African society. African communalism connotes a sense of community (or brotherhood) marked by life of communion or collectivity, solidarity, complementarity, and harmonious relationships that marks traditional African society off from western society characterized by individualism.

Nyerere articulated family-hood or common humanity through *Ujamaa* Socialism. He claimed that *Ujamaa* Socialism is not restricted to the ties of kinship, but rather it extends to the entire African society and humanity at large. It aims at the enlargement of individual freedom, enhancement of human well-being and dignity, common good, human flourishing and self-realization.[1] Such socialism he refers to as a distinctive nature of traditional African society is simply an attitude of the mind that consists in altruistic view of wealth.[2] For him, in traditional African society, each member has an access to the means of acquiring wealth, mainly land, and the acquisition of wealth is intended for the good of a community, and thus every member of the community is mutually helpful, contributing in the production of goods that are collectively owned: "Nobody starved, either of food or of human dignity, because he lacked personal wealth; he could depend on the wealth possessed by the community of which he was a member."[3] *Ujamaa as* love is extended to all people as members of the same human family. Here, a human person is seen and treated as an end in itself rather than solely as a means to an end.

In Nyerere's thinking, African socialism in traditional African society is built on *Ujamaa* humanistic and socialist principles of equality, freedom and solidarity.[4] Traditional African society that is founded on *Ujamma* Socialism, for Nyerere, is an egalitarian and classless society that is devoid of injustice, class struggle, exploitation, and discrimination characteristic of capitalism.[5] Similarly, Senghor maintains that traditional African society is socialist and communitarian in nature and that individual member of the society is made for the purpose of communal life.[6] For him, an indigenous African has an intrinsic altruistic attitude to life, as they are at one with the rhythm of the other, including objects. Nyerere's reasoning in respect of the other is intuitive and sympathetic. He feels the other rather than distance himself

---

[1] Julius K. Nyerere, *Freedom and Socialism* (Dar-es-Salaam, Tanzania: Oxford University Press, 1967), 137. See also Chukwudum B. Okolo, *African Social and Political Philosophy* (Nsukka, Nigeria: Fulladu Publishing Company, 1993), 32.

[2] Nyerere, *Freedom and Socialism*, 240. See also Okolo, *African Social and Political Philosophy,* 31; Josephat O. Oguejiofor, "African Philosophy and the Function of Socio-political Criticism: A Skeptical Consideration," *UCHE* 10 (2004): 23-37.

[3] Julius K. Nyerere, "The Basis of African Socialism," in *African Socialism*, ed. W. H. Friedland and C. G. Roseberg (Stanford: Stanford University Press, 1964), 240-42.

[4] Okolo, *African Social and Political Philosophy,* 32

[5] Ibid., 30. See also Oguejiofor, "African Philosophy and the Function of Socio-political Criticism," 27.

[6]Léopold. Senghor, *Prose and Poetry*, ed. and trans. J. Reed and C. Wake (London: Oxford University Press, 1965), 32.

from them.[7] He is deeply and passionately engaged with the other, and disposed to die 'to himself to be reborn in the Other. He does not assimilate, he is assimilated.'[8] This form of participation in being forms the basis of African ontology and world-view.

Iroegbu identifies belongingness as a constitutive mode of Africans' being (existence) and a defining principle of African communalism.[9] Belongingness is a 'synthesis of reality and experience of belonging,'[10] that is, the experience of being part of a community. A thing is said to be in so far as it belongs, and thus belongingness defines the reality of whatever. As he puts it: "To be is to belong. To belong is to be."[11] I am because I am being-with-others: God, gods, other human beings, the spirits, and other entities.[12] Africans do not simply exist as something-given like objects; their existence is meaningful through their mutually beneficial relationships. This can be better comprehended in Mbiti's famous dictum: 'I am because we are and since we are, therefore I am.'[13] The identity of a being lies in belongingness, in community ties with established structures (laws, customs, traditions, values, ideals formally or less formally) which impose obligations on the being.

As a communitarian being, an indigenous African is also tied to all members of the community - both the living and the dead.[14] His being is ontologically and intimately linked with them. Africans conceive of reality in terms of 'a universe of forces that are linked together, and are in constant interplay with one another.'[15] All beings (both humans and spiritualized beings) in African cosmos are inextricably bound up with one another; they are woven together in the chain of forces.[16] There are harmonious and complementary relationships between the living and the dead. The Supreme God (*Chukwu* in Igbo) has representatives and those who act as intermediaries between Him and the living taken to be deities and

---

[7] Senghor, *Prose and Poetry,* 29-30.

[8] Ibid., 32.

[9] Pantaleon Iroegbu, *Metaphysics: The Kpim of Philosophy* (Owerri: International Universities Press Ltd, 1995), 374.

[10] Iroegbu, *Metaphysics,* 374.

[11] Ibid.

[12] Ibid.

[13] John Mbiti, *African Religions and Philosophy* (Nairobi: East African Educational Publishers Ltd., 1969), 108.

[14] Mbiti, *African Religions and Philosophy,* 113.

[15] Izu M. Onyeocha, "Africa's Idea about the Nature of Reality," *Maryland Studies* 3 no 5 (2006): 89-105.

[16] Placide Tempels, *Bantu Philosophy* (Paris: Presence Africaine, 1959), 29.

ancestors.[17] Spiritual beings like deities and ancestors are, therefore, part of the African universal community. A being belongs to, and is known by, the community by what it does in relation to other beings directly or indirectly.

For Iroegbu, the communal solidarity of being which a 'We' relationship entails in African communalism transcends one's immediate and direct community to encompass the entire human community: in his conceptualization, community includes neighbors, visitors, strangers, passer-by and aliens, for they are all humans.[18] This implies that the relationship does not end in immediate community, but rather continues till the end of the world 'both spatially and temporally. It does not egoistically neglect anyone, nor does it limit itself to its epoch. It continues.'[19] An individual flourish within his community. The ontological dimension of this communal relationship (belongingness) is expressed in the Igbo proverbial dictum: *Egbe bere ugo bere* (literally translated as: 'Let the kite perch, let the eagle perch') that depicts community–individuality relationship. The dictum suggests that both the kite and the eagle are in the process of becoming; they are potential beings in need of plenitude. To attain fullness of being, each must not deny the other the right to perch on a tree which is their world. It goes to show that to belong functionally is to 'live and let live' or 'be and let be'; the existence of one therefore implies the existence of the other. One denies oneself of one' existence when one denies others of their existence.[20]

Nevertheless, indigenous Igbo communities and their circumstances, that is, structures (laws, standards, conventions, protocol and institutions) as well as Igbo religious philosophies and ethics and their socio-cultural practices have some particularistic, exclusive and discriminatory strains that are in direct contradiction to African communalism and its principles upon which the traditional Igbo world-view claims to be founded. For instance, double standards are applied in their treatment of in-groups and out-groups, and their religious and moral codes cannot be invoked for an offence committed by an in-group member against an outsider (an out-group member). Besides, the philosophy that underlies and underpins African religious ethics and socio-cultural practices reinforces and encourages

---

[17] Bolaji E. Idowu, *Olodumare: God in Yoruba Belief* (London: Longman, 1962). See also Emefie I. Metuh, *God and Man in African Religion: A Case Study of the Igbo of Nigeria* (London: Chapman, 1981). Iroegbu, *Beyond Materialism and Spiritualism* (Ibadan: Hope, 2002).

[18] Iroegbu, *Metaphysics,* 380.

[19] Ibid.

[20] Ibid., 379.

voluntarism and egocentrism at the expense of others, including in-group members. All these make some Igbo communal and religious codes and moral values and their associated socio-cultural practices non-universalizable, and hinder the realization of human flourishing and welfare in traditional Igbo communities.

Against this backdrop, this paper proposes philosophies of *Ubuntu* and *Sam-ae* Spirit as frameworks and social praxis for addressing particularistic and exclusive codes, ethics and ideologies in indigenous Igbo communities. It will expose some particularistic religious and communal ideologies and ethics that play out in Igbo religious and socio-cultural practices. It will posit that the applications of *Ubuntu* humanistic philosophy and a tripartite concept of love enunciated in *Sam-ae* Spirit in indigenous Igbo communities are pathways to attainment of universal humanhood bound by agapeic love in the communities.

THEORETICAL FRAMEWORK—*UBUNTU*

The word 'Ubuntu' is common among Southern African Bantu speaking which is inclusive of all things include nonhuman beings. It is often translated as 'humanness towards others.' In the Zulu aphorism, *Umuntu ngumuntu ngabantu* [a human is a human through other humans].[21] As a philosophical term, *Ubuntu* is the 'belief in a universal bond of sharing that connects all humanity.' It is encapsulated in common humanity through which an individual is linked to the collective so as to become an authentic and complete human person. The philosophy of *Ubuntu* is couched in the dictum: "I am because we are." As a human being, one *is* because of others; one's humanity or personhood is fostered in relation to other humans. Humanness is not a possession of any individual. It is a virtual that is always derived from or given by others. A person functions effectively in society and survives and attains full humanity through his relationship with others and participation in being. This implies that one needs the other in order to be fully human.

Ubuntu is an indigenous African epistemic and ethical mode of life that embodies the metaphysics of oneness with all beings: the spiritual and the physical, the human and the non-human, and the living and the living-dead

---

21 Desmond M. Tutu, *God Has a Dream: A Vision of Hope for Our Time* (London: Rider, 2004), 25-26.

in the chain of forces.[22] It is viewed as a traditional African spiritual ideal and way of being that is organic and collectivistic in nature, as opposed to detached, materialistic and individualistic character of Western perspectives and thoughts.[23] As a humanistic value, it is an expression of unconditional and absolute love untrammeled by any ethnic, religious, regional, political, or cultural differences. It extends to all humanity and spontaneously seeks to restore human dignity and achieve organic unity of human persons through harmony, solidarity and complementarity with one another as members of the universal community bound together by shared humanity. All ontological and interhuman values such as love, altruism, empathy, hospitality, caring, compassion, generosity, sharing, respect, honesty, dignity, equity, justice, right conduct/action and collectivity are epitomized in *Ubuntu*. *Ubuntu* therefore espouses an altruistic mindset that focuses on caring for not only oneself but also others and the environment as the cornerstone of sustainable development.[24]

SAM-AE SPIRIT

The concept of *Sam-ae* Spirit was created by Rev. Pai Min-Soo [Pae Minsu (1896-1968)], an ordained Korean Presbyterian minister, during Japanese colonization of Korea (1910-1945) as both a theory and a method for realizing a Korean vision of modernity centered on religion so as to negotiate the challenges of materialism and individualism-oriented modern capitalist state. *Sam-ae* embodies tripartite love, namely, the Divine-love (love for God), the neighbor-love (love for community/people/humanity) and the work-love (love for work/occupation). The spirit of *Sam-ae* is therefore the spirit of this inextricable and inseparable tripartite love. *Sam-ae* Spirit is a theory and a method for making sense of religion in the context of emerging colonial modernity.[25] It provides a frame on which new forms of agency and

[22] Samuel Ebale and Benson A. Mulemi, "The Spiritual Philosophy of Ubuntu as Path to African Renaissance," in *Dialogue on African Philosophy and Development: Proceedings of the 2022 International Conference of the Association for the Promotion of African Studies (APAS)*, ed. Ikechukwu A. Kalu, Ejikemeuwa J. O. Ndubisi, and Jude I. Onebunne (Maryland: APAS, 2022), 77-95. See also Tempels, *Bantu Philosophy*, 29-30.

[23] Dalene M. Swanson, "Ubuntu: An African Contribution to (Re) Search for/with 'Humble a Togetherness,'" *Journal of Contemporary Issues in Education* 2, no. 2 (2007): 53-67. https//doi.org/10.20355/C5PP4X

[24] Bernard Mayaka and Rory Truell, "Ubuntu and Its Potential Impact on the International Social Work Profession," *International Social Work* 64, no. 5 (2021): 1-14. https://doi.org/10.1177/00208728211022787

[25] Chammah J.Kaunda and Sang-man Kim, "'Samae Spirit' Assist toward 'Ubuntu Spirit' Model for Rural Adult Christian Education in Zambia," *Religious Education* 117, no. 1 (2022): 33-49.

social order that foster equality, justice and human values could be established in a modern society so as to have a meaningful and valuable social life and successfully navigate the capitalist modernity.

The forces of capitalism (*chabonjuŭi*) in the wake of modernism in Japanese occupied Korea occasioned 'new developments and violently upset social and cultural fabric that materially and ideologically clothes the daily lives of peasants.'[26] The disintegration of the fabric of Korean society, especially in the countryside, is exemplified in the reconfiguration of harmonious social relations and the fracturing of social unity, erosion of traditional ideas, values, institutions and practices, as well as disruption of traditional sources of livelihood and locally self-determined ways of life in rural Korea. Capitalist mode of production with its associated industrialization, mechanization of labor, and urbanization became the source of alienation, social exclusion and poverty in Japanese occupied Korea. Thus, everyday life (*ŭisikchu*) in rural Korea was replete with agony, abject poverty and misery, despair and strife.[27]

Capitalism brought about excessive materialism that deteriorated and relegated morality and social relationship, as it made people get lost in material desires, love gold and become enslaved by it.[28] Under the new capitalist economic system, Koreans were desperate to overcome material insecurity and thus were desirous of accumulation of material wealth and maximization of profits even at the expense of the other. High premium was put on money that dominated the life of the people and controlled every other thing. As a result, Koreans pursued material wealth, whatever the cost. The law of the jungle was the order of the day. Pai observed that people were commodifying members of their kith and kin in a desperate bid to make money and accumulate more wealth.[29] Money became the blood that supplied life to people. As Pai put it: "By worshipping gold and accumulating wealth, men make merchandise of the flesh and blood of their fellow-men."[30] Accordingly, both the affluent and the poor lost control over their lives and became controlled by materialistic desires, and hence material possessions or riches became a measure of success

---

[26] Albert K. Park, "Reclaiming the Rural: Modern Danish Cooperative Living in Colonial Korea, 1925-37," *Journal of Korean Studies* 19, no.1 (2014): 115-51, https://doi.org/10.1353/jks.2014.0007.

[27] Ibid., 116.

[28] Park, *Building a Heaven on Earth: Religion, Activism and Protest in Japanese-Occupied Korea* (Honolulu: University of Hawaii Press, 2015), 109.

[29] Ibid., 109.

[30] Min-Soo Pai, as quoted in Park, *Building a Heaven on Earth,* 109.

and fulfillment in life.[31] In the final analysis, the forces of capitalism in colonial Korea conditioned and dictated people's consciousness and behavior, and thus humanity was utterly lost.

Accordingly, the rise of modernization and secularization in the wake of Japanese colonization of Korea posed a challenge to Koreans who needed a theological framework for guidance and support in order to negotiate the forces of modernity. Against this backdrop, Pai sought to supersede unhealthy social practices and relationships, which hindered rural social transformation and progress, by desirable culture founded on the spirit of *Sam-ae.*[32] *Sam-ae* Spirit was a response to that clarion call in that it served as a valuable framework that sought to inextricably link religion with society/community,[33] to marry religious values with communal ethos such as mutual support, sharing, caring, cooperation and concern for the other in such a way that religion retained its significance and simultaneously had some bearing in socio-economic and political ordering in colonial Korea for the common good. Pai proposed a reconstruction of economic and socio-cultural life of Koreans on the basis of *Sam-ae* Spirit in order to build a heavenly paradise (*nagwŏn*) in Korea and negotiate the forces of capitalist modernity.

To imbibe and cultivate the spirit of *Sam-ae* was not to be estranged from capitalist modernity, but rather to ground new forms of economic thought, behavior and practices associated with capitalism in *Sam-ae* Spirit. Neighbor-love and work-love were expressions of Divine-love; they were clear demonstrations of Koreans' genuine love for God. They required that each person be industrious, productive and committed to work (labor), and work in harmony with his co-workers/laborers to ensure high productivity levels in economic and commercial activities such as farming, trading and industry. In the spirit of *Sam-ae*, Koreans were required to embrace modernity by acquiring requisite productive skills and knowledge for the production and exchange of goods and services designed not only as a legitimate source of income and wealth, but also to meet the Korean demand for commodity for survival. After the Korean war (1950-1953), Pai, with some support from his Presbyterian Church, organized an agrarian-based rural reconstruction campaigns[34] that were anchored in the cooperative system (*hyŏptong chohap*) as an alternative path to development.

---

[31] Park, *Building a Heaven on Earth,* 109.

[32] Pai, *Who Shall Enter the Kingdom of Heaven?*, 350.

[33] Ibid., 395.

[34] Park, "Reclaiming the Rural," 138.

Cooperative agriculture modelled on the cooperative system of Denmark – a communal economic organization that entails pooling the labor and resources of individual peasants (or producers) to negotiate the challenges of capitalist modernity and survive – was aimed at creating moral economy and economic democratization (*Gyeongje minjuhwa*) in Korean society as a response to the rural crisis occasioned by forces of capitalism. Cooperatives were ideal and effective social mechanisms for revolutionizing production and consumption in a manner that guaranteed material security, economic sustainability, and self-fulfillment in rural Koreans.[35] The cooperative system promoted egalitarianism (economic equality) and democracy and ensured high economic productivity and financial security. It 'sought to protect and raise life above profit and money…'[36] and enabled farmers 'to live rich, moral, spiritual and cultural lives.'[37] According to Hong Pyŏngsŏn, cooperatives 'fostered community based on the moral principle of improving the quality of human life.'[38]

In the Danish cooperative, unlike capitalism, members committed themselves to improving the livelihood of one another, placing their communal interest above their self-interest. The purpose of cooperatives was to establish an organic community of individuals in order to enhance each member's life. The ethic of mutual cooperation (*sangho pujo*), solidarity and support inherent in such a cooperative system epitomized the ideal community a German-Jewish existentialist philosopher, Marin Buber referred to as a real community where "members have a common relation to the center overriding all other relations."[39] For Park, the Danish cooperative system was designed to stabilize the agricultural and rural sectors and form a new community of farmers and rural inhabitants who would be economically secure and morally upright.[40] So, working cooperatively in the spirit of *Sam-ae* under the system did not only help to attain Koreans' material security, but also help to enhance their moral lives for the healthy development of

35 Pai, "The Rural Evangelistic Movement," *The Korean Mission Field* (1935): 148-50.

36 Park, "Social Renewal through the Rural: Agricultural Cooperatives in South Korea as a form of Critiquing Capitalism," *Global Environment* 9 (2016): 82-107. https://doi.org/10.3197/ge.2016.090105

37 Park, "Reclaiming the Rural," 126.

38 Hong Pyŏngsŏn, as quoted in Park, "Reclaiming the Rural," 127.

39 Martin Buber, 1970, as quoted in Paul Mendes-Flohr, "The Desert Within and Social Renewal: Martin Buber's Vision of Utopia," in *New Perspectives on Martin Buber*, ed. Michael Zank (Tübingen, Germany: Mohr Siebeck, 2006), 219-230.

40 Park, "Social Renewal through the Rural," 92-93.

modern Korea. While in capitalism wealth is accumulated by exploitation and dispossession (of the other), in cooperatives wealth is accumulated by pooling resources and labor together for the common good. On the whole, through Denmark-based cooperative agriculture imbued with the spirit of *Sam-ae,* rural Koreans forged communal bonds and became self-reliant which enabled them to negotiate the forces of capitalist modernity.

PARTICULARISM IN INDIGENOUS IGBO COMMUNITIES

In the introductory section, we expressed that communalism, which is widely believed to be the intrinsic character of traditional African society, is rationally and universally appealing in that it claims (that) the sense and ties of brotherhood are not limited to *ụmụnna* (family, kinsfolk and kindred), but are rather extended to humanity at large for the welfare and the common good of all people. However, indigenous Igbo communities, whose communal and religious ideologies, ethics and ways of life typify the sort of highly acclaimed communalism many contemporary African scholars enunciate and propagate as being essentially African, have some particularistic, exclusive and discriminatory ideologies, codes, norms, and practices that are inconsistent with the spirit of African communalism.

The practicalities of communalistic and religious philosophies, codes, ethics, and practices in some indigenous Igbo communities show that their communalism is designed exclusively for in-groups within the Igbo society (family, kinsfolk, kindred, clan, town, community, tribe, and so forth). Significant severe sanctions are inapplicable to a breach of ethical injunctions in respect of out-groups (other subcultures, communities, tribes, or ethnic groups). An individual member of traditional Igbo community is under no legal obligation to apply or not to apply his communalistic ethics trans-communally, trans-tribally, or trans-racially that is more universal.[41] Hence, he is free to apply or not to apply them universally; he can restrict the application of communalism to his in-group members and be absolutely indifferent to, and exhibit unconcern attitudes to, out-groups. Such a particularistic and exclusive outlook finds expression in the meanings and applications of traditional laws and moral codes.

For example, the first commandment in 'Ten commandments of the *Nze na Ọzọ*' (a conglomeration of chieftaincy title holders known as *Nze* or

---

[41] Joseph C. A. Agbakoba, *Development and Modernity in Africa: An Intercultural Philosophical Perspective*, eds. K. Eichmann and R. Voben (Cologne: Rüdiger Köppe Verlag, 2019), 173.

Ọzọ) of the Ụmụezearọlị clan of Onitsha (a city in Igbo land) is that 'one must respect his *Ọkpala* (the father figure and representative of the ancestors); must not seek to supplant him; must pay homage to him and must stand by him at all times.'[42] The last part of the first commandment means that one is legally obligated to stand by one's *Ọkpala*, regardless of whether *Ọkpala*'s actions are morally right and praiseworthy, or he is in the right. In other words, one is obliged to protect one's *Ọkpala* (or father) at all costs.

Again, the commandment on sexual intercourse for the *Nze na Ọzọ* stipulates that no one must indulge in any sexual relations with a female within the *ụmụnna* circle,[43] that is, a sister – one's sister from nuclear or extended families – a kinwoman, any daughter of the endogamous *ụmụnna* circle or a lady married into such a circle. But the injunction is silent on its application to females outside the *ụmụnna* circle. Thus, one is free to be licentious when dealing with females one has no blood ties with. Well-to-do, influential or powerful men could exploit this discriminatory and exclusive indigenous moral code and capitalize on their status or prestige to court wives of the poor at whim, or employ whatever means possible to take away others' wives at will outside the *ụmụnna* circle. Noting sexual proclivities and licentiousness one could display, Okwechime asserts:

> If a man was stronger than another man who was known to be courting a girl who may even have been betrothed to the suitor, the stronger man could beat him up and disgrace him publicly by defeating him in a wrestling contest to ward him off the girl. He then took over the girl. There was nothing wrong in seducing another man's wife and taking her over if a man was stronger than the husband but adultery was forbidden particularly for women and incest was considered an abomination.[44]

The application of double standards in the treatment of in-groups and out-groups also cuts across indigenous Igbo communities and towns. A case in point is a grotesque situation in Ọkpụnọ, a town in Igbo land. There is a man who is infamous for homosexual escapades with young lads. He usually lures the lads into having sex with him with money large enough to resist. He has been successfully enjoying this behavior considered in Igbo land as anti-natural, sexually deviant, aberrant, abhorrent, uncivilized, and unwholesome, and abusing boys sexually for donkey's years, and freely walking the streets

---

[42] Ben Chukwudebe, ed., *Onitsha Quo Vadis*, 2nd ed. (Owerri, Nigeria: B. N. Chukwudebe, 1986), 40.

[43] Ibid.

[44] Chudi Okwechime, *Onicha-Ugbo through the Centuries* (Lagos, Nigeria: Max-Henrie and Associate, 1994), 67.

with impunity. It is ludicrous, outrageous and totally unacceptable that the same town that has previously exposed and punished (or banished in most cases) deviants, who are non-indigenes, allows the man to get away scot-free. The reason for allowing him to freely walk the streets with impunity is not far-fetched: he is an indigene, pure and simple.

Another instance is a recent development in Awka, a city in Igbo land. In the face of killings and worsening insecurity in the city, one village employed a security outfit popularly known as 'Bakassi Boys' – a powerful and deadly vigilante group that has magical powers to reveal and arrest suspected criminals and bandits. The village had considerable success in fighting crime such that the neighboring villages formed an alliance with the village in order to combat crime in the city. The security outfit was to operate from the village of its employer as the base, while it launched manhunts and apprehension in other villages often at night or at the wee hours. Village leaders were to divulge to the vigilante group the whereabouts or homes of suspects. Unfortunately, the village leaders were selective in divulging the homes or whereabouts of suspects, as homes or whereabouts of the non-indigene suspects were mostly invaded. It was also observed that non-indigene crime syndicates were mostly captured, while some other notorious criminal elements that were indigenes were shielded by way of stealthily furnishing them with valuable information that aided and facilitated their escape before the vigilante group rescue operation in many villages commenced.

Particularistic mode of life in Igbo traditional communities also takes the form of pursuit of riches (material possessions) by fair means or foul which reinforces egocentrism, voluntarism – a principle that places too much emphasis on self-preservation and the perfection of the ego as the highest or supreme good in a struggle for domination – and the rule of personality rather than the rule of law or moral precepts.[45] The pursuit of personal wealth, whatever the cost, has its roots in the notion of vital force. The Igbo, like the Bantu, believe that everything (living and non-living) possesses and manifests vital force (*ike* in Igbo) as the supreme value.[46] A divine being (*chi* in Igbo) is generally the efficient cause of a person's procreative vital force or spirit *(mụọ* in Igbo) that outlives the body. Beings in this world and netherworld are connected in the chain of forces, interacting with, and influencing, one another. The spirit world is an extension of this material

---

[45] Agbakoba, "Values and Developing Administrative Instruments for the African Cultural Environment," *UCHE* 16 (2010): 1-17.

[46] Tempels, *Bantu Philosophy*, 22. See also Agbakoba, *Development and Modernity in Africa,* 158.

world. In other words, Life in the hereafter is viewed as an extension and continuation of this-worldly life. The spirit world is therefore seen as ethereality, that is, spiritualized materiality – materiality extended to the spirit world.[47] At death, procreative force or spirit of the deceased leaves to reside in the spirit world exerting powerful spiritual influences on the living.

The power of a person lies in his force and the concrete manifestation of the force is measured in terms of material possessions in this world. Hence, In Igbo land, a person who has riches is usually extolled when referring to his/her wealth in this way: "*I bu ike*" or "*I pa ike*" (You carry force). When he/she is being discussed elsewhere, a reference is made to his/ her wealth in commendation in this way: "*O bu ike*" or "*Ọ pa ike*" (He/she carries force). A person who possesses abundant wealth is regarded as a person of abundant and strong vital force. Abundant material possessions are viewed as a symbol of attainment of potential and full vitality of the person's specific spirit (*mụọ*).[48] This explains why the Igbo commend wealth in their naming culture, religious philosophies (ideologies), and proverbs. Such names as *Ụbaka* (wealth is greater), *Ụbanọzie* (wealth has taken the proper position), and *Ọbịanujuakụ* (the one that comes in the abundance of riches) lend credence to prominence given to riches in Igbo land.[49] An affluent person is considered to be a successful person whose earthly status would continue in the spirit world after death since life hereafter is part of a continuum of life on earth. It is therefore not surprising that the Igbo bury a wealthy deceased person with great pomp and pageantry and with his wealth in the grave so as to be accorded a rightful place in the ancestral land.

The high premium placed on wealth as a measure of one's force (*ike*) and the perception of blessings and success as a symbol of possessing strong vital force occasion the identification and classification of people according to the force and power they possess and display. The affluent, irrespective of whether their wealth is ill-gotten, are highly extolled and respected for having supposedly strong force, while the poor and the needy only deserve sympathy for possessing seemingly diminutive force. Given that wealth or riches are a symbol of strong vital force, people are urged by their contemporaries, colleagues, peers, and kith and kin to strive to acquire wealth, with little or no emphasis on its acquisition by legitimate means. The implication of this philosophical (ideological) underpinning of vital force is

---

[47] Agbakoba, *Development and Modernity in Africa,* 157.

[48] Ibid.

[49] Oguejiofor, "African Philosophy and the Function of Socio-Political Criticism," 34.

that individual subjective will with its concomitant voluntarism and particularism trumps general objective and rational will, including that of an in-group to which an individual belongs. Consequently, Igbo society keeps churning out voluntaristic and egocentric individuals who have the proclivity to accumulate personal wealth, acquire power, exploit and dominate others (including their in-group members) by any possible means to gain and enhance their prestige.

Ritual killings for personal aggrandizement – acquiring and gaining political power, riches, and prestige – which are rife in Igbo society of today are underpinned and reinforced by the religious ideology of vital force. An infamous Ọkịja shrine in Umuhu Ọkịja, in Igbo land where unscrupulous elements offer human sacrifices for power, wealth, fame and fortune, comes to mind. For instance, on 4 August 2004, Ọkịja shrine was raided by some fifty officers of the Nigerian police, in the course of which 83 corpses consisted of 63 headless corpses and twenty skulls were discovered in the deity's grove.[50] In the shrine, the police found three registers that recorded names of visitors that had allegedly offered human sacrifices in the shrines for the past five years.[51] The shrine is believed to be the meeting-place of a secret society – to which leading Igbo politicians are members – for the execution of nefarious religious practices like ritual killings in order to acquire spiritual and political power and wealth[52] as a concrete manifestation of strong vital force.

A SEARCH FOR UNIVERSAL HUMANHOOD AND SELF-FULFILLMENT IN INDIGENOUS IGBO COMMUNITIES

In the preceding section, we demonstrated that Igbo traditional laws, moral codes, religious ideologies and ethics, and their associated religious and socio-cultural practices are exclusive and applicable to in-groups – a tiny section of humanity. Moreover, particularism in Igbo society exists in the form of voluntarism and egocentrism underpinned by the religious philosophy of vital force, and it finds expression in one's utilization of the other (even a member of one's in-group) as an instrumental means to one's own ends – self-interest. All these strains of particularism make some

---

[50] Remigius N. Nwabueze, "Dead Bodies in Nigerian Jurisprudence," *Journal of African Law* 51 no. 1 (2007): 117-50. https://doi.org/10.1017/S0021855306000234

[51] Obed Minchakpu, "Human Sacrifices Redux," *Christianity Today* (1 December 2004), accessed 13 October 2022. https://christianitytoday.com/it/2004/december/16.22.html

[52] Stephen Ellis, "The Okija Shrine: Death and Life in Nigeria Politics," *The Journal of African History* 49, no. 3 (2008): 445-66. https://doi.org/10.1017/S0021853708003940

communalistic codes and modes of life in indigenous Igbo communities non-universalizable. Their non-universalizability stifles the development of human potential and hinders the enhancement of human well-being and the attainment of self-realization. *Ubuntu* and *Sam-ae* Spirit serve as frames on which healthy social relationships, which will allow people to experience spiritual love and achieve spiritual wholeness, can be constructed so as to achieve universal humanhood that will pave the way for self-realization in traditional Igbo society.

Ubuntu expresses that one's humanity is inextricably bound up with the other[53] and thus calls for mutual cooperation, friendly, harmonious and complementary relationships between a person and others and their responsibility to one another as the very essence of being human. Stanlake J. W. T. Samkage states the following principles as being deeply embedded in the philosophy of *Ubuntu*:

- To be human is to affirm one's humanity by recognizing the humanity of others and, on that basis, establish respectful human relations with them.
- If and when one is faced with a decisive choice between wealth and the preservation of the life of another human being, then one should opt for the preservation of life.[54]

Senghor's assertion of mutual relation of *I* and *Thou* as the hallmark of authentic African communalism captures other-regarding attitudes and actions enunciated in *Ubuntu* philosophy which should form the basis of Igbo socio-cultural and religious orderings:

> Our subject abandons his *I* to sympathize and identify himself with the THOU. He dies to himself to be reborn in the Other. He does not assimilate, he is assimilated. He does not kill the other life; he strengthens his own life through it. He lives with the Other in a communal life, lives in *symbiosis*: he is born-with and thereby knows the Other. Subject and object are dialectically confronted in the very act of knowing one another. It is a long caress in the night, an intimacy of mingle bodies, the act of love, from which the fruit of knowledge is born.[55]

Buber rightly remarks that such mutual love in *I-Thou* relation is devoid of objectification and exploitation of the other: "Love does not cling

---

[53] Desmond Tutu, *No Future without Forgiveness* (New York: Doubleday, 1999), 31.

[54] New World Encyclopedia, s.v. "Ubuntu (Philosophy)," accessed 15 Oct. 2022, https://www.newworldencyclopedia.org/entry/Ubuntu_(philosophy).

[55] Senghor, *Prose and Poetry,* 32.

to the *I* in such a way as to have the *Thou* only for its content, its object; but love is between *I* and *Thou*."[56] A disciplined environment of mutual cooperation, complementarity and beneficence enunciated in *Ubuntu* would ensure that individuals utilize money and other material possessions for loving service to others and for maintaining healthy social relations rather than upsetting the relation. This is consistent with Nyerere's claim that in traditional African society, wealth is acquired not for exploitation and domination of others, but in order to be of service to others.[57] In genuine communal mode of life in traditional African society, reciprocal relationships between all beings are underlain by organic unity of forces. It is only in communion with others, which entails mutual love and respect for the being of others, can an individual attain full humanity. In the words of Ekei:

> The fundamental assumption of African philosophy is that existing thing or reality is a life force, or reality is a life force, or that every reality possesses its life force. In other words, everything has something in common by virtue of life force. Following this onto-ethical presupposition, man seems to find humanity in the being of another, which helps his disposition to share, to care and to accept.[58]

The institutionalization and cultivation of the ethic of *Ubuntu* in indigenous Igbo communities will create a just and open society free from all sorts of discrimination, and where natives will be open and available to others (non-indigenes), participate in, and share, the universal brotherhood of love.

The spirit of *Sam-ae* is congruent with the community spirit and bond that is expressed by Africans as *Ubuntu*. Like *Ubuntu* spirit, *Sam-ae* Spirit enunciates the principle of mutual cooperation which is manifestly demonstrated in loving and helping one another as members of universal community bound together by agapeic love. Through mutual cooperation individuals collectively establish economic security and ascend to the higher plane of spirituality necessary for the experience of God's presence here on earth.[59] Thus, concrete realization of Divine-love, for Pai, is possible through mutual cooperation.[60] The principle of mutual cooperation should be at the base of all economic and social standards in indigenous Igbo communities.

---

[56] Buber, *I and Thou*, 2nd edition, trans. R. G. Smith (New York: Charles Scribner's Sons, 1958), 14-15.

[57] Nyerere, "The Basis of African Socialism," 240.

[58] John Ekei, *Justice in Communalism*: *A Foundation of Ethics in African Philosophy* (Lagos: Realm Communication, 2001), 194.

[59] Park, *Building a Heaven on Earth,* 110.

[60] Ibid.

In the spirit of mutual cooperation, valuing life and dignity of others, caring for, and having consideration for, them are the desirable ethical mode of life. When Igbo socio-economic and cultural system is undergirded by the *Sam-ae* Spirit that is concretized in the ethic of mutual cooperation and caring for the other, one would no longer see the other as an alien (an outsider), but as an ally and companion whom one is morally obligated to love and show concern about his problems and well-being.

Ubuntu recognizes God as the Fountain of life in which all things participate, and as the Giver of vital force in whom the attainment of plenitude of all other beings is guaranteed. However, *Sam-ae* Spirit goes beyond the acknowledgement of God as the ground of being to advance the frontiers of neighbor-love and work-love as an effective means of demonstrating Divine-love and concretizing it in social relations, institutions and practices so as to be a force immanent in the world. The connection of Divine-love with socio-cultural relations, interactions and events ensures that everyday life is the ground for encountering God who is love[61] For Pai, "the world… is where the heavenly kingdom resides and is exhibited."[62] Socio-cultural structures and practices, for Pai, are sites of concrete manifestations of *Sam-ae* Spirit.[63] *Sam-ae* Spirit is meaningful and useful when it is made manifest in social institutions, relations and practices.

It therefore becomes a significant force for universally and rationally appealing religious and communal ideologies and ethics and their associated socio-cultural practices in traditional Igbo communities when Divine-love is concretely translated into actions in socio-cultural affairs and inter-human relations. Just as Divine-love in Japanese occupied Korea served as a revitalizing and inspiring force that drove and propelled Koreans into neighbor-love and work-love that brought about authentic and holistic development,[64] the application of *Sam-ae* Spirit in indigenous Igbo communities will ensure that Divine-love provides the motive for loving the other (neighbor-love) that means loving all humanity (both in-group and out-group members), and loving one's work, profession, or occupation (work-love) which entails full commitment and dedication to one's calling, including the work of love for the other; working in cooperation with, and living in

---

[61] (RSV, I John 4: 8, 16).

[62] Pai, as quoted in Park, *Building a Heaven on Earth,* 104.

[63] Chammah J.Kaunda and Sang-man Kim, "'Samae Spirit' Assist toward 'Ubuntu Spirit' Model for Rural Adult Christian Education in Zambia," *Religious Education* 117, no. 1 (2022): 33-49.

[64] Kirsteen Kim, "Christianity's Role in the Modernization and Revitalization of Korean Society in the Twentieth-Century," *International Journal of Public Theology* 4, no. 2 (2010): 212-236, https://doi.org/10.1163/156973210X491903.

solidarity and harmony with, the other in all spheres of Igbo society for the improvement of human existential condition and for the betterment of Igbo society in general. In *Sam-ae* Spirit, neighbor-love and work-love are effective means of maintaining and promoting good relationships with the Supreme God (*Chukwu* in Igbo). They form the basis of Divine-love; they are foundational to one's encounter with the Supreme God. The relationships between the trilateral love in *Sam-ae* Spirit are demonstrated in the diagram below:

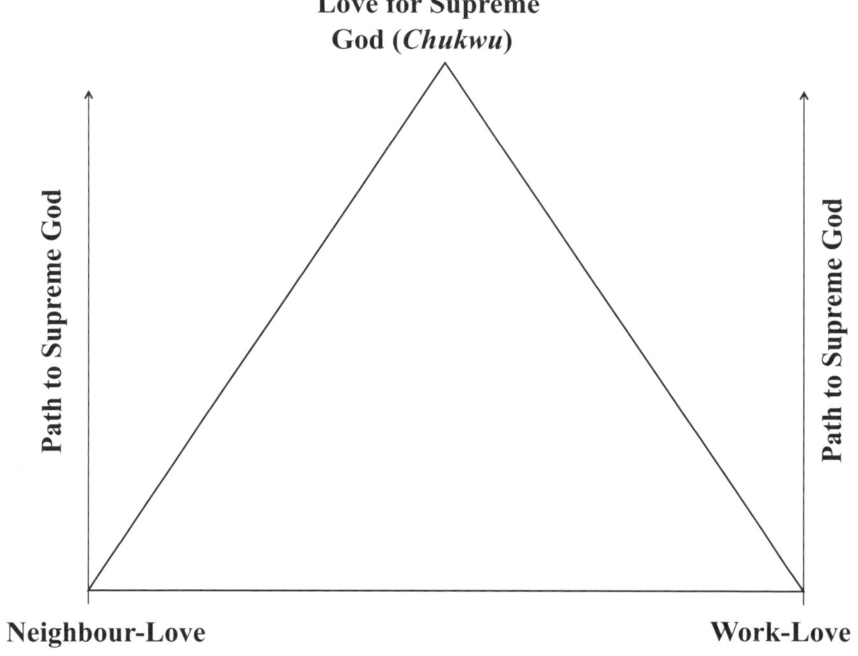

The love for the intrinsically impartial, objective, perfect, good, loving, life-affirming and abstract Supreme Being (God) is concretized in the love for one's neighbor, including out-group members, that is made manifest in concrete social institutions and relations and socio-cultural practices. Maintaining that neighbor-love is a precondition and index of Divine-love, Pai asserts: "He who loves God must also love other people and he who does not love other people who can be seen cannot love God who cannot be seen. Therefore, to love God is to obey and put into practice the law that God has commanded. Loving others is at the center of God's principle and truth, which will open the path to your life."[65]

Sam-ae philosophy is in harmony with Saint Paul's theology of love, in his first letter to the Corinthians, that equates love with benevolence, forbearance, and right conduct,[66] indicating that neighbor-love is the essence of Divine-love (love for God). Loving Supreme God is nothing short of loving one's fellow humans (neighbor-love) and being devoted and committed to enhancing their well-being (work-love) through the institutionalization and promotion of equity and justice in Igbo religious and socio-cultural codes, norms, and socio-political institutions, relations and practices. For the Igbo to respond to the demands of a universal, Supreme God, they must be responsible not only to in-group members, but also to the entire humankind over which God presides. It requires that the principle of equity and justice is not restricted to in-groups, and that the spread of beneficence and other affective (dispositional) attitudes and actions towards others such as altruism, love, care, sharing, kindness, benevolence, compassion, empathy, tolerance, concern and consideration for others is not constricted to members of one's family, kinsfolk, kindred, community, or religion.

There must be consistency and truthfulness in the spread of beneficence and other-regarding attitudes and actions to live out the spirit of *Sam-ae* in Igbo society. This implies that the spread of such desirable other-regarding attitudes and actions must have rational and universal appeal; it must demonstrate trans-communal or trans-racial applicability. It also suggests that there must not be partiality, discrimination, and double standards in the treatment of in-and-out groups with respect to traditional and communal codes, socio-cultural norms and practices. What is sauce for the goose is sauce for the gander. There should be equal treatment for all people, regardless of one's tribe, race, region or religion. Communal laws and moral codes should rule as common standards for all people residing in the Igbo ethnic community.

Given that for the Igbo, life hereafter is an extension of this-worldly life; the living on earth are the future ancestors of posterity, the Igbo should set new criteria for gaining admittance to the ancestral land by devaluing mere material possessions and emphasizing acquisition of wealth through legitimate means and deploying one's wealth for service to others, in keeping with the demands

---

65 Minsoo Pai, *The Kingdom of God and Rural Korea* (Seoul: Yonsei University Press, 2017), 121.

66 (RSV, I Cor. 12: 4-7).

of neighbor-love, as preconditions for offering a deceased person a rightful place in the ancestral land. When such other-regarding attitude and action in respect of the acquisition of wealth is institutionalized, imbibed and internalized, future ancestors, who are presently the living on earth, will be naturally disposed to rightfully admit any deceased person on the basis of the criteria. On the whole, *Ubuntu* and *Sam-ae* Spirit provide philosophico-theological frames on which new forms of social organization and interaction can be structured in indigenous Igbo communities so as to establish desirable order and social unity which will pave the way for religious experiences in everyday life that connect people to eternal sacred forces.

CONCLUSION

In this paper, we have demonstrated some particularistic strains in indigenous Igbo structures, religious philosophies and their associated socio-cultural practices. The much-vaunted communitarian spirit in indigenous Igbo society tilts toward particularism. This is because the nature of societal structures, religious ideologies and socio-cultural practices does not reflect any sense of brotherhood that has trans-communal, trans-tribal, or trans-racial applicability and thus cannot be universalized. We propose rejigging traditional Igbo structures and socio-cultural practices by underlying and imbuing them with the universalizable philosophies of *Ubuntu* and *Sam-ae* Spirit to make them rationally and universally appealing. Achieving this call for concretization of *Ubuntu* and *Sam-ae* Spirit in societal structures, ideologies and practices by adopting neighbor-love and work-love as the bedrock and index of love for Supreme God that is foundational to indigenous African religions which indigenous Igbo communities profess and practice.

This will spur the entire Igbo society to run on the universalizable principles of equity, justice and truth that have trans-communal or trans-racial applicability and validity since neighbor-love and work-love cannot be lived out without building the whole Igbo society around the principles. *Ubuntu* and *Sam-ae* Spirit are therefore effective philosophical and theological frameworks for spiritualization of socio-cultural, political and economic life and for throwing people off the yoke of particularism, voluntarism, egocentricity, and excessive materialism in indigenous Igbo communities for human welfare and the common good. They must be the spirit of religious and social structures and practices in indigenous Igbo communities so as to build a heavenly paradise in Igbo land which is a sine qua non for communal development, human flourishing and self-realization.

CHAPTER 6

SAM-AE SPIRIT AND FOLKLORE: LOCAL THEOLOGY AS LISTENING TO THE VOICE FROM THE SOCIAL MARGINS

IZAK Y. M. LATTU & IRENE LUDJI

INTRODUCTION

The voice from the rural area and margin has been neglected in the theological conversation for many decades because many scholars understand theology as the discourse involving elite and textual-based conversation. However, the concept of *Sam-ae* – "love, mercy, and compassion for the rural and the people on the margins" from Rev. Pai Min-Soo would open an avenue for engaging local knowledge in theological conversation.[67] Many theologies emerge from the Global South, however, only a few focus on local knowledge because most theologians emphasize academic works from the North. As a result, theological discourse situates folklore in the margins and mutes local voices. This research employs the *Sam-ae* concept to create a space for the rural living texts in theological conversations; it borrows the orality perspective from Walter J. Ong and Gayatri Spivak to "let subaltern speak" in theological discussions.[68] This paper employs ethnography research to explore folklore and develop a theological reflection from the social margins. This research argues that the *Sam-ae* concept can create ample space to engage marginalized voices and bring the rural perspective into theological discourse in the Global South, especially in Indonesia.

We employ an interdisciplinary approach to integrate the study of local theology, folklore, and sociology of religion in this article. The interdisciplinary approach integrates the concept of *Sam-ae*, folkloric studies that explores local knowledge as a cultural text to encapsulate people's

---

[67] Chammah J. Kaunda and Kim Sang-man, "'Samae Spirit' Assist toward 'Ubuntu Spirit' Model for Rural Adult Christian Education in Zambia," *Religious Education* 117, no. 1 (2022): 40, https://doi.org/10.1080/00344087.2021.1990474.

[68] Walter J. Ong, *Orality and Literacy* (London: Routledge, 1982); and Gayatri Spivak, *Selected Sub-Altern Studies* (New York and Oxford: Oxford University Press, 1988).

theology in the quotidian, and the sociology of religion – to provide room for a critical analysis to accept voices from the margins within theological discourse. The concept of *Sam-ae* itself has already has an interdisciplinary aspect as Rev. Pai Min-Soo retained social analysis and awareness in creating engagement between theology and subaltern ideas: voice of the laboring rural underclass.

Rev. Pai Min-Soo's theological position resonates with people's struggles in many social spheres and contexts. *Sam-ae* also speaks to different contexts and other parts of the globe because the concept is based on the perennial philosophy and lived theology of accepting and respecting people regardless of social backgrounds. Viewing *Sam-ae* from through the lens of Indonesia, we can discover the spirit of *Sam-ae* in Indonesian local knowledge and folkloric texts: a theology of the margins. This theology drawing from marginalized Indonesians draws substance from everydayness and orality. Marginalized Indonesians have preserved knowledge in oral traditions, through storytelling, rituals, and symbols. Although people have encountered written texts since the age of commerce during the spice trade, people predominantly stored their knowledge in the oral tradition of social remembrance.

This article argues that *Sam-ae* has the potential to contribute to creating a theological foundation to develop a theology from the social margins where people store local knowledge and experience the presence of logos in the mnemonic text. Therefore, we provide the basis of our main arguments that define *Sam-ae,* the spirit of three loves, as a voice of the social margins, when viewed from the Indonesian theology of the marginalized.

THE SPIRIT OF 'THREE LOVES': *SAMAE* [삼애]

When the powerful, dominant voice in the community becomes the sole interpreter of what the community needs, there is no hope for change that promotes and stands with those powerless in social margins. As the dominant voice, the influential member of the community sets the social norms and uses them to judge the position and choices made by the powerless. Rev. Pai Min-Soo, a twentieth-century Korean Christian,[69] understood the relation between the powerful dominant and the powerless

[69] Rev. Pai Min-Soo was born in 1897 at Cheongju, Chungbuk Province, Korea. "About GIT: Rev. Pai Min-soo," Yonsei University, accessed September 1, 2022, https://git.yonsei.ac.kr/git/about/samae.do.

in the margins, hence saw the need for a movement that addresses the problem and is able to effect a change rooted in the Christian virtue of love. Pai Min-Soo was born in the late nineteenth century, a time marked by the human and civil rights movement that transformed all spheres of life. Consequently, Pai's idea represents the spirit of respect towards human rights at the beginning of the twentieth century, as it appeared in his conscious decision to side with the powerless suffering of those pushed to the margins of Korean society.

From a young age Pai demonstrated his interest in standing against the powerful, dominant voice of Japanese colonialism. This interest led him to establish a secret society called the "Chosun Nationalist Association" that focused on the independence movement to free Korea, then called Chōsen (朝鮮), from Japanese oppression.[70] Even after he was sentenced to prison, Pai continued to speak up against the injustice in his community. In developing his social justice interest, Pai was remarkably influenced by Mr. Mansik Cho,[71] whom he called "the Korean Lincoln or Gandhi."[72] Cho was well known as an independence activist who worked in the rural Korean area to educate people to stand against unjust treatment from the oppressor and unfair customs in the community. In his own words, as quoted by Pai in *Who Shall Enter the Kingdom of Heaven?*, Cho preached to the rural community:

> Here in our country, men go first. You think you are too dignified to eat with women. Therefore, you take a small table alone and let the women and children eat together. When any woman walks from the opposite direction, the woman has to stop walking and stand still toward the other side until the man goes by. On the other side, women work harder. They cook meals three times a day. They make clothes and take care of their children. They wash and clean their homes and work in their gardens. It is a most unfortunate thing to be born a female in Korea. But as long as the women are looked down upon, your life cannot be happy or civilized. There is no democracy as long as you mistreat your wives and women.[73]

Through his work in the rural Korean area, Cho sided with those who were marginalized. It is these characteristics of promoting and standing with the powerless in the community, as demonstrated by Cho, that Pai carried on through his further work. Under Cho's guidance, Pai focuses his passion on

---

[70] "About GIT: Rev. Pai Min-soo," Global Institute of Theology, Yonsei University, accessed September 1, 2022, https://git.yonsei.ac.kr/git/about/samae.do.

[71] Ibid.

[72] Minsoo Pai, *Who Shall Enter the Kingdom of Heaven?*, 1st ed., trans. Nowon Park (Seoul: Yonsei University Press, 1952), 301.

[73] Ibid., 305

fighting against the powerful, dominant voice thru a "Rural Movement."[74] This rural movement is crucial because Pai observed that "about eighty percent of the people would be or whole population consisted of rural people."[75] Scholars have acknowledged the observation made by Pai as factual.[76] The spirit behind Pai's rural movement is the empowerment of the rural people so that they can support themselves.

Pai's rural movement established a strong tie to the Christian virtue: love, in the concept of *Sam-ae* (삼애). *Sam-ae* refers to "three loves–the love of God, labor, and farming."[77] In his personal experience, Pai has seen how love in practice can transform the pain and suffering of the marginalized part of the community. One of Pai's fondest memories of the impact of love was based on his encounter with the half-blind old lady who was living alone in a small tent.[78] In this encounter, Pai purposely decided to find and share resources that could provide money, food, and clothes for those in need.[79] However, the significance of his experience with the half-blind old lady goes beyond physical support. For Pai, the engagement with the half-blind old lady made it possible for him to understand the meaning of interdependence and solidarity, as he was later called "the son" of the half-blind lady.[80] Pai began from a genuine intention in relationship with others and ended with the empowerment of others and himself – this is known as the process of solidarity where there is a constant readiness to act with others and fulfillment for both parties in the relationship.

Faith in Christ plays a vital role in Pai's identity. Thus, it was crucial for Pai to find ways to "link the line between spiritual and practical life, the Kingdom of God on earth and Kingdom of God in heaven, and the church and the society."[81] He believes that ministers and missionaries are obligated to preach and teach and lead a life that sets an excellent example for the people they serve.[82] This personal goal to connect the spiritual and practical life would set Pai on the quest to find a meaningful connection between being a faithful follower of Christ and being an active doer of Christian

---

[74] Pai, *Who Shall Enter the Kingdom of Heaven?*, 301.

[75] Ibid.

[76] Kaunda and Kim, "'Samae' Spirit Assist toward 'Ubuntu Spirit' Model," 40.

[77] "About GIT: Rev. Pai Min-soo."

[78] Pai, *Who Shall Enter the Kingdom of Heaven?*, 306.

[79] Ibid.

[80] Ibid.

[81] Ibid., 315.

[82] Ibid.

teaching. As a result, when Pai started the program "Teaching of Christ and the idea of the Rural movement" through The Christian Rural Research Association,[83] he was able to include projects that answered the need for contextualization of Christian teaching. Projects such as Rural Leaders Training and Rural Adults Education that were conducted in the spirit of *Sam-ae* transformed the rural community's uni-fragged[84] and impoverished condition into a united front of citizens who were ready to collaborate for the common good.

Chammah J Kaunda and Sang-man Kim observe in "'Samae Spirit' Assist toward 'Ubuntu Spirit' Model for Rural Adult Christian Education in Zambia," that Pai's "hermeneutical point of departure was to engage and transform the mindset that shaped the imaginations of rural people in order to empower them to understand their struggles and move to issues of rural development through embracing the samae spirit."[85] *Sam-ae* represents the foundation for a social community that enlivens the Biblical call to love one's neighbor (Matthew 22: 35–40). In response to that call, Pai thought of the need to "feed the hungry, clothe the naked, and help the needy ones as Jesus commanded" as the way to bring the Kingdom of God to rural Korea.[86] Pai's liberating movement was relevant because the members of the Korean rural community, even though they represented the majority in number, could not stand for themselves in the face of the oppressor. The social change in Pai's rural movement arises from his faith in Jesus, characterized by love, and displays the vision of the Gospel. Like the one promoted by Pai, a Christian liberating movement begins with examining of the powerful, dominant voice in the community and offers a critique on how it was not used to promote love and solidarity. Pai's work shows consistency between his faith and his action – his integrity – that brings the hope of liberation in the context of the rural community.

Sam-ae, understood as three loves, represents the three essential aspects of the rural community at that time: Focus on the love for God, labor, and farming. Within *Sam-ae* is the hope for a redeemed life in Christ based on love for God, which inspired the moral duty to love the work (labor) God

---

[83] Pai, *Who Shall Enter the Kingdom of Heaven?*, 348-9

[84] 'Unifragged' refers to the condition of being united yet fragmented within. This term was first introduced by Steve Jones in his article "Understanding Micropolis and Compunity," in *Culture, Technology, Communication: Towards an Intercultural Global Village*, eds. Charles Ess and Fay Sudweeks (Albany: State University of New York Press, 2001), 55.

[85] Kaunda and Kim, "'Samae' Spirit Assist toward 'Ubuntu Spirit' Model," 40.

[86] Pai, *Who Shall Enter the Kingdom of Heaven?*, 347

provided and be responsible for doing it (sustainable farming). The rural community accepted the three loves idea of *Sam-ae* because it was characterized by respect towards God, others, and the planet. In answering Pai's question, "but what did I have to help and give to the poor?"[87] *Sam-ae* represents the spirit of interdependence, collaboration, and solidarity among the powerless in the margins, who then effect change in the community. *Sam-ae* is the call to love rooted in the spirit of constant readiness to act together with others – the spirit of solidarity and interdependence.

VOICE FROM THE SOCIAL MARGIN: THE IDEA OF SOLIDARITY IN *SAM-AE* AND THE MARGINALIZED RURAL COMMUNITY

Rev. Pai Min-Soo's approach to the struggling context of the rural community is characterized by the twentieth-century idea of solidarity. In his most famous work in classic sociology, The Division of Labour in Society, Emile Durkheim discussed solidarity as a moral phenomenon with a moral goal.[88] According to Durkheim, the moral goal of solidarity is to live in a peaceful and harmonious community where members are responsible for each other.[89] Durkheim's analysis of social solidarity brought to light several vital themes in social theory, including the connection between solidarity, justice, and equality, the power of the law in integrating members of society, the development of individualism, and the relationship between similarity and difference.[90] Durkheim examines solidarity as an act that relies on the individual willingness and ability to reason, as much as the willingness to accept the state's moral authority.[91] In Durkheim, the state plays a vital role in ensuring that specific moral rules are observed.[92] Solidarity is understood as being closely related to equal participation from each community member in relation to the state's authority.

According to Durkheim, there are two forms of solidarity: mechanical solidarity in traditional society and organic solidarity in modern society.[93] Even

---

[87] Pai, *Who Shall Enter the Kingdom of Heaven?*, 306.

[88] Emile Durkheim, *The Division of Labor in Society* (New York, NY: Simon and Schuster, 2014), 52.

[89] Ruud ter Meulen, *Solidarity and Justice in Health and Social Care* (Edinburgh: Edinburgh University Press, 2017), 5.

[90] Steinar Stjernø, *Solidarity in Europe: The History of an Idea* (Cambridge: Cambridge University Press, 2005), 35.

[91] Meulen, *Solidarity and Justice*, 5.

[92] Ibid.

[93] Stjernø, *Solidarity in Europe*, 33.

though Durkheim uses the term mechanical, he did not mean to show that the connectedness in this type of solidarity is achieved through mechanical or artificial ways. Instead, the term mechanical is used to show the interconnectedness between community members compared to that which unites a thing to a person.[94] Mechanical solidarity develops in a traditional society where homogeneous social structures and members are connected based on their living conditions, culture, beliefs, rituals, etc.[95] In traditional society, even though families or clans are independent of each other and can produce their needs by themselves, the tie of solidarity is strong because of the homogeneous aspect of community life.[96] Over time, traditional society developed, and the increase of individualization created an imbalance in the community because each member started to focus on individual goals and best interests. Hence, a need arose for a new form of solidarity to ensure that society still held together as a moral community. In modern society, a new mode of solidarity appeared – organic solidarity. Durkheim called it organic solidarity because he compared the interdependency between individuals to the unity among the parts of a single organism.

Mechanical solidarity is expressed in Pai's rural movement, emphasizing the interconnectedness between rural community members and the homogeneous aspect of rural life. It is of utmost importance that mechanical solidarity is conducted to ensure the harmonious rhythm of social life because, in mechanical solidarity, the collective consciousness overcomes the individual consciousness. Accordingly, Sam-ae can be interpreted as a tool to ensure the formation of collective consciousness in the rural community. The outlook brought by Sam-ae made it possible for the rural community to move toward their shared goal of community empowerment. In short, it was the spirit of *Sam-ae* that pushed forward the vision of quality social life for the rural community.

Pai's brilliance lies in his ability to link the characteristic of social theories of his time with his religious beliefs. In particular, Pai's work showed the interconnectedness between mechanical solidarity in the community and Jesus's solidarity in the Bible. Miguel de la Torre, professor of social ethics and human rights movement activist, remarked "Jesus is in

---

[94] Emile Durkheim, *Selected Writings,* ed. Anthony Giddens (Cambridge: Cambridge University Press, 1972), 139.

[95] Stjernø, *Solidarity in Europe,* 33.

[96] Meulen, *Solidarity and Justice*, 57; Stjernø, *Solidarity in Europe*, 33.

solidarity with the very least of humanity."[97] Jesus's church cannot practice solidarity without the willingness to stand with the marginalized members of the community. To be sure, "Jesus can never belong to the oppressors of this world, for he is one of the oppressed."[98] Pai's faith in Jesus was embodied in his rural movement's work. The concept of love in *Sam-ae* identified by Jesus's solidarity made it possible for Pai's rural movement to pass the test of biblical fidelity.

Pai's method of empowerment in the rural movement that resulted in social transformation includes two substantial aspects. First, focus on the margins, the weak, and the powerless. Only from "the margins of power and privilege can a fuller and more comprehensive understanding of the prevailing social structures be ascertained."[99] Moreover, only those who have been marginalized can explain "what it means to be a marginalized person attempting to survive within a social context designed to benefit the privileged few at their expense."[100] The voice of those powerless in the margins disappears in the face of a powerful, dominant voice. Thus, providing space for the powerless in the margin to be empowered and to empower others is the only way to promote change.

Second, focus on local knowledge to promote actions with solid moral bases. In Pai's work, he uses *Sam-ae* in the rural movement "to help the needy ones."[101] Within Pai's *Sam-ae*, love is achieved through a genuine act of solidarity. This solidarity in *Sam-ae* is not only solidarity with others but "solidarity of others."[102] The wording of the concept "solidarity of others"[103] itself was first offered by Anselm K. Min, a Korean theologian. "Why solidarity of others, and not solidarity with others?"[104] Min believes that "solidarity with others implies some privileged vantage point from which I or we look at others as other and choose which others to enter into solidarity with."[105] Consequently, we see others "only as victims needing my or our

---

[97] Miguel A. de la Torre, *Doing Christian Ethics from the Margins* (New York: Orbis Books, 2014), kindle edition loc. 361.

[98] de la Torre, *Doing Christian Ethics from the Margins,* loc. 361.

[99] Ibid., loc. 398.

[100] Ibid.

[101] Pai, *Who Shall Enter the Kingdom of Heaven?*, 351.

[102] Anselm K. Min, *The Solidarity of Others in a Divided World: A Postmodern Theology after Postmodernism* (New York: T & T Clark International, 2004), 82.

[103] Min, *The Solidarity of Others*, 82.

[104] Ibid.

[105] Min, *The Solidarity of Others,* 82.

assistance; we tend to be paternalistic."[106] "Solidarity of others, somewhat colloquial but grammatically perfectly correct, implies that there is no privileged perspective, that all are others to one another, that we as others to one another are equally responsible, and that all are subjects, not objects."[107]

These two key aspects are united through Pai's good ethical intention, which is grounded in his Christian faith. For Pai, belief in the Kingdom of God is characterized by love and justice, and must enable followers to practice love and create justice in the world: "Pai believed that contributing to rural emancipation was fulfilling the will of God."[108] Two substantial aspects of Pai's method of empowerment will be used in discussing the importance of folklore as a subaltern theological voice in Indonesia. Theological discourse situates folklore in the margins and mutes local voices. Pai's *Sam-ae* creates a space for the rural living texts to be considered in theological conversation.

INDONESIAN THEOLOGY AND THE VOICE FROM THE MARGIN

Christianity's relationship with Indonesia can be viewed as four different episodes and encounters with local culture: (1) 'Introduction' in the pre-colonial era, Nestorian Christianity was brought to the archipelago located between Asia and Australia continents. (2) 'Domination' is a phase of coerced Christian presence maintained through colonialism and the spice trade. (3) 'Acceptance' the stage where Christianity as a religion from the West recognized the presence of local culture. (4) 'Mutual transformation,' the era where Christianity and local Indonesian culture transform – and are transformed by – each other. These encounters of Christianity with Indonesia highlight the theological understanding of local cultures in Indonesia.

The relationship between Christianity and culture in Indonesia has undergone a dynamic juncture. For a hundred years, Christianity, through its European-centric theological lens understood local culture as – to borrow a term from Foucault – 'subjugated knowledge.'[109] The banishing of the local language in Christian services during colonial times betrays the dominant culture at work within Indonesian Christian religious life. Local knowledge and indigenous theology have become covert voices in Indonesia's church

---

[106] Ibid.

[107] Ibid.

[108] Kaunda and Kim, "'Samae' Spirit Assist toward 'Ubuntu Spirit' Model," 41.

[109] Michel Foucault, *Power/Knowledge: Selected Interviews & Other Writings 1972-1977*, ed. Colin Gordon (New York: Vintage Books, 1980), 82.

services and theological discourse. European-centric Christianity pushed local theology to the margin and framed it as inappropriate knowledge.

The path of Indonesia's colonization is as follows: Pax Portuguesiana, Pax Nederlandica, Pax Javanica, Pax Indonesiana. After Pope Urban II announced and blessed the journey to discover the 'Spice Islands' in the southern part of the world, Western powers took steps to sail the ocean in search of 'black pearl': clove, nutmeg, and sandalwood. In 1513, the Portuguese landed in Ternate, North Moluccas, and quickly started its '3M Program' (merchant, military, and mission).[110] In his research on the colonial history of Moluccas, Leonard Andaya writes that when the Portuguese encountered the local people, the Europeans saw the Moluccans as monsters because of their physical appearance, modes of consumption, and textile materiality. The Portuguese perception of locals mirrored the Europeans' understanding of people from the Global South during the colonial era: the natives are less human than Europeans.[111] Therefore, the European changed the native people's worldview, faith, identity, and quotidian practice.[112]

The Dutch came to Indonesia in 1602, bringing Protestant Calvinism to replace Portuguese Catholicism. Dutch missionaries introduced Calvinism to the natives, while also forcing their language and sidelining native culture. The Dutch acquainted Calvinism through the Heidelberg Catechism translation from Dutch to Malay in Malaka.[113] Prior to colonialism, the Malay language had been the merchant's means of communication. The Dutch merchants, military, and missionaries used the same language to interact with locals. Calvinist Church employed Malay as the congregational and liturgical language. We visited many old churches from colonial times in Moluccas, where we encountered countless documents from the Dutch era written in Malay. However, the Dutch Missionaries had pejoratively considered the native language as means to communicate with devils and ancestors. Since Dutch colonial times, there has hardly been any practice of language and culture in local churches.

---

[110] Izak Y. M. Lattu and Tedi Kholiludin, Nusantara Pasca Kristeninsasi (Semarang, Indonesia: eLSA Press, 2021).

[111] Leonard Andaya, *The World of Maluku: Eastern Indonesia in the Early Period* (Honolulu: University of Hawaii Press, 1993).

[112] Izak Y.M. Lattu, *Rethinking Interreligious Dialogue: Orality, Collective Memory, and Christian-Muslim Engagements in Indonesia*. (Leiden, Netherlands: Brill Schöningh, 2023).

[113] John Roxborogh, *The History of Christianity in Malay* (Kuala Lumpur: STM Press, 2014).

When Indonesia gained its independence from the Dutch and Japanese, Sukarno, the first president of Indonesia, endeavored to unite the archipelago into a nation. Before Independence, the archipelago was a group of separate peoples and states under the Dutch East Indies colonial government. In his research on founders of pre-independence conversations, the Indonesian scholar John Titaley argues that Indonesia is a "new phenomenon."[114] Before August 17, 1945, no such formal political entity called Indonesia existed. Indonesia only came into being when representatives of the various 'nations' in the Dutch East Indies, agreed to unite and establish a new nation named "Indonesia." With this spirit, Sukarno launched "the national and character building" campaign to develop public awareness of nationhood. The Christian presence in Indonesia during the nation- and character-building process was to set an example of unity. In 1950, Churches in Indonesia established an ecumenical organization named Dewan Gereja-Gereja Indonesia (the Council of Indonesian Churches). Johannes Leimena, a prominent Christian figure from the Indonesian Christian Party (Parkindo) and Sukarno's best friend since colonial times, once stated that an Indonesian Christian has two nationalities: belonging to Heaven and Indonesia.[115]

Although the church played a central role under the Sukarno presidency, with the appointment of its second president, Suharto and his "New Order" administration, Indonesia underwent "de-Sukarnoization" from the 1970's, where the country was increasingly pushed towards forced Javanization. Here, predominantly Christian areas were forced to give up local culture and assimilate Javanese refinement. Local Christians who were previously coerced to westernize under Portuguese and Dutch colonial rule, similarly had to endure extreme Javanization under President Suharto. The Suharto administration's "nationalist spirit" campaign also banned local churches from receiving foreign aid. While those of the religious majority enjoyed prosperity brought by Suharto and petrodollars, Christians experienced double marginalization: the loss of local culture and global support.

INDONESIAN THEOLOGICAL DISCOURSE: EMBRACING MARGINALIZATION

As a method to embrace unfortunate people in the margins, theology brings hope and strengthens human attachment to God in any situation. Rev. Pai

---

[114] John Titaley, *Nilai-Nilai Dasar yang Terkandung dalam Pembukaan Undang-Undang Dasar 1945* (Salatiga, Indonesia: Fakultas Teologi Press, 1999).

[115] F. B. Litaay, *Pemikiran Sosial Johannes Leimena tentang Dwi-Kewargaan di Indonesia* (Salatiga, Indonesia: Satya Wacana University Press, 2007).

Min-Soo's *Sam-ae* concept criticizes an unbalanced world where the dominant group becomes the theological arbiter possessing sole knowledge. *Sam-ae,* which is based on a triune love of God, labor, and farming, proposes a deconstruction of conventional theology—the locked theology formulated in seminary libraries far away from any true reflection of society outside the center. Theology disengages with Indonesia's social and cultural context but mainly uses theological works from North America and Western Europe. This theology perpetuates colonial domination in Indonesia that underestimates local text and knowledge. In colonial times Dutch masters, including missionaries, upheld the Dutch perspective and experience as the sole source for theological reflection. The Dutch 'masters' understood human relations in accordance to skin color and physical appearance. According to Dutch law of the East Indies (*Vreemde Oosterlingen*), the people in colonial Indonesia were divided into three categories: Europeans, Eastern Asians, and Middle-Eastern Locals. The Dutch placed whites on the top of the social pyramid and browns on the bottom.[116] Consequently, the locals' (*pribumi*) theological experience could not partake in colonial Christian reflection.

The *Sam-ae* concept criticizes theological reflection that leans towards the dominant class. Rev. Pai Min-Soo understood that this type of theological domination was injustice and violence against human rights. *Sam-ae* pushed back on a theology based solely on seminary and scholarly works. Rev. Pai Min-Soo's encounter with a half-blind old lady leads to a deeper understanding of *Sam-ae*: that logos also dwells within the quotidian lives of marginalized people. *Sam-ae* invites Indonesian scholars to cross theological borders to develop reflection from life and, borrowing Nancy Ammerman concept, lived religion of the marginal people.[117] *Sam-ae* deconstructs the colonial theological trap and unpacks the epistemic violence of Christian domination of Western European and North America in Indonesia.

Marginalization of local theology marks European perceptions of native people. In colonial theology, both in colonial time and postcolonial times, theologians place theology as the knowledge from the West European and North America.[118] Colonial theology situated theological texts as valid Christian knowledge when it comes from giant theology from the Global

---

[116] Eleazar Zorab, *De Publiekrechtelijke Toestand Der Vreemde Oosterlingen: In Nederlandsch Oost-Indie, 1890* (Amsterdam: Kessinger Publishing, 2010).

[117] Nancy T. Ammerman, *Studying Lived Religion: Contexts and Practices* (New York: NYU Press, 2021).

[118] Pui-Lan Kwok, *Postcolonial Politics and Theology: Unraveling Empire for a Global World* (Louisville, KY: John Knox Press, 2021).

North. Theology, as such, undermines texts and theological exercises from the local community. Until hitherto theological discourse, many scholars remain trapped in this theological paradigm. Because of Western European and North American theological glorification, local texts and theological exercise underwent inappropriateness.

Located as inappropriate knowledge, local theology, for many decades, suffered disregard because Christianity relied on textual knowledge. Theology, as for textual understanding, comes into being as a body of knowledge because it is placed in the form of writing. According to this perspective, Christian life is one spent in the realm of the written world with an ink horizon. Many elders in the Eastern part of Indonesia, where Christian culture is a strong presence in people's religious practices, would only participate in Christian rituals when holding a book regardless of its sacredness. Our autoethnographic experiences in Moluccas and Timor, show the book's influence on religious rituals: some elders would instead bring school books to the church than present them in the sanctuary without any canon.

Canonical influence in Christian life highlights the imperialism of ink in Church services and Christian practices. Ink defines theological foundations and shapes theological meaning in Christian life. Lattu has written elsewhere that ink defines theological meaning in Christian life. Christian theologians frame Christianity as a religion of the book. In this context, Christians celebrate the presence of logos within the realm of ink as if God's word only fits the sacred canon. However, Christianity believes that logos entered the material world in the flesh, not through the word of ink.[119] Jesus is logos and someone who never put the word to ink, but rather spread his gospel orally through narratives, parables, and practice. In the early decades of the first Christian community, people memorized the theology and circulated Jesus's teachings by word of mouth. Christian teachings only embraced the world of ink and became predominant when Paul the Apostle addressed Christian communities in Near East through his apostolic letters.

The world of ink views theology as being in the domain of the learned and elite in world Christianity. Theology belongs to people on top of the social pyramid who communicate with fellow human beings and express the 'Ultimate Concern' through written words. Studying the experience of the Black community during slavery in American history, James Cone discovers the

---

[119] Izak Y. M. Lattu, "Teologi Tanpa Tinta: Mencari Logos Melalui Etnografi dan Folklore," in *Membangun Gereja Sebagai Gerakan Yang Cerdas dan Solider* (Yogyakarta, Indonesia: Sanata Darma University Press, 2020).

enslaved people practiced theology through storytelling and oral narratives. At the same time, the White masters were practicing theology printed in ink. For Cone, this theology of ink served the needs of the bourgeoisie and the elite. Therefore, theology in oral forms is relegated to the margins and viewed as a peripheral community.[120] In the Indonesian context, a wave of local theology has pushed Indonesia theologians and sociologists of religion to embrace indigenous knowledge, cultural texts, and local narratives into their theological discourse.

CONCLUSION

Sam-ae is the invitation to embrace and accept peripheral theology based on a triune aspect of love: love of God, labor, and farming. In the context of twentieth-century Korean life, members of the laboring and farming class in rural areas suffered being marginalized socially. *Sam-ae* is believing that the love of God is equal to the love of labor and farming. This theological understanding of the *Sam-ae* concept inspires theologians and religious scholars to open avenues to explore the presence of logos in an everyday – as well as an everybody – context. God presents and dwells in the lives of people in the social periphery in the Korean context and beyond. *Sam-ae* believes that the love of God and logos live beyond social boundaries, physical sanctuaries, and academic buildings.

Sam-ae Spirit resonates with folkloric theology, creating room for accepting mnemonic text and orality in the theological discourse. Folklore, as local knowledge in conventional theological discourse, experiences marginalization because theologians and religious scholars have curved logos in the canonical frameworks and academic atmosphere for many decades. *Sam-ae* idea accommodates the spiritual voice from the social margin as much as folkloric theology searches in the religious-cultural discussion. As it is for *Sam-ae that* respects labor and farming, folkloric theology respects the *logos spermatikos* (divine seed) and the voice of God in everybody and quotidian contexts. Theological understanding, in this sense, represents solidarity and respect for people in the social margins.

---

[120] James H. Cone, *God of the Oppressed* (Maryknoll, NY: Orbis Books, 2000), 40.

CHAPTER 7

SAM-AE SPIRIT AS A MIRROR: ANNIE CHIKANJI'S *UBUNTU* LEARNING HUB IN POST-1990 ZAMBIA

NELLY MWALE

INTRODUCTION

Although the Zambia National Policy on Climate Change advocates for improved participation of women, youth and children in climate change programs,[1] the contributions of women have not been adequately addressed in scholarship. Additionally, the efforts of women in ecological wellness grounded in indigenous knowledge systems in Zambia have hardly been linked to similar knowledge systems elsewhere. Of particular interest is Pai Min-Soo's *Sam-ae* Spirit grounded in the Korean context which relates to a threefold spirit of love – comprised of the love for God, the love for people/ community, and the love for work.[2] Therefore, this chapter seeks to demonstrate dialogue between *Sam-ae* Spirit and Indigenous Knowledge in Zambia which finds expression in the concept of *Ubuntu*. This is done by addressing the following research question, 'how does the *Ubuntu* learning hub contribute to ecological wellbeing and a sustainable future from a gendered perspective'?

The research question is anchored on the recognition that though female participation in agriculture is increasing worldwide,[3] the contributions of women in the sector as informed by indigenous worldviews remain unexplored in many contexts. It is also anchored on the need for dialogue between indigenous knowledge systems such as *Sam-ae* Spirit and the work of *Ubuntu* learning hub in ecological wellness for purposes of not only contributing to emerging studies on *Sam-ae* Spirit and *Ubuntu* in

---

[1] Government of the Republic of Zambia. *The Zambian National Policy on Climate Change* (Lusaka: GRZ, 2016).

[2] Chammah J. Kaunda and Sang-man Kim. "'Samae Spirit' Assist toward 'Ubuntu Spirit' Model for Rural Adult Christian Education in Zambia," *Religious Education* 117, no. 1 (2022): 33-49.

[3] M. Niaz Asadullah and Uma Kambhampati, "Feminization of Farming, Food Security and Female Empowerment," *Global Food Security* 29 (2021).

Zambian scholarship,[4] but also for enriching scholarship on environmental care from a gendered perspective.

Additionally, the research question is grounded in the notion of *Ubuntu* as understood in African Indigenous thought. In this regard, it is related to a unified community in which it is believed that life belongs to a community (in which the value is strongly linked to the concept of wholeness). This entails that a human being finds fulfilment in the total community of their fellows in whose existence they participate. African thought emphasizes that individuals can only exist when they are part of a group: 'they are because they belong'[5]. Therefore, while it is acknowledged that the notion of *Ubuntu* may have different words to describe it, it is used to refer to a collection of values and practices that Africans view as making people authentic human beings.[6] Although these values and practices vary across different ethnic groups, they all point to the idea that an authentic individual human being is part of a larger and more significant relational, communal, societal, environmental, and spiritual world.

BRIEF CONTEXT

The chapter is situated in post 1990 Zambia which is among other things characterized by the liberalisation of the economy. The liberalisation of the economy had implications on many spheres of life, including negatively impacting on the environment and the poor. For example, the Environmental Council of Zambia observed that the liberalization of the Zambian economy contributed to the rate of ecological degradation in the country.[7] This was through the high electricity tariffs and reduction of the fiscal support to the forestry department, which heightened deforestation levels.

Additionally, the chapter is situated in an agricultural setting, a sector not only impacted by economic trends, but also climate change whose effects affect the poor and marginalized groups differently. For example, the economic emphasis on agribusiness resulted in the use of mechanized commercial farming that is dependent on chemicals which are hazardous to

---

[4] Kaunda and Kim, "Samae Spirit' Assist toward 'Ubuntu Spirit' Model."

[5] Thaddeus Metz, "Ubuntu as a Moral Theory and Human Rights in South Africa," *African Human Rights Law Journal* 11, no. 2 (2011): 532; S.A. Thorpe, *African Traditional Religions: An Introduction* (Manualia didáctica, 16) (Pretoria: University of South Africa, 1991), 120.

[6] Jacob Rugare Mugumbate and Admire Chereni, "Now, the Theory of Ubuntu Has Its Space in Social Work," *African Journal of Social Work* 10, no. 1 (2020): 1.

[7] "State of Environment in Zambia ," Environmental Council of Zambia (Lusaka: ECZ, 2001).

ecology and marginalized the poor. The growing effects of climate change also affect the poor more, as observed by the United Nations that climate change was one of the greatest challenges of our time as increases in global temperature, sea level rise, ocean acidification and other climate change impacts were seriously affecting coastal areas and low-lying coastal countries, including many least developed countries and Small Island Developing States.[8] The Zambia National Policy on Climate Change also acknowledges that climate change has significantly affected rainfall patterns, a situation that has resulted in crop failure and a further reduction in economic growth.[9] This scenario entailed that the post 1990 was characterized by neo-liberalization which resulted in inequalities and contributed to social divisions between the haves and have-nots.[10] These inequalities are also gendered as observed by some scholars that gender is an important consideration in discussions of agriculture as high levels of women's participation in urban agriculture are recorded in many developing world cities.[11] As such, the entry of female personalities such as Annie Chikanji and her *Ubuntu* learning hub could be understood in relation to liberative initiatives and gender dynamics which can be extended to contributing towards wellness beyond one's immediate needs, but the wider community.

THEORY AND METHODS

Theoretically, the chapter is framed in Pai Min-Soo's threefold love (the love for God, the love for humanity, and the love for work). While a comprehensive biography of Rev. Pai Min-Soo can be read elsewhere,[12] it will suffice to stress that Pai's trajectory was characterised with works of love, mercy, and compassion for the rural and marginalized people in the Korean context. This approach to life was centred on seeking solutions to human, social, and political challenges in the wake of Japanese

---

[8] "2019 Climate Action Summit," United Nations, New York, https://www.un.org/en/climatechange/2019-climate-action-summit.

[9] "The Zambian National Policy on Climate Change," Government of the Republic of Zambia (Lusaka: Government of the Republic of Zambia, 2016).

[10] Nelly Mwale, "Ethics and Morality in a Religious Educational Community: The Self-Understanding of Catholic University Education in Zambia," *Journal for Islamic Studies* 38, no. 1 (2020): 107.

[11] Godfrey Hampwaye, Etienne Nel, and Christian M. Rogerson, "Urban agriculture as local initiative in Lusaka, Zambia," *Environment and Planning C: Government and Policy* 25, no. 4 (2007): 553-572.

[12] Kaunda and Kim, "Samae Spirit' Assist toward 'Ubuntu Spirit' Model."

colonialization of Koreans and resulting mass economic, social, and cultural problems. In turn, Pai opted to go against mainstream conservative Christianity to formulate Christian ideas that could help transform a fragmented and materially distressed rural society.[13]

Although situated in a Christian Korean context, the 'threefold loves' is used as lens to relate the work of *Ubuntu* learning hub which has attributes of working with the marginalized and nature. Both Pai and Annie had a religious background (vocation) although in different Christian denominations. While *Sam-ae* Spirit was closely linked to colonialism, the chapter links *Ubuntu* with elements of neo-liberalization as mirrored in the post 1990 Zambia. Despite these differences in personalities, contexts and vocation, their work is brought in conversation to draw lessons contributing towards ecological wellness through one's love for work, God, and humanity.

In this case, *Sam-ae* Spirit is brought in conversation with *Ubuntu*, here viewed as a philosophy based on generic life values of justice, responsibility, equality, collectiveness, relatedness, reciprocity, love, respect, helpfulness, community, caring, dependability, sharing, trust, integrity, unselfishness, and social change.[14] It emphasizes that people's identities are continuously developing in the context of their reciprocal relationships with others, and thereby, through supporting and nurturing others, one's own identity and life quality are enhanced. *Ubuntu* focuses on the inclusivity of everyone within a community, their responsibility to others and to the wellbeing of the environment to ensure success for their own and future generations. *Ubuntu* is, therefore, timeless in the sense that the knowledge and the practice have been passed from previous generations and apply to yet un-born generations; everything is connected.

The chapter trails the work of *Ubuntu* learning hub through personal interviews with Annie Chikanji and the analysis of documents in the form of newspapers, videos, and social media engagement. It particularly employs a narrative research design (in which the unit of analysis was purposively selected, and documents were chosen based on the availability criteria). Accordingly, *Ubuntu* learning hub and Annie Chikanji were purposively chosen. The inclusion and exclusion criteria included being a female promoter of naturally grown foods, employing religious discourses and

---

[13] Kaunda and Kim, "Samae Spirit' Assist toward 'Ubuntu Spirit' Model."

[14] Bernard Mayaka and Rory Truell, "Ubuntu and Its Potential Impact on the International Social Work Profession," *International Social Work* 64, no. 5 (2021): 649-662.

community outreach in the sphere of ecological care. As such, the narrative is for purposes of providing understanding on how *ubuntu* learning hub could be related to *Sam-ae* Spirit.

The collected stories about the *Ubuthu* learning hub and Annie Chikanji were analysed through restorying in which stories were gathered, analyzed for key elements of the story (e.g., setting, plot, and scene), and then rewriting the stories to place them within a chronological sequence.[15] Ethical issues surrounding informed consent and privacy and guidelines for using documentary sources were kept in check as recommended by scholars.[16]

BRIEF BIOGRAPHY OF ANNIE CHIKANJI

Annie Chikanji is the name behind *Ubuntu* learning hub. This brief biography was gathered from her own account of her life story in September 2022. Annie was a Religious Sister for 15 years and asked to leave due to the health of her brother in 2011. She is now a married woman. Having been an orphan at an early age (5 years old), Annie grew up with her uncle through whom she was introduced to Catholicism at a young age. She was an active choir member at church and recalled having learnt to play drums with the inspiration from her Uncle:

> Farming was his livelihood. He was converted to Catholicism and the entire family followed him. I loved him very much and I followed him to the Catholic Church. He would ask me to beat drums because he had one hand, so I would play, and he would sing, and the entire house became a choir. So, I became very strong in the church.[17]

She attended her primary school education at Muchinshi Primary in Chingola. She did her Grade 8 and 9 at Chikola Secondary school and Ibenga Girls Secondary School, respectively. She had to return from Ibenga when her sister fell ill and thus completed her secondary education at Chingola High school. During her time at Chingola secondary school, she came into contact with an International Catholic Religious group of Sisters, the Sacred Heart Sisters of Jesus and Mary. Having observed the language

---

[15] Jo Anne Ollerenshaw and John W. Creswell, "Narrative Research: A Comparison of Two Restorying Data Analysis Approaches," *Qualitative inquiry* 8, no. 3 (2002): 329-347.

[16] Alan Bryman, Social Research Methods (Oxford: Oxford University Press, 2004); John Scott, *A Matter of Record: Documentary Sources in Social Research* (Cambridge: Polity Press, 1990).

[17] Personal Interview, Annie Chikanji, 29 Sept. 2022, Chongwe.

challenges which, the sisters encountered in their outreach activities, Annie promised to join sisterhood:

> Due to language barrier, the sisters would always ask for girls to help with interpretation, and I would always be the first one to volunteer. I saw how they were struggling, and I said to myself; these people are working in our own country and struggling like this… as soon as I finish school, I will join them.[18]

She thus became the first Zambian and African to join the Sacred Heart Sisters in 1994. In 1996 she became a sister and studied Pre School teaching at Rugambwa in Kabwata. From 1997 to 2011,[19] she was sent to work in different countries: UK, Ireland, Wales, El Salvador and Uganda. One of her memorable experiences was her encounter with the rebels in Uganda:

> I chose to go to Uganda for my Development studies, we had to answer the question, {What is Development?} this was a place I had never been before. I stayed in a camp called Pabo in Northern Uganda near Sudan. I had to learn a new language. I had an encounter with the rebels, including experience of poverty.[20]

She returned to Zambia to finish her BA in Development studies from Ireland in 2011. For her Bachelors' degree research paper, Annie returned to Zambia for her research whose focus was on ICT and development. Through this research, young people were trained in ICT. She was then the Lusaka coordinator of the computer project Camara,[21] and worked with all headteachers in Zambia.

Being a finally professed Sister, she had to have a good reason for leaving sisterhood and the only person who would allow or give her that permission to leave was the Pope from Rome because International Religious Sisters are under the Pope:

> When I asked the Mother Superior to leave the Organisation, she said write to the Pope and see if he will give you that permission. So, I wrote to him, that time it was the late Pope John Paul the Second. I gave him

[18] Personal Interview, Annie Chikanji, 29 Sept. 2022, Chongwe.

[19] When she was in Zambia as a sister, she worked in the Home-Based Care section as a Coordinator at St. Lawrence from 2007 to 2009.

[20] Personal Interview, Annie Chikanji, 29 Sept. 2022, Chongwe.

[21] Camara is an international charity organization which was founded in 2005 in Dublin, Ireland. It focuses on a model of education delivery that is both sustainable and highly scalable by inviting companies give them computer equipment they no longer need. In 2012, a total, 1,851 computers were dispatched to 166 educational institutions and 826 teachers were trained. In February, Camara Zambia opened a sub-hub at SOS Children's Village in Lusaka, responding to the demand from educational institutions in the Lusaka Province for Camara services (Camara, 2012:20).

> the reason of my uncle who looks after my mentally sick brother is getting old now. It was my turn to look after my brother. I assured the Pope that I will continue to do good works even in my country since the poor are everywhere. 3 days later I got a reply from the Pope and he gave me permission to leave Sisterhood.[22]

When she was an ordinary lady in 2012, she also lectured (part time) in Gender and Human and Social Psychology at YMCA. During her time at YMCA, she recalled having contributed to the development of Mahopo Community:

> When I took a walk there, I saw houses which were not fit for human habitation. I said, this place is only 5 kilometers from Chilenje! I cried and wondered what was wrong? This place was called Mahopo because settlers (there) used to work as locomotives, trees were cut in logs to be used in trains. They used to hip them in bundles. So, people were saying we are going to Mahopo. Mahopo was operating as a village with the headman. I wanted to know more about it and the situation of poverty. So, the question of development came in, how do I develop with them. I used the method of going to the people, work with the people and with the best leaders, the people will say, We, have done it ourselves. YMCA asked me to do a social work class so that I could practically show students how to develop the community. I started by assessing the community, taking their story and gave back the information to the community. I told them not to let any other organisation or person who comes to ask them again about their story, they can say that their story is already with one person called Annie and they can contact her. Together with the community leaders, we formed the Mahopo Community Association. I mentored the leaders together with Mr. Given Lubinda, the MP for Kabwata Constituency that time. The needs of Mahopo were listed and the first one was housing. Leaders of Mahopo and myself used to attend housing meetings and formed the first ever Housing cooperative in Zambia. This helped them to get ownership of their land and they started building their houses. Education was the second on the list and I helped them to apply for Japanese grant for the school. We used Civic Forum to monitor the grant and build the school. The Government also gave them a clinic, Police post and now Mahopo is well developed as a Township. Sadly, the community part died, and people live as individuals. The market part did not really work out as we advised the women to be selling food in their homes.[23]

She also served as an assistant researcher for the biodiversity community network (BCN-Zambia) in which she was involved in documenting crop

[22] Personal Interview with Annie Chikanji, 29 Sept. 2022, Chongwe.

[23] Ibid.

characterization, report writing and collecting data from farmers. Additionally, she was the knowledge manager for the Revival NGO.

Prior to establishing *Ubuntu* learning hub, Annie worked as the Schools and Colleges of Permaculture Programme (RESCOPE) network's national coordinator in Zambia from 2018 until her resignation in 2021. Zambia did not have schools and colleges in permaculture and thus she became the first one to be trained. ReSCOPE, sought to revive African youths' interest in their land, food and culture. By introducing hands-on agricultural education into the academic curriculum, RESCOPE sought to promote a "whole school" approach in more than 50 schools and communities across Africa. The focus was on Youth and smallholder farmers championing farmer seed systems and agroecology to enhance food sovereignty and nutrition in 5 countries in East and Southern Africa.

She describes herself as a problem solver, seeking to provide solutions, and her passion remained to undertake developmental work focusing on and fostering the grassroots.

A BRIEF DESCRIPTION OF *UBUNTU* LEARNING HUB

Ubuntu learning hub is located around Kasisi area, in Lusaka and defines self as a piece of land where all are welcome to explore and experience living and eating healthy food, including learning the permanent way of doing things. Although a recent establishment (2 years), it has created an imprint on the ecological wellness discourses in the country. This initiative came into fruition when Annie decided to focus on permaculture by way of creating a learning centre given that there was no practical centre where people would appreciate the permaculture way of life in Lusaka. She recalled that permaculture, "is seeing resources with new eyes. It has opened me to see that there's nothing to throw . . . in the land of plentifulness, why are we suffering?"[24]

She recollected that *Ubuntu* learning hub came into existence because of her own life experiences. She had observed that people had become filled with jealousy and individualism:

> When I saw what was happening in Zambia – like when you ask for directions they would say, give me money for water and I asked myself where is *Ubuntu* here? We have lost that togetherness. So, I developed the idea of I am because we are. I had wanted to call the centre *Mwana*

[24] Personal Interview with Annie Chikanji, 29 Sept. 2022, Chongwe.

> *alilenji* – everything you want is there, no none should go hungry but settled for *Ubuntu* – I am because we are.[25]

The centre had a special option for the young people, women and those living with disabilities. For example, young people were offered life skills and given opportunities to use their skills at the learning centre. Similarly, women were engaged to learn life skills. In the case of those living with disabilities, the learning centre infrastructure was built with them in mind in which case, it was an inclusive centre. Annie recalled that her inclusive approach to life was influenced by her uncle who could not use stair cases after he survived a fatal locomotive accident while working on the mines.[26]

The centre was anchored on the permaculture way of life and focused on offering local practical solutions to problems. *Ubuntu* learning hub will be offering learning opportunities to rural communities and other interested persons through workshops, field trips and online sessions. "We share what we know because knowledge is power. Every month we try to share on agro ecology on different topics. As a small-scale farmer, I believe that we have a lot to share . . ." [27]

UBUNTU LEARNING HUB IN CONVERSATION WITH *SAM-AE* SPIRIT

Ubuntu learning hub was engaged in numerous works for ecological wellness which mirror the threefold loves in different ways:

LOVE FOR WORK

To start with, *Ubuntu* learning hub grew in a context which had experienced climate change. She recalled that the land on which *Ubuntu* learning hub was established was bought in an area with drought and that people were abandoning the place:

> Trees around this village have been cut for charcoal so it never rains here. We only had rain for one month. We have had 3 years of drought. People are abandoning the place and we said this is the land we want to buy so that we can bring back life. Climate change is serious and all the water which was in the shallow wells is gone. [28]

The centre was also attempting to contribute to ecological wellness by controlling life. She emphasised that there was need to work more with

---

[25] Personal Interview with Annie Chikanji, 29 Sept. 2022, Chongwe.

[26] Ibid.

[27] A. Chikanji, Facebook posting, 22 June 2022.

[28] Personal interview with Annie Chikanji, 29 Sept. 2022, Chongwe.

nature than against nature. This was by managing natural elements to meet different needs. For example, *Ubuntu* learning hub was harvesting water and teaching others how to utilise the available resources from a permaculture perspective. The infrastructure was constructed using local resources, including the solar dryers, cold storage and accommodation facilities which embraced the concept of dry toilets. The lay out of the hub also followed the permaculture design of having ecological zones.

Ubuntu offered knowledge on growing food naturally, including value addition. This was done through different methods such as webinars, field visits and workshops. For example:

> Farmers are learning the life skills as they spend some time with *Ubuntu*. Sometimes they come and are given space to practice making *bochashi* at *Ubuntu* farm or *Ubuntu* reaches then where they are. Topics covered under value addition included introduction to natural herbs, herbal worldview, practical herbal making, teas, ointments, oil and tinctures, management of community ailments, local healing plants, soap making practical, and herbal garden designs.[29]
>
> On 19th August, we were in Kitwe sharing knowledge on natural farming. A natural farmer prepares the field just after harvest. The land should be slashed, mulched, and covered by anthill soils if that is locally available. A natural farmer should always know many ways of making the soil fertile. What is sustainable is to grow your own fertiliser by including trees in the fields such as *musangu*, *Lucerna* and T*ephrosia*, etc. We learnt the importance of protecting our good seed from diseases and that coating makes our seed to germinate 100% therefore giving us more yield. We learnt how to dry in a simple solar dryer. With liquid fertilisers we learnt that the smaller the animal, the stronger the fertiliser. . . .[30]

Ubuntu also embraced syntropic farming to enhance biodiversity. This was complimented by involvement in tree planting and local seed growing in villages. This was in the quest to achieve input reduction. For example, *Ubuntu* reflected the success story of the local seed growing initiative as follows:

> Local seed was grown using natural methods and farmers proved that it was possible to be seed sovereign in Zambia. The farmers grew their own seed after a workshop for trainers. . . . Mr Michelo never buys maize seed, he saves his seed.[31]

---

[29] *Ubuntu* Learning Hub, Facebook posting, 13 Sept. 2022.

[30] Ibid., 22 Aug. 2022.

[31] Ibid., 10 June 2022.

Local seed was not only grown but shared with others. She insisted that seed comes back, a reflection of the *Ubuntu* principle of sharing and caring for others. *Ubuntu* learning hub was also passionate about tree planting:

> Climate change is real, but we can help to be that change. We can cool down our surroundings by planting trees to meet all our needs. Trees that this generation and the future generation will find.[32]

The initiative in local seed could be closely linked to the quest to fight the dominant love driven by the promotion of seed from multinational companies at the expense of local (indigenous seed). As observed by Farnworth and Hutchings, indigenous communities are being locked into relationships with monopoly driven multi-national seed companies that are forcing dependence on GM seed and chemical fertilisers.[33]

This involvement in ecological wellness through promoting the growing of food naturally suggest that the creation of the *Ubuntu* learning hub was a way of problematizing the dominant self-love and providing an alternative love centred on empowering communities through offering natural wellness education services and growing organic food. In a context where the liberation of the economy in the 1990s had an impact on the wellness of the Earth and as the use of chemicals to increase yields became the norm in the agriculture sector, Annie went against the dominant trends by adopting earth friendly practices. This closely resonated with Pai Min soo's stance to turn against mainstream conservative Christianity to contribute towards transforming rural communities.

LOVE FOR HUMANITY

Annie's love for humanity was further mirrored in her passion to serve the marginalized communities in ways which affirm the idea that people are meant to be of service to others and the environment. Anchored on the very notion of *Ubuntu*, the *Ubuntu* learning hub was driven by the quest to deliver development at the grassroots level and with members of the grassroots. This literally reflected the understating of *Ubuntu* as humanity to others. As spelt out by Tutu, a person is a person through other persons.[34] This love for humanity was expressed through retrieving and sharing indigenous

---

[32] *Ubuntu* Learning Hub, Facebook posting, 31 July 2022.

[33] Cathy Farnworth and Jessica Hutchings, "Organic Agriculture and Women's empowerment," *IFOAM, Germany* 86 (2009), 25. https://www.wocan.org/sites/default/files/gender-study-090421.pdf

[34] Desmond M. Tutu, *No Future Without Forgiveness* (New York: Doubleday, 1990).

knowledge on natural agriculture. In this regard, young people, women and other interested persons were taught how to use locally available resources for sustenance. These included making solar dryers, seed storage facilities, including being introduced to natural foods. For example, she taught children aspects of natural farming as was she case on 8th October 2022 where children learnt about natural farming at the showgrounds in Lusaka.

Her love for humanity was also shown through her option for young people, women, and children:

> I always uplift young people, their mothers, and children. For me, my people are these young people, they understand development and I understand them well. But mostly because young people understand any situation better, and if you want to bring any change, target the young people, they are change agents. The gap I see in young people is how they can be enabled to understand real issues and how to support themselves. For women, it is because of vulnerability. When I see them, they have no control, so I usually teach them to be in control of the situation, not to depend on their husbands. If I have my own money, I will look after my needs. There's big gap on how we are brought up-dependency. For people with disabilities, I have been inspired by own uncle.[35]

Her option for the marginalized groups (especially women) which pointed to retrieving the inherent potential and skills in these groups closely resonates with the observation by Rocheleau, that the marginalization of indigenous women's skills, needs and knowledge in agriculture is directly related to the unequal power relations inherent within the ideologies of colonization, capitalism and globalization.[36] By retrieving indigenous values and practices of *Ubuntu* through a special option for women, the *Ubuntu* learning hub not only demonstrated love for humanity but also an alternative love in a context where the visibility of women and their work, interest and knowledge were obscured. This was extended to offering to help the farmers access markets:

> We are facilitating the selling of soya beans/Maize/Groundnuts from anywhere in the country delivered in Lusaka at K2.80 per kg soya beans, Maize K85, Groundnuts K11 per kg – less 10% facilitation and in addition we are providing a free truck transportation with only own fuel by farmers with payment within 24 to 48 hrs of delivered business.[37]

---

[35] Personal interview with Annie Chikanji, 29 Sept. 2022, Chongwe.

[36] Dianne E. Rocheleau. "Gender, Ecology, and the Science of Survival: Stories and Lessons from Kenya, *Agriculture and Human Values* 8, no. 1 (1991): 156-165.

[37] "Annie Chikanji is Facilitating the Sale of These Commodities," Zambia Farmers Hub, 15 June 2017, https://zambiafarmershub.wordpress.com/2017/06/15/annie-chikanji-is-facilitating-the-sale-of-these-commodities/.

Ubuntu learning hub further encouraged the use of local resources in farming in ways which point to the quest to retrieve indigenous knowledge in a context where dominant western knowledge was perceived important. For example, organic fertilisers were manufactured using local materials (such as charcoal, dried grass or leaves, maize bran, ash and rocks) before being distributed to the farmers. Thus, as argued by Siwila *Ubuntu* learning hub could be seen to be contributing towards responding to ecological issues.[38] Annie's account further points to discourses of how African women embedded ecological spirituality could be retrieved and transformed for the liberation of both women and nature. This is line with Farnworth and Hutchings' conclusion that women in organic farming were contributing to rewriting the paradigm of ecological wellness from a woman's perspective as imprinted with life and spirituality.[39] Her option for women and the marginalized also resonated with Pai's focus on empowering the farming communities of women. She linked her passion to serve humanity to her own experiences:

> I was an orphan at a young age. Mom died when l was 5 years old, I was told to be strong and not to cry. I am the third born and both my elder sisters died. Being the third born, I became like the first born and I had to take care of a baby for my sister who was 6 months at the time. I also became responsible for my brother who was mentally sick. Situations like that make you sensitive and responsible, so I grew up not liking people to suffer.[40]

Her love for humanity was also seen through her quest to promote culture and traditional foods:

> We had this system of sitting together and uncle would tell us stories. So that culture concept for me is rich. For me, culture is very important because you are nothing if you don't have a culture. How do you keep it alive? Through food grown and cooked but we are losing culture. We are running away from healthy foods. So, nutrition and healthy foods is important, and parenting is key as children will eat what they are served if they see what we eat and that way they will get to know their culture.[41]

The stance on traditional and healthy foods is a pointer to providing an alternative for humanity through speaking against GMOs and unhealthy

---

[38] Lilian Cheelo Siwila, "'Tracing the Ecological Footprints of Our Foremothers': Towards an African Feminist Approach to Women's Connectedness with Nature," *Studia Historiae Ecclesiasticae* 40, no. 2 (2014): 131-147.

[39] Farnworth and Hutchings, "Organic Agriculture and Women's Empowerment."

[40] Personal interview with Annie Chikanji, 29 Sept. 2022, Chongwe.

[41] Ibid.

eating habits. As concluded by Chen et al., the increasing control of multinational corporations over the food environment, the unregulated operations of the fast-food sector and the extensive advertising of high-status fast foods has resulted in an environment saturated with unhealthy and cheap food with implications for public health, hunger, and nutrition.[42] Her promotion of traditional foods was not only a direct way of promoting healthy lifestyles but also upholding the identity of the indigenous communities through the food culture.

HER LOVE FOR GOD

Her work and service to humanity was also anchored on the love of God which inspired her to engage with farmers and rural communities, including nature. For example, her work was related to God as she attributed all creation to God. This cannot only be understood in light of her being a Catholic, but also one who could be said to put her social teachings of the church in practice. She recalled that she was motivated to do what she was doing because of her experiences and religious life. Her experiences with the church and in the church also enabled her to reach out and serve the community with passion:

> I used to sing a lot in the choir and wherever there was a funeral, I would be there. I was very active in the church, and I was brought up like that…. As a religious sister, I was also given groups to work with…. I have worked with different groups, as was the case in South America and Uganda where I tried to offer solutions to problematic situations.[43]

While she attributed part of her success to her religious life, she was also critical of the Church:

> I don't go to church every Sunday, I go once in a year and at times once in three years because I have graduated. It's time to internalise what faith means. . . . When I was asked as First Zambian Sacred Heart religious sister to decide for young sisters in the congregation, I decided that we do away with the veil. When you work with the poor, you don't need a uniform, but an option was given for those who wanted to put it on special occasions to do so. I was a rebel from day one. In instances where

---

[42] David Sanders et al., *At the Bottom of the Food Chain: Small Operations versus Multinational Corporations in the Food Systems of Brazil, Mexico and South Africa* (Cape Town: Economic Justice Network, 2016), https://foodsecurity.ac.za/wp-content/uploads/2018/04/FINAL-REPORT-MNCs-8-August-2016-SP2.pdf

[43] Personal interview with Annie Chikanji, 29 Sept. 2022, Chongwe.

> blacks were not respected, I could protest, including through a hunger strike.[44]

Her critical mind enabled her to challenge powers that be as was the case in her religious life so that she could fulfill her passion to foster local development. This is closely related to Pai's account where he had to let go of conversative Christianity to stand with the poor.

EMERGING LESSONS

The narrative of Annie and her *Ubuntu* learning hub brings to the fore lessons on women's contributions to ecological wellness and strides to provide alternative loves for work, humanity and God. For example, her trajectory seems to be a journey of always searching for ways to serve others. This journey resonates with the *Sam-ae* Spirit and underscores how an individual's experiences can have a bearing on ecological wellness. Her passion which was derived from her own experiences in life enabled her to rebuild relationships with both humans and nature. As such, she exemplifies that while agriculture is a gendered space, women could make significant and life changing contributions. This view is also supported by Farnworth and Hutchings who have argued that indigenous women have played a key role in biodiversity management through their vast knowledge on seeds and their selection and vegetative propagation among other roles.[45]

Her account also shows that ecological wellness could be enhanced using the available resources. This not only contributed to safeguarding an indigenous identity but was an opportunity to celebrate the distinct knowledge inherent in women. Jiggins observes that the concern of some women for the health of the environment is closely connected to their perception as sustainers and nurturers of life, as embedded in their distinctive knowledge (daily lives, experiences, interactions, and perceptions of reality).[46] Using an example of planting in succession, she stressed that there should be continuity in life. *Ubuthu* learning hub was a space that was contributing to passing on the heritage from one generation to another using different methods. As concluded by Hosken, the stories shared by women in their own words of how they were actively working with their local communities, reviving seed diversity, and regaining their leadership role

---

[44] Personal interview with Annie Chikanji, 29 Sept. 2022, Chongwe.

[45] Farnworth and Hutchings, "Organic Agriculture and Women's Empowerment."

[46] Janice Jiggins, *Changing the Boundaries: Women Centred Perspectives on Population and the Environment* (Washington DC: Island Press, 1994).

reflected how they saw their work as a duty to future generations and a responsibility that brought with it much joy.[47] For Annie, the transmission of the knowledge, skills and economic opportunities was facilitated through the practical educational facilities and sessions which could be deemed as avenues for empowering present and future generations.

Additionally, her account affirms that despite the presence of numerous power structures, the communities were appreciative of the strides made by women like Annie: initiative is a first of its kind in the region, and smallholder farmers have been eager to get involved. They soon appreciate that farming in agro-ecological manner is in sync with nature, rather than against it and that it is more cost effective and sustainable. It yields healthy food for their families and the market and replenishes their degraded soil in the process.[48] It demonstrated the strides to fight the dominant powers on food and seed choices. As observed by Shiva, the replacement of traditional crops with crops grown for the global markets – and more recently genetically modified crops – is undermining biodiversity, the relationship of indigenous peoples to that biodiversity, and thus the ability to maintain sustainable agricultural practices and retain and use indigenous knowledge. [49]

CONCLUSION

The chapter sought to demonstrate dialogue between *Sam-ae* Spirit and Indigenous Knowledge in Zambia using the ways in which *Ubuntu* learning hub contributed to ecological wellbeing and a sustainable future from a gendered perspective. Anchored on *Ubuntu* as a guiding philosophy, Annie's love for work (seen through her passion to foster development at the grassroots level), love for God (appreciation of God's gifts of creation) and love for humanity (retrieving and sharing indigenous knowledge on sustainable agriculture) affirms that her quest is to empower marginalized groups in the Zambian context. This was achieved through using different methods such as practical field visits, webinars, and workshops and tapping into indigenous methods of farming. As such, she drew on natural farming,

---

[47] "Celebrating African Rural Women: Custodians of Seed, Food and Traditional Knowledge for Climate Change Resilience," African Biodiversity Network and The Gaia Foundation Research Report, 2015, https://www.gaiafoundation.org/post-library/celebrating-african-rural-women/

[48] "Training a New Generation to Create Resilient Livelihoods Through Permaculture Farming," One Earth, https://www.oneearth.org/projects/training-a-new-generation-to-create-resilient-livelihoods-through-permaculture-farming/.

[49] Vandana Shiva, *Tomorrow's Biodiversity* (London: Thames and Hudson, 2000).

sharing knowledge and advocating for ways and practices which were environmentally friendly to empower communities at the Ubuntu learning hub. Annie's love for work, humanity and God not only mirrors the principle of togetherness but also closely resonates with the *Sam-ae* Spirit. Therefore, the chapter has argued that that indigenous knowledge systems do not only offer an alternative to addressing contextual realities but also provide an avenue for a gendered dialogue with the threefold loves in the Zambian context.

CHAPTER 8

SAM-AE SPIRIT IN THE CONTEXT OF GLOBAL MIGRATION

SHAKESPEARE SIGAMONEY & FRANS BEST SOMA MARPAUNG

INTRODUCTION

The movement of people is as old as humanity itself and is not a new phenomenon to humanity, but this century is witnessing what has been termed as a 'large scale migration'[1] in an unprecedented level. Stephen Castles and Mark J. Miller argue, "While movements of people across borders have shaped states and societies since time immemorial, what is distinctive in recent years is their global scope, their centrality to domestic and international politics and enormous economic and social consequences."[2] People migrate for various reasons such as war, economic crises, threat to life and Ecological crises. In the first-place people will not migrate if they had a decent life in the soil they were born. The Afghan war, ongoing war in Ukraine, the unstable government in Sri Lanka and Myanmar are some of the recent examples from where people migrate. On the Other hand, most states are not willing to accept migrants as a result we see dead bodies floating every now and then in the seas. This sight has become so common that at times one can become numb and at times avoid the discussion on migration since it is disturbing.

Global migration has been one of the serious issues that the world has been facing. The relation between wars and mass migrations are complex. The various of violent conflicts and wars such as the war on terrorism in Iraq and Afghanistan, civil wars such as in Myanmar, China, or Sri Lanka, and the recent war between Russia and Ukraine have produced a massive humanitarian loss and refugees. On one hand, these various conflicts, wars and migration did not only impact on local condition but also influence a global change. On the other hand, the forced migrants face multiple new problems and crisis in the way to survive. The issues of discrimination, racism, classism, environmentalism, and poverty are increased. This

[1] Stephen Castles, Hein De Haas, and Mark J. Miller, *The Age of Migration: International Population Movements in the Modern World*, 5th ed. (New York: Guilford, 2014).

[2] Ibid., 1.

condition has challenged our humanity approach to overcome the problems of migration and wars.

The sufferings of the migrants call the Church to rethink mission in the context where migrants are dehumanized by the structural violence. Migration has become a worldwide, multi-directional phenomenon which is reshaping the Christian landscape[3]. The question is: What resources can we draw from the *Sam-ae* Spirit in response to global migration?

This article aims to construct a missional praxis. To explore this research issue, this article will elaborate the concept of *Sam-ae* Spirit to address the issue of global migration. Rev. Pai Min-Soo is the Korean theologian who introduced the concept of *Sam-ae* Spirit. *Sam-ae* Spirit is the concept of God's love developed in a rural Korean context. The concept of *Sam-ae* Spirit brings together the theological teaching and praxis that encourages and empowers the rural people to transform the society. The dialogue between the concept of the *Sam-ae* Spirit with the issue of migration will develop the concept of Christianity mission to transform the society.

THE *SAM-AE* SPIRIT OF PAI MIN-SOO

According to Chammah Kaunda and Sang-man Kim, "Hermeneutical point of departure was to engage and transform the mindset that shaped the imagination of the rural people in order to empower and to understand their struggles and move to issues of rural development to re-embrace the *Sam-ae* Spirit."[4] This understanding illustrates the theological action of Pai in empowering the rural people. As a Christian, Pai started to transform the rural community by recognizing the rural people as subjects of the mission. In his theological reflection, Pai introduced three concepts of God's love. To begin with, the presence of Christians is to love the neighbor. If people cannot love the neighbor who they see and live together with them, so how could the Christians love the unseen God? Therefore, the Christians must recognize the presence of the other or the neighbor as God's face. To love God means to obey and to practice the communion with God by keeping the commandments to love the neighbor. In short, loving others is at the center of God's principle and truth, which will open the path to human life.[5]

---

[3] Jooseop Keum, ed., *Together towards life Mission and Evangelism in Changing Landscapes* (Geneva: WCC Publications, 2013).

[4] Chammah J. Kaunda and Kim Sang-man, "Samae Spirit' Assist toward 'Ubuntu Spirit' Model for Rural Adult Christian Education in Zambia," *Religious Education* 117, no.1 (2022):40.

[5] Minsoo Pai, *The Kingdom of God* (Seoul: Yonsei University Press, 2017), 121.

In addition, the Christians need to practice the love of the rural area. Pai understood that the Gospel of the Kingdom of God arose in the rural context of Jesus time, where the poor live. During the time of Pai, farmers in Korea where economically struggling community that was poor. He was convinced that the rural Korea is the place where God calls to show the Love Christ by working to uplift the farming community. While people usually tend to move to the city for development but Pai, focused on developing the rural Korea, by introducing modern farming techniques. He was inspired from the nineteenth century cooperative movements in Europe that paved way for a just economic society. The communal way of life, brings holistic development to the community and not just the individual development. Furthermore, the love of labor is the last concept. During Pai's time, scholars were respected and were considered as the elites while the hard labor was look down upon. In this discriminative context, Pai advocates the dignity of labor. He insisted that to develop the nation love of neighbor is very significant.[6] The love of labor is the way to propose human equality that opens way to develop cooperative work. As a result, the love of labor encourages people to work together and recognize that the society is an interdependent and interconnected societal life.

The concept of *Sam-ae* Spirit is a contextual theology approach. The context of poverty, injustice, suffering, discrimination and poverty had challenged Pai to construct the concept of God's love that can be implemented to transform the society. The three concepts of love: love for God, love for agriculture and love for labor, had become a model for a missional act. This was in the context of Korea's independence movement and developing of the independence by restoring the individual worth, and dignity of the common people.

In today's context we can see that the migrants are one of the struggling communities at the bottom of the society. Though the concept of *Sam-ae* Spirit was developed in the Korean context, however it can be applied globally. There are several issues in the world that affect human worth and dignity, and one among them is migration. Addressing the issue migration by interpreting the parable of the good Samaritan with the *Sam-ae* Spirit can be helpful to develop a theology of mission relevant in the context of migration.

---

[6] Pai, *The Kingdom of God,* 123.

THE MIGRANT AS THE SUBJECT OF MISSION

Jesus used the parable of the good Samaritan to answer the crucial question about what meant by the word "neighbor." Jesus challenged the people to love beyond geographical borders, cultural conception, religious dogma or human perception. William R. Herzog pushes the readers of the parables to read in the social economic context.[7] In the passage the identity of the victim of violence is not based on race, political or religious affliction but a wounded man. His condition is that:

1. He is wounded and bleeding: The bandits have robbed him and beaten him, he is bleeding and if someone doesn't take him to hospital he will die soon.
2. Immobile: He is struck because of his injury and unless moved by someone he cannot get back to social life.
3. He is homeless: He is in a strange land as he is traveling and his home is not probably nearby since no one who passes by knows him on the high way. He is on the way as he has left home and is traveling for some purpose but now is lying in between.
4. He is deprived of Human dignity. The robbers have taken his clothes and have left him naked.
5. He is in hunger and thirst as he has lost blood and has been lying in hot sun.

According to the social order of Jesus time, the third person must be an Israelite but, Jesus does something one cannot even imagine during his time. To the shock of the lawyer, the third person who enters the scene is a Samaritan who has a broken family line, direct enemy of the Jewish society. Obviously, the audience does not expect a Samaritan to do any good when it was not possible for a Priest and Levite. His entry is same as that of the priest and Levite, but he makes a difference by saving the life of half dead man. The dead man, even if he is a Jew, is not in a position to say 'no' when a Samaritan helps him. The main difference between the Samaritan and the others who passed by is 'compassion.' There is a huge space given for the Samaritan, explaining in detail what he does. He pours the olive oil, bandages his wounds, puts him on his own vehicle, pays for his stay, and thus takes complete care.

---

[7] Culpepper R. Allen, ed., *The New Interpreter's Dictionary of the Bible,* vol. 4 (Nashville: Abingdon Press, 2009), 376.

The good Samaritan does all that is needed to bring the deserted man back into the human community from the place where he was deserted and left to die. The Samaritan pours wine and oil, and puts the man on his own vehicle. The Samaritan probably walked alongside on the road, bringing the man to inn. The Samaritan gives him first aid and does what is immediately needed. Being a physician, Luke is keen to give detailed description of the medical aid given. The Samaritan has done all that is needed to save the wounded man. He leaves him in the hands of the inn keeper to continue to care for him, paying him two Denarii – enough to provide for boarding and lodging for two weeks.[8] An outsider is made hero of the story and this is very significant for us today as nation states look down on refugees as an unwanted 'Other.' Looking at the story from the perspective of one in dire need, it is the practice of mercy that transforms the traveler into a neighbor. Jesus tells the lawyer to love his neighbor with this new understanding provided by the concrete expression of compassion shown by the Samaritan. The Samaritan becomes a neighbor by putting compassion into action – this action stems from viewing the whole situation from the point of view of the victim. The parable of the good Samaritan becomes for us a paramount foundation in defining the concept of loving one's neighbor and community.

Laws relating to the neighborhood have great importance in the East. The number of customs and regulations associated with the neighborhood is second only to those relating to family. The reason for this is that one's "neighborhood" or community was not an incidental, but a necessary aspect of social life. Here, social life cannot be understood without understanding neighborhood. In the villages, when the peasants go out for work, it is usually the neighbors that are left to safeguard their house. The Arab word "*karib,*" like the Hebrew word "*karobh,*" used for both neighbor and relative – means "near." One of the features of communities in the East was that the villagers lived a closely-knit life, where they had common interests and intimate knowledge of one another's affairs. One of the common activities among neighbors was to safeguard each other's goods during absence – and also, lending and borrowing money and valuables. The great purpose of true religion is the perfecting of social life. The commandment, "Thou shall love thy neighbor as thy self" (Lev.19:18), is viewed as the highest expression regarding one's neighbor among the Israelites.[9]

---

[8] John Nolland, *Word Biblical Commentary,* vol. 35b, (Dallas: Word Book Publisher, 1993), 596.

[9] James Hasting, ed., *A Dictionary of the Bible* (New York: Charles Scribers and Sons, 1900), 511.

The story teaches compassion – to rescue and show love to the half-dead man, when others failed to do so – rather than stressing some behavior that conforms to some covenant obligation. The wounded man is a person who is half-dead and to help him may evenincur some personal risk. In the context of today's busy world, it is not easy for family members to spend time with one another, but giving one's time for a stranger is unfathomable. The parable challenges us value and practice expression of love, even outside the bounds of group solidarity. Jesus's answer to the question of the lawyer suggests that we should answer the question from a vantage point of one in desperate need and isolation, and then make use of the same answer when we face the question from a position of strength, when it is within our reach give favor rather than receiving them.[10]

It is important to note that the central figure is the wounded man as the story is told from his perspective and not from the perspective of the Samaritan. Towards the end, the wounded man gains a loving neighbor. The story challenges the reader to take up the perspective of the victimized. Throughout the history of interpreting this parable, Jesus has usually been identified with the Samaritan – as he is the one who plays the saving role. As Christ is our savior, one is easily tempted to interpret the parable in the traditional way. In the context of church sermons, this interpretation may teach a valuable lesson. However, in situations of conflict, hatred, or violence – as relating to migration – it may be more apt to view Christ as the wounded person. In Luke 9:51-10:54, as Jesus's coming fate in Jerusalem has been foreshadowed, a commitment is required to follow Jesus, who is heading to Jerusalem to suffer. There is an ever-growing importance attached to Jesus's message regarding the Kingdom of God.[11]

MISSIONAL PRAXIS OF LOVE FOR ONE'S NEIGHBOR

From the dialogue between the concept of *Sam-ae* Spirit and the concept of neighborly love shown by the good Samaritan, I propose the idea of "becoming neighbor" and "amazing love" as the missional praxis of Christians. This concept aims to overcome the issue of migrants and wars. In constructing this missional praxis, we need to recognize that the migrants are victims of structural violence and all the above conditions of the victim in the passage of good Samaritan are also the struggles of migrants. Migrants are naked, hungry, bleeding, victims of violence, rejected, denied human

---

[10] Nolland, *Word Biblical Commentary,* 597.

[11] Ibid., 576.

dignity, and treated as untouchable. Hence it is important to become a neighbor to the *other.* Love of God is expressed by the act of loving one's neighbor. For instance, love of neighbor extends the action to love, help and share with the unknown *other*, or a complete stranger.

First, neighbor is not *being* but *becoming*. This becoming is not possible if struck in being. Becoming a neighbor is a pilgrimage that takes us to unknown terrains instead of familiar ground – it is an Abrahamic journey. Becoming a neighbor is not affirming what one already knows or confirming one's pre-existing knowledge, but journeying with a stranger in a strange land, because one cannot predict what will happen on this journey. The risk is worth taking, as Jesus says, "Whoever tries to save his life will lose it, but whoever loses his life will preserve it" (Luke 17:33; John 12:25; and Matthew 10:39). This action emphasizes God's amazing love. Love of God and love of one's neighbor are not separated from each other. As Melba Maggay underscores,

> We cannot truly love our neighbor without, at the same time, loving God. There is no force on earth, besides the grace of God, that can deliver us from the insatiable appetite for profit, or many subtle ways by which we use 'the greater good for the greater number' to camouflage our interests and eliminate competition or opposition.[12]

Thus, God's amazing love ought to be reflected in our love for a stranger.

The encounter with people leads the Christians to practice the action of "becoming a neighbor" to others. In the action of "becoming a neighbor," Christians must show God's amazing love in order to transform the society. I propose four concepts of amazing love. First, *unconditional love***.** It means that there are no conditions laid to show love. This unconditional love is grounded on God's love to the world as it is said "God so loved the world that he gave his only begotten Son that whose ever believes in him shall have eternal life" (John 3:16). God just loves the world without any conditions. The compassion is the key in the parable of good Samaritan.[13] The Hebrew word for *mercy* or *compassion* comes from the root word which means 'womb,' a sibling feeling or a motherly feeling. How would one react if the other person was one's sibling or if the other was born from one's womb? God's mercy can be manifested in different ways in forgiveness where a

---

[12] Melba Maggay, "To Respond to Human Need by Loving Service," In *Mission in the 21st century: Exploring the five marks of Global Mission*, edited by Andrew Walls and Cathy Ross (New York: Orbis books, 2008), 46-52.

[13] E. R. Achtemeier, *The Interpreters Dictionary of the Bible* (Nashville: Abingdon Press, 1962), 352- 354.

person or a nation was restored to relationship with God. Compassion was the proof through an outward act that God loves, cares, and protects His covenant people. In the Hebrew community, mercy was found among the family and where family is, there is mercy. In the Old Testament, it was extended to the close community, neighbors and friends deserving of help. Those that were dependent on community like the poor, widows aged, and fatherless had special claim to mercy. In the Old Testament, one of the worst characteristics of armed conqueror was one's lack of consideration for the poor and needy. Human mercy in Old Testament is like that of God's mercy which is understood in a context of relationship. In short, human relationship becomes a part of relationship to God.

Human mercy in the New Testament is similar to that of the Old Testament. It is manifested in acts of giving aid to a fellow member. The New Testament gives new meaning with its instruction to show mercy to others who do not belong to the same community. This is a major difference between the Old Testament's understanding and The New Testament's understanding regarding human compassion. For the latter, it does not matter who the person is. Although they may be a scribe, Pharisee, tax collector, or sinner – they are all to give love and aid to one another. Jesus has shifted focus from the boundaries of required neighborliness to the essential nature of neighborliness. A neighbor is defined not passively, but actively. The word 'neighbor' in the beginning of the discourse was an object, but toward the end it becomes the subject of the narrative. At the end of the narrative, the word 'neighbor' undergoes a radical change from the sender-receiver relationship that was announced in the beginning.[14]

Second, *the stranger love*. The lawyer's question to Jesus was asked in this context: his neighbor can only be of the same religion and ethnicity. In the question of "who is my neighbor?" – there underlies a claim to membership in the covenant community. The issue is whether claims of neighborly love should be allowed in the case of people who were not part of the covenant community.[15] A neighbor is one who will reciprocate help in some form as someone living in the same locality. It is not possible for a Jew to view a stranger as a neighbor because the other person may not be a Jew and it is not safe to interact with strangers. Jesus's parable of the good Samaritan is a paradigm shift in the understanding of one's neighbor.

---

[14] John Dominic Crossan, ed., *Semia 2: The Good Samaritan* (Montana: Scholars Press, 1974), 34.

[15] Nolland, *Word Biblical Commentary,* 590.

For a Jew, a neighbor was a fellow member of the covenant community. Hence love is restricted to the covenant community.[16] Thus, the wounded traveler's covenant status is irrelevant according to the dynamics of the story. Neighborly love is towards the stranger and not the kith and kin belonging to the same race, color, religion or any other affiliation. To do God's mission is becoming stranger in a new land. Anthony Gittins says:

> If a new comer honestly presents herself or himself as a stranger, thus showing respect for the hosts and allowing them to take certain necessary initiatives, this facilitates the interaction, even though the price may be some uncertainty and powerlessness on the part of the stranger. But only by doing this will missionaries be able to indicate their openness, integrity, and willingness to engage in relationships.[17]

For Christians, outsiders can become an ethical category with a practical imperative. According to Orlando Costas, the outsider is important even for the salvation of the insider. He argues, "Salvation lies outside the gates of the cultural, ideological, political and socio-economic walls that surround our religious compound and shape the structures of Christendom."[18] Furthermore, Costas affirms his soteriological perspective focusing on the death of Jesus. He argues "that with the death of Jesus there came a fundamental shift in the location of salvation since Jesus died in the wilderness among the outcast and disfranchised."[19] Costas uses this perspective to critique Christendom, which for him is the vision of a society organized around Christian principles and values with the church as its manager or mentor. In Christendom people are divided between "insiders" and "outsiders."[20] He sees this module of Christendom as something which prevents the church from receiving the outsider. According to Costas:

> As a 'historical project,' Christendom dominates the church's mental structures. It causes the church to see society as an extension of itself and its inner life as a reflection of its culture. Therefore, those who lie outside its ecclesiastical compounds, those who are not heirs of the 'appropriate' religious traditions, those who do not have the same cultural background, those who do not speak the same language," even if they call themselves Christians do not share in the spiritual socio economic and political

---

[16] Ibid., 589.

[17] Anthony J. Gittins, *Gifts and Strangers: Meeting the Challenges of Inculturation* (New York and Mahwah, NJ: Paulist Press, 1989), 132.

[18] Orlando E. Costas, *Christ Outside the Gate: Mission Beyond Christendom* (Maryknoll, NY: Orbis Books, 1982), 191.

[19] Ibid., 189.

[20] Ibid., 190.

> blessings of salvation. They are not insiders but outsiders. for all practical purposes, they share the same fate as everyone else in the wilderness': they are lost.[21]

The challenge for Christians in the context of the migrants' crisis is to transcend this boundary of insider and outsider and embrace the outsider. Costas underlines that Christian mission means "encountering the crucified Christ in the world of the outsiders and sharing in his suffering for the rejects and the outcasts. When this happens all the traditional aspects of Christian mission must be interpreted from the perspective of the periphery."[22] On the basis of this argument, the refugees are the periphery. They should be the center of our missional praxis.

Third, *unquestioning love*. Humanity is placed as the criteria and no other identity is sought for. A Person in need is not questioned about documents and administrative requirements. The victims are not questioned for any qualification for instance, whether the person belongs to a particular race, nation, language group, or any kind of identity does not become the qualification for love and responsibility. Therefore, this love does not question, who the *Other* is? Does not focus on the being of the person. One cannot set conditions to become neighbor. The only criteria are that we belong to one common humanity that binds us. All people are created in the image of God.

It is the love of God that calls for responsibility towards the *Other*. It is in recognizing the humanity of the *Other* we affirm our own. It is that bleeding face of migrants from which we hear "love thy neighbor as thy self." The suffering of the other is bounded to my humanity, as me and the other are in the image of God. We can compare the love for other with Africa and Asia cultures. The concept of Ubuntu and Hospitality in Tamil culture are some resources, where humanity is placed above all differences. Ubuntu is the interrelatedness of human being irrespective of identity and differences. The Zulu concept of Ubuntu is a challenge and calls to realize one's relationality to the world of others. In the context of refugees where people are dying in the seas because they are not accepted and the nation-state is very exclusive. Ubuntu offers a way to go beyond individualism and to realize the interdependence of humanity.

Archbishop Desmond Tutu who placed an active role in the reconciliation process in South Africa said:

---

[21] Costas, *Christ Outside the Gate,* 191.

[22] Ibid., 192.

> Ubuntu… means that my humanity is caught up, is inextricably bound up, in theirs. We belong in the bundle of life. We say a person is a person through other people… I am human because I belong, I participate, I share. A person with Ubuntu is open and available to others, affirming of others, doesn't feel threatened that others are able and good; for he or she has a proper self-assurance that comes with knowing that he or she belongs in a greater whole and is diminished when others are humiliated or diminished when others are tortured or oppressed, or treated as if they were less than who they are.[23]

Tutu who has shown the richness of Ubuntu philosophy says, that when others are hurt or tortured, the self is diminished because of common humanity. This precious philosophy can save the future of humanity from narcissistic self-centeredness. Michael Eze rightly says of the relationality in Ubuntu:

> Humanity is not embedded in my person solely as an individual; my humanity is co substantively bestowed upon the other and me. Humanity is a quality we owe to each other. We create each other and need to sustain this otherness creation. And if we belong to each other, we participate in our creations: we are because you are, and since you are, definitely I am. The 'I am' is not a rigid subject, but a dynamic self- constitution dependent on this otherness creation of relation and distance.[24]

The interconnectedness of humanity is essential to overcome individualism and narcissistic self-centeredness. The cooperative community envision in the *Sam-ae* philosophy is an interconnected community where people leave their individual comfort zone and come together leaving in relation to each other.

Fourth, hospitality. In this part, love refers to the action of hospitality. This amazing love results in action towards the *other* who is marginalized. We see that God's love incarnated in Jesus. This love is not just a feeling, it can't but result in action even if it is risking Jesus's life. Love demands sacrificial life. Love can be translated in to action through hospitality. Levinas lived his life as a stranger in a strange land and enjoyed the hospitality in the community where he lived. Hospitality is "an interminable movement toward a future never future enough."[25] For Levinas, the other is an ambiguous stranger[26] who cannot be fully known at any point of time. Thus, hospitality is the way to come in contact with the strangeness for Levinas. Levinas in his preface to totality and infinity says:

---

[23] Desmont Tutu, *No Future Without Forgiveness* (London: Rider, 1999), 34-35.

[24] Michael O. Eze, *Intellectual history in contemporary South Africa* (Palgrave: Macmillan, 2010), 190.

[25] Emmanuel Levinas, *Totality and Infinity* (Pittsburgh: Duquesne University Press, 1969), 254.

[26] Ibid., 152-155.

> This book will present subjectivity as welcoming the other, as hospitality; in it the idea of infinity is consummated. Hence intentionality, where thought remains an adequation with the object, does not define consciousness at its fundamental level. All knowing qua intentionality already presupposes the idea of infinity, which is pre-eminently non-adequation.[27]

For Levinas hospitality become the work of justice.[28] Enrique Dussel calls the Levinesian hospitality as Levinasian politics of hospitality a liberating act.[29] The political community of Hobbes excludes the stranger while Levinas hospitality provides space for strangeness. In politics, Levinas places anarchy beyond politics resisting totalization beyond the modern state sovereignty therefore strangers have space.[30] Levinas shows the importance of the completely other saying that which is completely other:

> And it is only man who could be absolutely foreign to me–refractory to every typology, to every genus, to every characterology, to every classification. . . . The strangeness of the other, his very freedom! Free beings alone can be strangers to one another. Their freedom which is 'common' to them is precisely what separates them.[31]

The human rights as a product of modernity have failed in the case of refugees and Levinas' hospitality opens a new space forward in maintaining the tension between the self and the other with responsibility and hospitality beyond charity. Subjectivity is not a fixed one, subjectivity is based on interrelatedness, the welcoming of the refugee has the potential to transform subjectivity. The subjectivity of the refugee interacts with that of the host and subjectivity is in constant transformation as it is an ongoing process.

From the explanation above we can see that incarnation is an act of dialogue. God – who was above, unseen and powerful – becomes human to converse on equal terms with us, without having an upper hand to power. Mission, then, is to become like the kenotic love of God expressed in action. Kenosis is self-emptying to identify with the last in social hierarchy and reverse the existing social order, not to oppress again but to celebrate life in fullness together. To proclaim "the Kingdom of God" with our actions, is to struggle for justice, in solidarity with those who are denied dignity,

---

27 Ibid., 27.

28 Ibid., 28.

29 Enrique Dussel, "'Politics' by Levinas: Towards a Critical Political Philosophy," In *Difficult Justice: Commentaries on Levinas and Politics* edited by Asher Horowitz and Gad Horowitz (Toronto: University of Toronto Press, 2006), 80.

30 Emmanuel Levinas, *Otherwise Than Being or Beyond Essence* (London: Kluwer Academic, 1997), 99.

31 Levinas, *Totality and Infinity,* 73-74.

oppressed and marginalized like the migrants.

Migrants are not on the receiving end of mission, but are rather agents of mission with a prophetic role that affirms life for the whole of humanity. Migrants are important partners in the mission of God. Since migrants are marginalized, oppressed and suffering, they have the gift to differentiate what news is good and what news is bad for them.[32] For mission to be life-giving and life-affirming, the voices of the migrants are very crucial. Mission should work for the transformation of the migrants' lives, and in the process, mission will continue the process of being transformed. Migrants are not the objects of mission, but rather, they are the subjects of mission. Migration is the context in which God calls us to do mission – in dialogue *with* migrants.

CONCLUSION

Sam-ae philosophy addresses the issues of those in the rural areas outside the city, where marginalized farmers struggle. These farmers relegated to the margins of rural Korea were considered by Pai to be very significant for the holistic development of the nation. The marginalized farmers have to be the subject of theology, in order for theology to be meaningful within the context of migration. The Western classics cannot be the sole source of theology any longer – which means that Asian and Latin American theologies need to take their proper and respective places. The struggles of refugees, people on the move, their life stories, the suffering of the migrant women and children ought to become the context for doing theology for theologians in Asia, Africa, Latin America, and the rest of the world – because Christianity is not a territorial religion if we understand the pain of one is the pain of all. The refugee phenomenon is humanity's problem since they are the image of God.

Pai put the love of God into action by advocating the love of one's neighbor through cooperative movements where everyone cares for everyone else. Rev. Pai Min-Soo's concept of *Sam-ae* Spirit has the very potential to derive a new mission praxis in the face of life-negating realities that exploit nature and weaker members of society. The good Samaritan teaches us God's love in respect to the sense of responsibility we should show to others. Those imbued with *Sam-ae* Spirit also seek to express the love of God through loving one's neighbor. The concept of *Sam-ae* Spirit has the potential, even today, to translate the gospel of Jesus Christ into action within the context of global migration.

---

[32]Keum, ed., *Together towards life Mission,* 39.

CHAPTER 9

MASS MOBILIZATION AS THE EXPRESSION OF POSTMODERN POLITICAL LOVE IN RUSSIAN ORTHODOX SOCIETY

OXANA MECHSHERSKAYA

INTRODUCTION

The Korean minister Pai Min-Soo mobilized Korean rural dwellers by appealing to *Sam-ae* Spirit (love of God, love of the neighbor, and love of labor) as a form of pre-modern political love in the context of Japanese colonization.[1] Utilizing this framework of thinking for current socio-political events in Russia, one would naturally be interested in attempting to perceive and understand the underlying and contributing factors that eventually have led towards recent developments. Having been trained in historical science, this researcher would suggest a certain framework of analysis that might allow us to look at those originating elements that have brought the Russian state to military action and also the flood of citizens hurriedly leaving the country after it announced mobilization. Considering the historical and social framework of research is insightful for understanding how love for one's home country could be understood, i.e., providing deeper awareness of the modern-day epistemology of love. The understanding of the socio-political milieu as one of the key components in investigating the subject matter allows for a more critical assessment, thus, may also suggest a means for creating other epistemological grounds and facets of the studied concept.[2] Hence, this paper suggests that the epistemology of love bears the tenets of socio-political and religious elements, and attempts to reveal those in order to provide a better understanding of postmodern epistemology in the Russian context.

Similar to Pai Min-Soo's context the philosophy of modernity suggests a closer look at the agendas behind every conception of love, dismantling political, social and religious ideologies that have been employed in

[1] Chammah J. Kaunda and Sang-man Kim, "'Samae Spirit' Assist toward 'Ubuntu Spirit' Model for Rural Adult Christian Education in Zambia," *Religious education* 117, no. 1 (2022): 33-49.

[2] Georg G Iggers, Q Edward Wang, and Supriya Mukherjee, *A Global History of Modern Historiography*, 1st ed. (Routledge, 2013)., 389

conceiving their certain perceptions, as 'working social conceptual models' necessary for a certain time period. As the research on historiographic schools points out, it was in the domain of the state to designate meanings and to create understanding for such social entities as an individual, a family, a marriage, a childhood upbringing, etc. Those were ingenious, culturally sustainable for the state teachings, philosophies and ideologies that promoted the agendas of the governing political body and its social policies.[3] Hence, love that is intrinsic to all the above-mentioned social relations is deprivitized and instead is politicized in the hands of social institutions. However, the age of pluralization is providing a person with new opportunities for creating their own epistemologies of love that are of private, quantitively individualistic, family oriented, and fluctuating nature. Therefore, if history is not approached as just a mere study of the facts of the past, but in the age of pluralism perceived through the unfolding of the dynamic of the object-subject referents,[4] then there appears a space for other epistemologies of love, instructive for an individual to embark on in order to produce their own hermeneutical and phenomenological journeys. As such this journey is to take a dismantling axis on the one hand and an exploring one, on the other hand.

This framework of research allows every individual to be liberated from the constraints of ideological version of love and to develop their own individual versions. The article will outline the object referent of the restraining domain, which is the systematic understanding of theological belief code, political ideologies and historical schools, as exemplified in major works of respective fields. This referential source will highlight the configurations of the socio-political, religious and historical background of the Russian modernity on the one hand, and will assist in investigating the epistemology of love within such a background on the other hand, which ultimately will help to understand the ongoing responses of the Russian citizens towards the order for a mass mobilization in the country.

DISMANTLING AXIS—RUSSIAN MODERNITY

There are various views as how to characterize and define Russian modernity depending on various ideologies that have been circulating within certain time space of this historic period. A few of those produced such versions as

---

[3] B. E. Ileritskiy and I. A. Kudryavtseva, *Istoriographia Istorii SSSR s Drevneishih Vremyon Do Velikoy Oktyabrskoy Revolyutsii* (Moscow: Bysshaya Schkola, 1971), 25-26.

[4] David Tracy, *Plurality and Ambiguity (*Chicago: University of Chicago Press, 1994).

Ethnic modernity,[5] Russian civilization modernity,[6] Totalism modernity,[7] Orthodox modernity[8] to name a few. It is necessary to underpin the fact that certain ideological versions had been propagated by the state representatives via various means of mass media and other channels of social communication. As such Russian social space could be characterized as less of fluctuating and fuzzy one, with various ideological ideas to be 'negotiated' and debated. Such is the nature of Russian ideological mechanism, which had previously been planted by totalistic regime and a very few opposing views of dissident nobility barely known to the public, had been attempting to propose the alternatives. President Putin's administration has reserved to a subtler and less conspicuous ideological mechanism, thus propagating and promulgating another state version of modernity. The modern ideological mechanism could be defined as a managerial state democracy that has been producing the version of Cultural Orthodox Modernity version.[9] One of the leading scholars on modernity are Anthony Giddens and Peter Berger. The former suggests the framework of modernity that focuses on industrialism and capitalism, that is constructed on the institutional axis in the form of machinery and production processes, followed by the axis of product market axis. These are constituting globalizing tendencies of modernity, which he suggests are to be supplanted with the local social activities represented in the process of self-reflexivity. Subtly he introduces the other important element into the contours of modernity, which is the Self.[10] Peter Berger, envisions the contours of modernity from the religious perspective, suggesting institutional axis of government regulation on the one hand, religious market on the other and individual faith as the decisive element of this social construct.[11] It is important to look into the configurations of

---

[5] See Andreas Buss, *The Russian-Orthodox Tradition and Modernity* (Leiden, Netherland: Brill, 2004).

[6] See Massimo Rosati and Kristina Stoeckl, *Multiple Modernities and Postsecular Societies* (London: Routledge, 2016).

[7] See Boris Solovyov and V. S. Jakim, *Lectures on Divine Humanity* (Hudson, N.Y: Lindisfarne Press, 1995).

[8] Alexander Ponomariov, *The Visible Religion: The Russian Orthodox Church and Her Relations with State and Society in Post-Soviet Canon Law, 1992-2015* (Frankfurt: Peter Lang, 2017).

[9] Oxana Mechsherskaya, "The Orthodox Church and the State in Russia" (PhD Dissertation, Yonsei University, 2017).

[10] Anthony Giddens, *Modernity and Self-Identity: Self and Society in the Late Modern Age* (Cambridge: Polity Press, 1991), 14-34.

[11] Peter L Berger, *The Many Altars of Modernity: Toward a Paradigm for Religion in a Pluralist Age* (Boston: De Gruyter, 2014).

Russian modernity in particular, by integrating the findings of both Western scholars. I argued that the contextual nature of Russian modernity to be Orthodox culturalism that instead of integrating the axis of the Self, demonstrates a different dynamic, that is of dialectics. Besides, she highlights that this ideology is creating the third axis of a collective, nationalistic identity – the sobornost. As such, Russian modernity is of Orthodox cultural sobornost.[12] The Self in postsecular Russia is only in a state of awakening into creating individual self-reflexivity of personal faith. Such process of revisiting the Self, looking into the construct it is becoming, having been exposed to socio-political realities is, in fact, inevitable due to the modern forces of pluralization. Furthermore, the epistemology of love is essentially connected with the Self, the socio-political aspects of it, which is displayed in the sphere of the Self, loving their motherland. Hence, this article is investigating the epistemology of love in the context of Russian modern situation as expressed in their response towards mass mobilization order issued by President Vladimir Putin on September 21, 2022. In his public address he stated that the mobilization was issued due to visible and tangible threats to the country's sovereignty, safety, and stability:

> I will be suggesting necessary and immediate actions towards the defense of sovereignty, safety and territorial integrity of Russia, the need for gaining support for disposition and determination of our fellow citizens to be able to define on their free volition their own future; and the aggressive policy of some of the Western elites, that are attempting to preserve their own hegemony by all means possible. They are trying to block and suppress any sovereign independent centers of development in order to further on grossly impose onto other countries and nations their own will and embed their own pseudo values.[13]

Positioning this research within the framework of social-political background it is feasible to discover the present-day nature of love, to which the majority of populace is subscribed to. As modernity is suggestively envisioned from the three axes, it is plausible to see the epistemology of love, on the one hand and to offer a working approach towards it if modernity is to be perceived as age of plurality, as proposed by P. Berger. Therefore, let us dive into the first, institutional axis, the nation-state, that promulgates historical legitimacy of the epistemology of love. What kind of love is expounded and is translated via mass media and other informative

---

[12] Oxana Mechsherskaya, "The Orthodox Church and the State in Russia."

[13] "Address of the President of the Russian Federation," *President of Russia*, 21 Sept. 2022, http://kremlin.ru/events/president/news/69390.

channels for the populace. It is possible to notice the character of love that is supported by the government, which refers to Russian classic and religious literary historic heritage represented in the works of Russian philosophers, writers and religious scholars.

DISMANTLING AXIS—RUSSIAN PHILOSOPHY

Russian philosophical thought has been deeply religious throughout its ages and though modernity could be laudably argued is the time of liberation of the secular from the sacred, the divorce of philosophical, epistemological secular thinking from the domain of faith and religious morality, yet Russian modernity had been still underpinned with religious sentiments, exactly because of its religious foundation. The secularizing process of modernity has challenged Russian religious philosophers to spur such facets in their philosophical outlook as holistic approach to reality with elements of morality and metaphysics, which is only feasible within the framework of religion. Hence, Russian modern philosophers pursue ideals of wholeness, synthesis, and integrity.[14]

One of the expressions of such philosophical features could be the concept of *sobornost*, which, not only on the one hand encompasses the ideals of collectivism, thus subtly neglecting individual voices but also dismissing love towards self, while rather advocating love towards one's neighbor. It could be suggested, then, that the concept of love within such philosophical framework is of messianic, universalistic and holistic nature, which is introduced in a classic Russian literature in the works of such Slavophile writers as L. Tolstoy, N. Gogol and F. Dostoyevsky. In the words of the later one: "If you destroy the community, the nation will immediately be corrupted within the single generation... Does not exist (in the community) the grain of something unique... the new future, an ideal... that we alone can realize, we alone can bring forth, as it will be no war, no revolt, but . . . great and universal harmony."[15] The universal brotherhood and unity advocated by Slavophile proponents in the works of Dostoyevsky and Solovyov was grounded on the faith in God and their messianic philosophical belief in the Russian society to be the nation that will bring consolidation and redemption to humanity, the harmony obtained by all unity. However, the Russian revolution swept the

---

[14] V. V. Zenkovsky, *A History of Russian Philosophy* (London: Routledge & Kegan Paul, 1953).

[15] Oleg V. Parilov et al., "Sobornost As The Basis Of Russian Identity: History And Current State," *European Proceedings of Social and Behavioural Sciences*, February 27, 2021, 754–60, https://doi.org/10.15405/EPSBS.2021.02.02.94.

focus of this religious ideology and instead of striving for universal truth and harmony, Lenin and Trotsky were aiming at obtaining land and freedom with the same global and universal philosophical ideology. "The Russian idea is a desire for a universal unity of mankind, for a universal fraternity of nations, for a better life not only for oneself but for everyone. . . . The great goal of the Russian concept is a universal unity, which should be rooted in a high-level social harmony . . . A perfect man of the Newest Age is a holder of a collective global sobornost."[16] Hence, social realities of certain age and time become the focal point the society is to fulfill, yet by same universalistic, messianic and holistic means deeply rooted in Russian religious philosophical thought. Latest version of such thought is expressed in the ideology of Orthodox culturalism, where the social realities of the society seek to fight off the individualistic Western pluralizing forces of disintegration and work towards integration both within and outside of the nation. Nationalism is expounded throughout the various channels of communication, thus justifying the military actions against Ukraine, in particular. Again, the same ideology of collectivistic, unifying, messianic nature is brought as legitimizing principles in stating, that territories of former Ukraine need help in liberation from Ukrainian sovereignty. "There had been residing over more than seven million people in Donetsk and Lugansk national republics, Zaporozhsk and Khersonsk regions at the start of military operation. Many of those were forced to become refugees and abandon their native lands. Those that had stayed, estimated at the number of five million people, are subjected to ongoing, constant artillery and rocket fire from the neo-Nazi militants. They strike over hospitals and schools, organize terrorist attacks against local civilians. We cannot and have not have any moral right to leave those that close to us in the hands of the tormentors, we cannot not to respond to their sincere desire to define their own fate themselves. The parliaments of Donetsk republic, as well as civic and military administrations of Khersonsk and Zaporozhsk regions have made a decision to hold referendums on the issue of the future of their territories and requested the assistance from us, Russia, to support this measure."[17]

DISMANTLING AXIS—RUSSIAN THEOLOGY

Russian modernity having been argued to differ from the Western one due to its religious philosophical underpinnings proves the fact that the 'capitalistic

---

[16] Parilov et al., "Sobornost as the Basis of Russian Identity."

[17] "Address of the President of the Russian Federation," *President of Russia*, 21 Sept. 2022, http://kremlin.ru/events/president/news/69390.

spirit,' the innate dynamic taken into consideration by A. Giddens in his configuring the Western modernity is not applicable in Russian context. Yet, P. Berger's approach, though of Western underpinnings as well, is still helpful in that regard that pluralization is a social force that has already arrived to the Russian society and is in the process of dialectic configuration with its contextual elements. Conspicuously, Russian modernity is guided by sobornost[18] and obshchina, accepting individualism at the subordinate level. Moreover, according to Kallistos Ware,[19] modern Orthodox theology is argued to be an ecclesiological one, which was emphasized and advocated by such towering figures as Alexis Khomiakov and Nicholas Afanasiev. In the words of the former "The Church is one, notwithstanding her division as it appears to a man who is still alive on earth. It is only in relation to a man that it is possible to recognize a division of the Church into visible and invisible; her unity is, in reality, true and absolute."[20] Such proposition highlights his arguing that the Church is the community of the faithful who is in unity to each other from the *sobornost*. This emphasis on the internal unity hints on the dismissal of an individual whose interests and opinions that could be different form the majority of the congregation are allowed to be ignored and neglected. Such theological tradition suggests that love it to be sacrificial, it is to surrender one's voice for the sake of common good. As such familial love is portrayed as submissive and an obedient one, giving up one's own.

OUTCOME OF IDEOLOGICAL EPISTEMOLOGY OF LOVE

Therefore, epistemologically love in Russian context is conspicuously politicized, reloaded and reinvented through the political lens of national culturalism, supported by the ecclesiological Orthodox tradition. Love is of subordinate, sacrificial, nationalistic nature, that pursues ideals of national patriotism and familial unity, at the expense of an individual and marginal voices. Love in Russian socio-political nature is less of religious character – "love of God and love of the self and love of the neighbor" as stated in the Scripture (Mark 12:30) or *Sam-ae* Spirit (love of God, love of neighbor and love of labor)

---

[18] The word *sobornost* was coined by Khomiakov, implying the quality of being in accordance with the unity of all, of the unity of humanity in God, which he nevertheless discussed mostly within the historical church rather than as a theological teaching. According to him, "the Church demonstrated abiding unity in the essential unity of her members, based on unanimity of soul and mind, under the sole authority of God."

[19] Kallistos Ware, *Orthodox Theology in the Twenty-First Century* (Geneva: World Council of Churches, 2012), 52.

[20] A. S. Khomiakov et al., *On Spiritual Unity: A Slavophile Reader* (Hudson, NY: Lindisfarne Books, 1998).

mentioned above, but rather, a deeply ideologically nationalistic one. One of the apparent and visible platforms where such a nationalistic nature of love could be perceived in the public arena could be the relation of a citizen to their country, i.e., one's love toward their country, their motherland. In particular, the national mobilization,[21] announced by the administration of the president Putin is an ongoing socio-political process, as this article is being written, is grounded in the ideas of nationalistic love, patriotism, that citizens ought to demonstrate by submitting to voluntary be enlisted and participate in the military operations in Russia-Ukraine conflict. "Within two weeks of mobilization at least 213.2 thousand people have been enlisted in 53 regions, estimated by '*Vazhnye istorii*' publishing editorial and by the analysts of Conflict Intelligence Team (CIT) group. The survey was published on Wednesday of October 05."[22] However, the reactions of ordinary citizens, who choose rather to immigrate to neighboring countries point to the disintegration of such patriotic ideals, that Russian government has been earnestly and tediously trying to implant into the mentality of its citizens. Such responses suggest that Russian society is not demonstrating wholistic sacrificial ideals, but rather individualistic, self-pursuing benefits, which is the result of pluralistic force that has been seemingly taking over the long established cultural social sentiments and beliefs. Pluralism allowed individual citizens to be liberated from collective nationalistic agendas of the church. Therefore, postmodern epistemology of love in Russian society could be argued is of collectivistic, national, culturally Orthodox sentiments, but not so ubiquitously anymore. The Orthodox church disseminates the teaching of abandoning of self-love and instead, pursuing and growing sacrificial filial love. In words of St. Nikolai of Zica "Loving only himself, a man loves neither God nor his fellowmen. He does not even love the man that is in himself; he loves only his thoughts about himself, his illusions about himself. Were he to love the man in himself, he would at the same time love God's image in him and would quickly become a lover of God and man, for he would be seeking man and God in other men, as objects of his love. Self-love is not love, but is rejection of God

---

[21] Number of mobilized citizens has surpassed that of earlier figures that had been announced by Sergey Shoigu, the defense minister of Russia. According to Shoigu, since the start of mobilization there have arrived for more than 200 thousand people to the armed forces of Russia. Besides 213 thousand people, that have been accounted by the researchers, the information on the number of those enlisted from 32 regions is absent, as 'Vazhnye istorii' states. They have used official count of people submitted by local authorities and officials, mass media reports and statements of military commissioners.

[22] Daniil Sotnikov, "Research: More Than 213 Thousand People Have Already Been Mobilized in the Russian Federation," *DW*, 25 Oct. 25, 2022, https://www.dw.com/ru/issledovanie-v-rossii-mobilizovali-uze-bolee-213-tysac-celovek/a-63341710.

and contempt for men, whether open or concealed. Self-love is not love but sickness, a serious illness that inevitably brings other illnesses in its train."[23]

EXPLORING AXIS—CONFIGURING SOCIO-POLITICAL LOVE

The investigation of the dismantling axis suggests the following configurations of the socio-political tenets of the love concept. Love nature that is promulgated in the social space by means of classic literature is shown to be permeated with religious philosophical thinking on the one hand, and by means of mass media channels, it is demonstrated to be supplanted with religious, nationalistic and messianic nature, on the other hand. One is to look out for the needs of the majority, sacrificing their own personal individual opinions in order to keep and protect the nation, which has a mission to defend their long-standing sovereignty and to assist neighboring Slavic minorities against the incursions of ideologies of Western countries. One of the expressions of such religious, socio-political epistemology of love is visible through the recent presidential order for the mass mobilization, where people are subtly obliged to submit to the participation in the military operation, thus demonstrating their love towards their motherland that needs protection of foreign enemies. However, the response of the citizens demonstrates the disintegration of the society in their perception of love, they refuse to blindly subscribe to the constructs of love that such social institutes as church and state publicly circulate. They choose to love their families, care for the safety of the loved ones, their own individual freedoms and future, thus taking matter in their own hands, rather than protect their state's sovereignty and sacrifice their lives for the agendas of the culturally Orthodox state. They choose to actively create their own history here and now, in constructing their individual epistemologies of love, rather than rely on the past history of the collective nationalistic state, which had put the objectives of the nation above those of minorities, nobilities and intelligentsia. Though, historically Russian state was able to safeguard its sovereignty and had a long history of not been occupied, yet it had come at a high price of the loss of many individual lives, especially of those who spoke against such measures. Modern Russians choose to immigrate and protect their lives, rather than endanger themselves in the war fought not on their lands even.

THE ORDER AND THE AMBIGUITY

The above presentation on the dismantling axis proposed the nature and the character of the epistemology of love in the postmodern Russian context, that

---

23 "The Poison of Self-Love . . ." Simply Orthodox, *Tumblr*, n.d., accessed 26 Oct. 2022, https://simplyorthodox.tumblr.com/post/37037792547.

is expressed in the object-referent of some of the above-mentioned documents and religious teachings, which, in turn is actualized in the recent order of mobilization and the social response to it. Yet, besides the aforesaid object referent sources from where the concept of love is constituted, there emerges another significant platform that is to be taken into consideration in order to understand a contemporary perception of the subject matter fully. As pluralizing forces have been disseminated due to the introduction of Western post modernizing forces of differentiation in political arena, tendencies towards individualism in cultural context, Protestant rationalism and scholasticism in the religious belief system, Russian netizens have opportunities to negotiate in their private, mental spaces as what love means to them, thus, creating their own epistemologies of love concept. Therefore, postmodern concept of love in this society is becoming less rigid, certain, and constant but is rather becoming more fluid, fluctuating and negotiating due to the involvement of the Self. In words of A. Giddens, "The coming of modernity, it might be accepted, brings about major changes in the external social environment of the individual . . . For social circumstances are not separate from personal life, nor are they just an external environment to them. In struggling with intimate problems, individuals help actively to reconstruct the universe of social activity around them."[24] Is there a chance for a socio-political nationalistic, religious love to be transformed with the arrival of pluralization? The refusal to follow the national mobilization is the answer to this question, introducing the individual, the power and the voice of the Self, the subject-referent to be constructive and crucial in reconfiguring Russian religious modernity and socio-political realities.

The Self is not only on the institutional level of the governing organs, or on the level of religious space, but also within the mentality of the Self that love takes upon different interpretations. Once pluralism has found its way via various means of communication and education, it has started to produce individualistic approaches and ways of 'doing life' in the Russian society. Due to other religious institutions that have emerged and brought other approaches to faith and social practices, the Russian citizens have been provided with options they could choose from as shown in table one.

---

[24] Giddens, *Modernity and Self-Identity*, 12.

Do you identify as a follower of any religion? If so, which one?

As %% of respondents

	Orthodoxy	Catholicism	Protestantism	Judaism	Islam	Buddhism	Hinduism	Other	None	Atheist	Refused to answer	Can't say
дек.89	27%	0%			3%			1%		70%		
фев.90	33%	0%			0%			0%		48%		19%
июл.91	53%	1%		0%	2%			1%		24%		20%
авг.93	52%	0%		0%	3%			0%		19%		25%
янв.03	73%	0%	0%	0%	5%	0%		1%	14%	4%		3%
янв.07	69%	0%	0%	0%	4%	0%		1%	17%	6%		3%
янв.08	73%	0%	0%	0%	5%	0%		1%	14%	4%		4%
дек.09	80%	0%	0%	0%	4%	0%		0%	8%	6%	1%	1%
дек.10	76%	0%	0%	0%	4%	0%		1%	10%	5%	3%	1%
дек.11	76%	1%	0%	0%	4%	1%	0%	1%	9%	7%	1%	1%
июл.12	76%	1%	0%	0%	5%	0%	0%	1%	9%	6%	1%	1%
авг.14	74%	0%	0%	0%	8%	0%	0%	0%	10%	6%	1%	1%
мар.15	76%	1%	0%	0%	6%	0%	0%	0%	8%	6%	1%	1%
фев.16	79%	0%	0%	0%	6%	0%	0%	0%	7%	5%	1%	1%
фев.17	79%	1%	0%	0%	8%	0%		0%	5%	5%	1%	1%
июн.18	75%	0%	0%	0%	7%	0%	0%	0%	10%	5%	1%	1%
июл.17	77%	0%	1%	0%	5%	0%	0%	0%	10%	6%	0%	1%
янв.20	65%	0%	1%	0%	7%	1%	0%	1%	18%	7%	0%	1%
апр.22	71%	1%	1%	0%	5%	1%	0%	1%	15%	4%	0%	1%

Левада-центр, @levada_center, принудительно признан иноагентом

Created with Datawrapper

Table 1. "Religiosity," *Levada Center*, 18 July 2017, https://www.levada.ru/2017/07/18/religioznost/.

Also, the appearance of other social agents, independent social organizations of political and social affiliations served as means to create for citizens their options to subscribe to other socio-political ideologies of their own,

> forms of civic resistance continue to reinvent themselves, despite being annihilated and persecuted. For Russians who remain in their country and wish to escape state propaganda, the migration to Youtube channels or the Telegram app are the only possibilities to stay informed and broadcast information about their real lived experience. Whilst some media and non-governmental organisations are trying to reorganise their work in exile – the independent TV channel Dozhd (TV Rain) has announced that it could broadcast from Riga – those who have remained whilst 'thinking otherwise' continue their ordinary acts of resistance on a daily basis.[25]

---

[25] Anne Le Huérou and Aude Merlin, "Russian Civil Society Put to the Test by the Invasion of Ukraine," *Alternatives Humanitaires*, trans. Juliet Poweys, 20 July 2022, https://www.alternatives-humanitaires.org/en/2022/08/17/russian-civil-society-put-to-the-test-by-the-invasion-of-ukraine/.

Therefore, the past three decades of democratization, though of managerial nature, yet have made a way for pluralistic forces to germinate and to produce individualistic voices of the country's citizens, which is still subjected to various means of control and suppression: "In 2006, when Vladimir Putin presented the law "on non-governmental organisations" as a major step forward against money laundering; Oleg Orlov, a member of Memorial, warned: "The margin of manoeuvre is worded so vaguely, it is so broad, that any bureaucrat can put our existence at risk, if they so wish."[26] Since that declaration, we can see in hindsight that virtually the entire free civil society in Russia has been undermined."[27] However, according to Burger,[28] the fact of spurring of various socio-political institutions that profess and promulgate various ideals and ideologies is enough for individual's mentality to be subjected to change and to search for personal response towards country's military crises, in particular.

Hence, the country could be characterized as the one guided by managerial democratization with the traits of a somewhat struggling civil society that equally coexists with not so rigid monolithic, nationalistic Orthodox culturalism. This can be perceived in the polar-opposite responses of the citizens to the mobilization, where those that have been upholding the program of nationalistic ideology have stayed and are willing to participate in the ongoing war.[29] While, on the other hand, those who have been

---

[26] David Ernesto García Doell, "A Fascist Regime Looms in Russia," *AK (Analyse & Kritik)*, 1 Apr. 2022, https://www.akweb.de/politik/putin-war-in-ukraine-a-fascist-regime-looms-in-russia/.

[27]"Huérou and Merlin, "Russian Civil Society Put to the Test."

[28] Tracy, *Plurality and Ambiguity,* 73.

[29] Researchers note that mobilization in different regions are organized irregularly. The highest numbers are in the Krasnoyarsk region with 28 thousand sent to war, with almost 5.5% being reservists. Whereas Sergey Shoigu claimed that "mobilization will affect only one per cent or maybe a little over 1.1% of reservists." The average number was also exceeded in Buryatiya with 3.7% of reserve conscripts; in Dagestan with 2.6%; and Kalmykiya with 2.2%. Analysts at CIT have commented, "It is observed that there is a correlation between the proportion of conscripted reserved men and the poverty of the regions. These regions must have had contract service men that have just recently finished their term. Often if not, the army in these regions is considered to be one of not so many employing organizations as well as the social conduit." In 23 out of 26 regions, where conscription at higher numbers than the percentage announced by Shoigu for reserves, the level of all-Russian income is lower, as researchers underline.

influenced by the pluralistic critical forces choose to immigrate and to avoid mobilization.[30]

Russian society as such is disintegrated, it is split in their understanding and expression towards love to their motherland. Love, on the one hand is of constant, wholistic, national, cultural, and collective epistemological notions but also, on the other hand is more of a fluid, individualistic, separatist, rational elements. Modern day Russian society is argued to face the period of clashing of former solidified and deeply grounded ideologies with recent, yet firm response and ideas of its individuals that are taking a firm stance as well in their right to choose and to profess their own beliefs. These are the times of opposition towards official political ideology and evolving, strengthening civil society, represented by emerging ideologies of the Self. Further on, we are to witness the dialectics of the two entities, the space of negotiating of the political establishment with its people, who have shown to be capable and assertive to withstand governing ideologies of love and to produce their own. The Russian society is evolving due to the forces of plurality that produce various institutional, religious and individual responses towards love, thus, inconspicuously creating new versions of this concept. Is it loving to stand for one's country and participate in the military conflict, or it could be also loving one's country when refusing to do so and rather demonstrate a civil disobedience and leave the country. The response of both Western and Russian scholarship and civil society in the interviews and publications is introduced here, in order to witness the influence of pluralizing forces that have been constructing the other axis of modernity. Ingeniously, pluralization uncovered different agendas of the collective society represented by the governing authorities and the individuals, gathered in the entity of the emerging civil society. The former above all pursues "the need for continued pressure on the system to protect Russian sovereignty against both immediate and longer-term threats, real and perceived. Security trumps economic efficiency," while the later seeks for personal physical security and

[30] Earlier, various mass media agencies have reported that 194,000 Russians have left for Georgia, Kazakhstan and Finland, the week after the announcement of mobilization. 98,000 of those have arrived to Kazakhstan. MIA of Georgia stated that 53,000 Russian citizens have arrived within a week, and daily the border is crossed over by 10,000 people, which is 40-45% higher than prior to September 21. Within the week, 66,000 Russians moved to EU, which is 30% higher than a week before, estimated by the Frontex EU cross border agency. The agency informed that most of those have arrived through Finnish and Estonian checkpoints, wherein, the number of those arriving via Finland has significantly increased after the announcement of mobilization.

well-being.[31] It is no longer about the nation, its history, grandiose or geopolitical position in the world, rather it is just a search for a peaceful coexistence, cooperation and simple search for content, individual security and love.

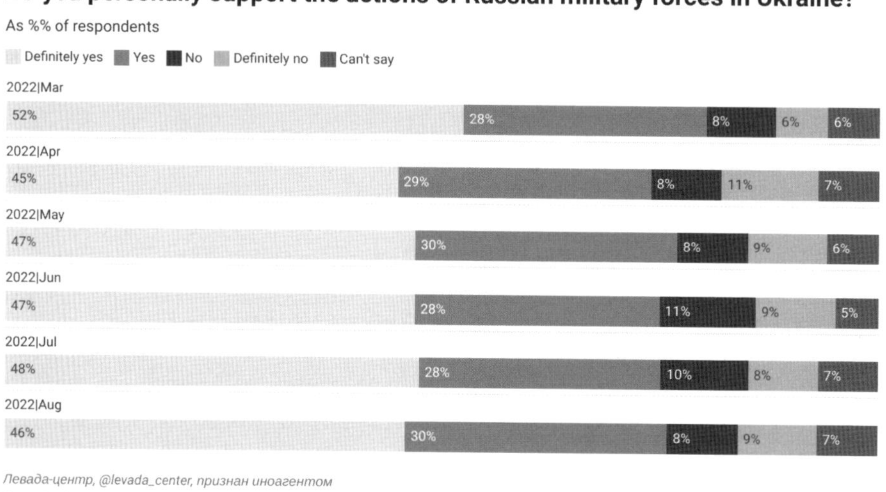

Table 2. "Conflict with Ukraine: August 2022," *Levada-Center,* 14 Sept. 2022, https://www.levada.ru/en/2022/09/14/conflict-with-ukraine-august-2022/.

The survey does prove the argument this paper outlines, naming the shifting response of the citizens towards the policy of its government. Within a little less than half a year of the ongoing military operation in Ukraine, almost 3% of the population took a negative stance on the matter while 2% became less convinced of the support for it and 1% couldn't identify their position. This change has happened at the time of the correspondents not actively been forced to participate in the conflict. The numbers of people leaving the country would only support the assumption of this ongoing negative response towards the events to increase. The social survey underlines the fact that on the one hand, people of Russia have lost their trust in the modern presidency to advocate their needs as democratic political structure presupposes, while on the other hand, the objectives of the official state historically prove to demonstrate that the opinions and interests of a

[31] Andrew Monaghan, *Russian State Mobilization: Moving the Country on to a War Footing,* (London: The Royal Institute of International Affairs, 2016), 29

political elite triumph individual voices. Nevertheless, as the numbers demonstrate, Russian populace is overwhelmingly supportive of the ongoing military actions on Ukrainian territory. The good news is that more and more Russians notice the diversification of the state and the people and understand that there still could be other means of dealing with perceived or even real threats. Thus, questions arise from the civic organizations as could it be possible to resolve the neighboring conflict by other means such as negotiating, seeking for more allies with other countries in order to get the support and have a better strategy in responding towards external pressure, instead of actions of cornering and intimidating. In general, could there be another response, the dialectical response of these pluralities allowing an opportunity to stay and disobey. As the present survey proves more and more people of their progressive age and education do support the ideals of non-military resistance and negotiation rather than voicing aggressive support towards Russian army itself and to the entire operation as a whole. "As for the opinion of Russian society as a whole, it seems very difficult to measure to a fine degree, with the polls gauging popular support for the "special operation" (the war cannot be called as such) at more than 80% to be taken cautiously, as should any measure of opinion in a non-democratic context."[32]

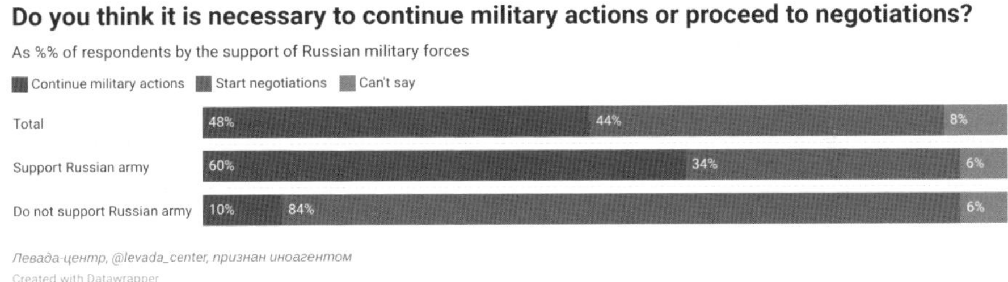

Table 3. "Conflict with Ukraine: August 2022," *Levada-Center,* 14 Sept. 2022, https://www.levada.ru/en/2022/09/14/conflict-with-ukraine-august-2022/.

[32] Huérou and Merlin, "Russian Civil Society Put to the Test."

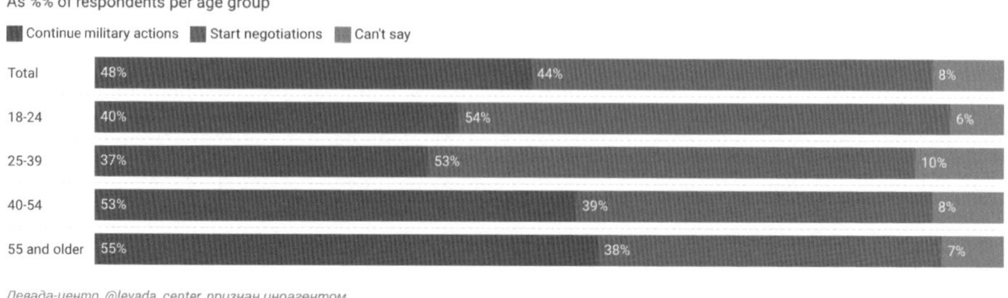

Table 4. "Conflict with Ukraine: August 2022," *Levada-Center,* 14 Sept. 2022, https://www.levada.ru/en/2022/09/14/conflict-with-ukraine-august-2022/.

As this recent survey demonstrates, the number of those that prefer their government to engage in the negotiating process is half of those that strongly back military action instead. Interestingly, the age groups with majorities preferring negotiations are those 25-39, the cluster of the populace that is usually a part of some educational institutions. At the same time those that strongly supporting Russian military actions come from the older generation of those aged of 55 and older, that polarizing the society on the issue with the later taking the lead with 4%. These numbers reveal that state propaganda in mass media – with its cultural ideology based on the historical precedents though – still appeals to the older generation. However, citizens that are younger, progressive, and better educated with access to other means of obtaining information have formed an opposite opinion. Again, with the later event of mobilization in the country that took place just a month after the survey it would only prove this tendency and even increase it, for it is not the elderly that will participate in the dangerous military operation. Therefore, the opinion of more than half of the population, those that are eligible for mobilization are not heard and considered. It does seem that all other options were not explored and instead, administration of President Putin acted rather uncompromising in order to demonstrate a great resolve and employed a 'power muscle' to prove its long-standing desire to display to the world that Russia is equal in its military and geopolitical power. Again, questions arise as whether this is necessary? Whether it is needed to respond to the historically similar issue by the same measure of the past. These are different times, with the arrival of mass media and internet revolution, where people are given options to choose, the power to exercise their individual rights, to organize their own communities, create civil society and demonstrate a civil disobedience by means available.

Contrary to the needs of the past, people seek peace not strife, and seek cooperation, instead of competition. Plurality, as a matter of fact, hints at the individual rights, needs and means to pursue what matters to a Self by means of a conversation, socialization, negotiation, the dialectics of the past and the present. It is an unstoppable force that needs to be reckoned with by historically established institutions and it is time for them to recognize the power of the individual over the weakening nationalistic sentiments, which are clearly waning – for the people are willing to change their citizenship, putting love for self above that of the collective. They redefine their love for their motherland by choosing to leave and retain their Russian heritage not geographically, but rather culturally – as there are still countries possessing 'Russianness' entailed in their social structures, by means of language, education, ethnicity, etc. One does not need to live in Russia to be Russian, one does not need to belong to the Russian Orthodox church in Russia to be religiously or culturally Orthodox. These realities have been developing for some time in such countries as Kazakhstan, Uzbekistan, Georgia, and others – and this new perspective has provided opportunities for many to explore. "On the 4th of October the head of the Ministry of Internal Affairs of Kazakhstan, Marat Akhmetzhanov stated that since September 21 there were 200,000 Russian citizens that have arrived to the country, while 147,000 Russians have left the country within the same period."[33]

Not surprisingly, Russian citizens flee to these countries in hopes to retain their cultural, ethnic and religious heritage, while at the same time strongly believing that the greatest expression of love is to protect themselves and their immediate families, rather than the nationalistic ideology of the elite governing their motherland. The order of the nationalistic state has been disrupted by the ambiguity, yet strong reality of the individual Self. National security is trampled by the personal well-being. The Self, that has been released through pluralization seeks for peace and cooperation which is found in dialects and a dialogue. Ongoing military conflict conspicuously suggests that the ideologies are found to be gradually dismissed, reconfigured in the age of pluralization and the emerging ideas that come to the foreplay. As such it is not about the transformations of the

---

[33] Elena Tofanyuk and Yulia Sapronova, "About 700,000 Citizens Left Russia after September 21," *Forbes*, 4 Oct. 2022, https://www.forbes.ru/society/478827-rossiu-posle-21-sentabra-pokinuli-okolo-700-000-grazdan.

'whats' of epistemologies of love, that we would argue, are undergoing configuration, but rather the 'hows' of expressing and actualizing those. There is no official data arising and no surveys undergoing on the subject of ones loving the country, yet still it is in the space of contest among the means, the actions and the expressions of it, that one is able to get a glimpse of the arising postmodern epistemologies of love in Russia, for both sides that support and those that oppose the military operation would argue to demonstrate their love as a motivating factor behind their actions.

CONCLUSION

Having applied the framework of thinking of *Sam-ae* Spirit (love of God, love of the neighbor and love for labor) in this paper towards the postmodern Russian context of mass mobilization, I can draw some conclusions on the epistemology of love. Firstly, Russian postmodernity unfortunately does not welcome the Self, as the love for oneself – both in Russian philosophy and theology – must submit to the common good, the *sobornost*, the nation, the motherland. Thus, the military actions initiated by the government are legitimized through the historical traditions of the Russian state. As a matter of fact, the geopolitical ideologies, which had been advanced in the imperial, soviet and quasi-democratic state policies via historical heritage both in political and classic literary works and philosophical treatises of Russian Slavophiles are still engaged with, revisited and modernized for the postmodern social military conflict. History and tradition are becoming the confines that eliminate the pluralizing voices of the younger, more progressive population that has been exposed to the Western ideals, Protestantism, capitalism and history by means of higher education, various other non-federal state channels. This is the social strata that is 'forced' to endanger their lives for the nation that is losing its appeal for its populace for it does not advocate, promote or pursue the very interests of peaceful coexistence with neighboring countries. Russian people do not want to be the part of the historically continuing practices of the Russian state in its expansionistic practices and policy. Thus, the ideological nationalistic epistemology of love that has been promoted and circulated by the state media platforms is less supported and instead, individualistic ideas of love that pursues peace and personal well-being comes to the foreground. As such the Russian society is becoming more polarized as the above-mentioned surveys have pointed out. The pluralizing force is proving to be potent in empowering individuals, the Self, the civil society to create their own epistemologies of love, even in such quasi-democratic state like Russia. As this paper demonstrates, the shift is on the way, now even historical tradition if treated not for ideological purposes but as one of the platforms to create individual ideals of love, social engagement, of which this paper is one of the attempts to do just that, then the long standing legitimizing foundation of geopolitical ideologies employed by the state could become the very avenue to do the opposite, to liberate from this ideological confines and be an active participant, maker of history.

CHAPTER 10

SAM-AE SPIRIT AS UNCONVENTIONAL LOVE: A POSTCOLONIAL FEMINIST READING OF MARI'S COLONIAL STORY

NITOLI SHEQI

"That she is herself
Is more difficult than
water is water . . ."
—*Kora Kumiko*[1]

INTRODUCTION

(Post)colonialism provides a lens to examine the identity of the subjects in terms of colonized/nativized, victim/hero, and oppressed/liberated. Love also situates within the alterity of such binaries. In his work, *The Location of Culture* (2004), Homi Bhabha identifies a border space as "the realm of the beyond."[2] Here, the beyond is an unconventional space, or a contested space, "the borderlines of the present."[3] Bhabha explains that this transit/in-betweenness is where space and time cross to produce complex figures of difference and identity, past and present, inside and outside, inclusion and exclusion.[4] The beyond represents, an unconventional space and disorientation, which lead to negotiation, particularly of meaning-making, without hegemonies and structures in the postcolonial condition. Homi Bhabha theorizes this state of disorientation as the Third Space; a space of displacement and contestation, within the context of postcolonialism.[5] Bhabha's theory develops and pushes beyond the ideas of Frantz Fanon and Edward Said.[6] The deep-rooted version of Bhabha's postcolonialism in the

[1] Cited in Kenneth Rexroth and Ikuko Atsumi (eds), *Women Poets of Japan* (New York: New Directions Books, 1977), 123.

[2] Homi Bhabha, *Location of Culture,* 2nd ed. (London: Routledge, 2004), 1.

[3] Ibid., 7.

[4] Ibid., 1-2.

[5] Nitoli Sheqi, "'(Un)becoming Herself': A Postcolonial Feminist Rereading of The Samaritan Woman in the Naga Context." PhD diss., (Yonsei University, 2022), 50.

[6] Edward Said, *Orientalism* (London: Penguin, 1977).

Third Space provides a space to contextualize and identify issues in a postcolonial state.

Spivak's essay "Can the Subaltern Speak?"[7] interrogates the perception of the colonial 'subject.' Spivak states that "the subaltern cannot speak." I contend that Spivak's remark lacks the aspect of whether the subaltern can be heard? In my opinion, the subaltern voice is continually looking for spaces to be heard.[8] For such voices to materialize, the question of agency becomes an important factor in creating space for narratives emerging from Asian perspectives. As Kwok Pui-lan writes,

> feminist theology in Asia will be a cry, a plea and invocation. It emerges from the wounds that hurt, the scars that hardly disappear, the stories that have no ending. Feminist theology in Asia is not written with a pen, it is inscribed on the hearts of many that feel the pain, and yet dare to hope."[9]

Mari's story emerges from this aspect of the struggle to find the space for unconventional love in the context of war. Therefore, this paper aims to engage how Rev. Pai Min-Soo's *Sam-ae* Spirit offers a space to reconceptualize unconventional love in Mari's colonial story in "the Third Space" – a love that transcends socio-political, cultural, and racial barriers. In so doing, the study will enable me to draw implications for the postcolonial feminist love in the context of war and displacement.

MARI — A COLONIAL LOVE TALE OF A NAGA WOMAN[10]

Mari is a story of a young Naga woman in Easterine Kire's novel, *Mari*.[11] The protagonist, Mari (as called by her fiancé) or Khrielieviu (Aviu) Mari O'Leary[12] in Kire's novel accounts the story of a young Naga woman who finds love amidst World War II (WWII) and its aftermath in the Naga hills

---

[7] Gayatri Chakravorty Spivak, "Can the Subaltern Speak?" in *Colonial Discourse and Post-Colonial Theory*, ed. P. Williams and L. Chrisman (New York: Columbia University Press, 1992): 104.

[8] Sheqi, "'(Un)becoming Herself,'" 57.

[9] Pui-lan Kwok, *Introducing Asian Feminist Theology* (Sheffield: Sheffield Academic Press, 1984), 228.

[10] This section is an excerpt from my PhD dissertation (unpublished) where I read Mari's story as a contextual inquiry alongside the story of the Samaritan woman in John's Gospel.

[11] Easterine Kire is a poet and a novelist. Mari happened to be Kire's aunt (her mother's eldest sister). Most of Kire's works predominantly features the Naga people, culture, tradition, and socio-political agendas in the form of narratives.

[12] An ethnic name, of the Angami tribe. Angami is one of the tribes in Nagaland of which Mari belongs.

(1943-1998).[13] Kire writes the story of Mari, who witnessed the cruelty of war, finds love, loses her loved ones, and lives on to recount the episode as a single parent. It is a story set in the real-time and space of WWII or otherwise known as "the battle of Kohima,"[14] the historical event which by far changed the contours of the Naga identity in general till today.[15] Kire's *Mari* echoes the reality of Naga women's struggles and aspirations to identify themselves (within their own existential space). It represents the cultural, sociopolitical, ethnic, and religious demography of the Naga society. The ongoing struggle of Naga women to find their space in today's patriarchal Naga context and neocolonial India is a testament that a (post)colonial and feminist appropriation is a viable approach particularly to find an interpretive voice of love for the Naga women and to understand Naga feminism.

For Mari and her family, the Battle of Kohima in 1944 altered their lives drastically in terms of their simple, traditional lived experiences. They had firsthand experienced of becoming refugees in their own land, with the presence of the British colonials and the Japanese invasion that follow suit. Mari's hometown became the blazing war zone during the battle. In the midst of war, Mari and her siblings (oldest brother, and two younger sisters) get separated from their family as they seek refuge in other villages. As much as Mari's story depicts the unsettling reality of people in war zone, the story predominantly speaks of the love story of this young woman Aviu or Mari and her fiancé, a British Staff Sergeant named Victor (Vic), who she lost to the war. Vic did not live to see his daughter and Mari became a widow and a single parent before she could become a wife.

Mari's lived experiences of love quickly draw the reader's attention as it presents itself in "betwixt and between."[16] Mari encountered Vic when she was seventeen. She narrates how the presence of Vic enriched her life during the time of war. A love that renders hope and liberty in the phase of war. As Mari asked herself, "Did people fall in love in wartime?"[17] Nevertheless,

---

[13] The Naga are an indigenous group of people, predominantly located in Nagaland, in the Northeastern part of India.

[14] Kohima, which is now the capital of Nagaland, was the battleground of World War II.

[15] Kire, *Mari* (India: Harpar Collins, 2010), vii.

[16] Victor Turner, a British anthropologist, explains this term as finding oneself in liminality, a contested space of shifting identities and cultures. In this space, the subject is in a transitional state, not defined by the past and the future that is yet to form. In other words, a state of fluidity. See Victor Turner, *The Forest of Symbols* (Ithaca and London: Cornell University Press, 1967), 97.

[17] Kire, *Mari*, 45.

Mari's love story is short-lived as her fiancé, Vic gets killed by a sniper's bullet during the battle at Kohima. This episode altered Mari's life completely. Having lost Vic to war, it left her as a single parent at the age of eighteen. Mari narrates the upheavals of her lived experiences, such as war, love, displacement, and lost. The story unfolds the ugliness of war and its aftermath in the powerful narrative of this young woman and her community, whose lives take a turning point in wartime. It transports the readers to see the different facets of love, loss, fear, heroic deeds, uncertainty, and displacement in the existential human predicament of war. After Vic was killed in a war, Mari finds herself with another British soldier, Dickie (who was a friend of Vic). She had a daughter with him, although they were never married, and he left for England after the war never to return. Mari later in life meets Patrick O'Leary, who becomes her husband for 42 years until he died in 1998.[18] Mari exemplifies that a passionate living and loving unreservedly gives sustenance, depth, and hope to our existence.

Mari's colonial love story entails an (un)becoming of a young woman, a love that blurs the sociopolitical, ethnic, and racial boundaries – an emancipatory love. A love in "the Third Space"[19] that begins to see cracks in the hegemonic power structures in the midst of hybridity and polarization. Mari's love finds itself in the binaries of ethnicity and sociopolitical upheaval. To find space for stories such as Mari requires a reimagination of love beyond the boundaries and social conventions. It raises the question of what it means to be attracted to someone as a locus of search for freedom and liberation? However, beyond Eros, the story also stresses the love for the neighbor amidst a political entanglement. In the budding stage of Christianity, the re-imagining of love that extends beyond one's own community was a significant force and Nagas in general upheld such communal love and respect for the other. Mari's narrative reflects this communal love and sentiment for their land. It enacts the notion of love in the context of colonization and war transcend sociopolitical, cultural, and racial boundaries. This re-imagination of love is not far from the polyvalent love concept of '*Sam-ae* Spirit.' Rev. Pai Min-Soo's *Sam-ae* Spirit deciphers a contextual inquiry which is answerable to colonialism and empowerment and emancipation of the marginalized.

---

[18] Ibid., 184.

[19] Bhabha, *Location of Culture,* 53.

POLYVALENT LOVE — *SAM-AE* SPIRIT

Rev. Pai Min-Soo (1896-1968), a Korean Presbyterian minister and a social reformer, pioneered a revolutionary movement in Korea post Japanese colonial rule. He was born in Cheongju, Chungbuk Province, Korea. He lived in a period of imperial turmoil, sociopolitical oppression, and economic meager. Undoubtedly, his theology engages such aspects of the Kingdom of God, where the spiritual(church) and the practical(society) life must coexist on the same axis. Emerging from the struggles of the people, Rev. Pai fervently presents 'love's multiplicity' – the love for God, the love for humanity, and the love for work.[20] This 'love's multiplicity' concept of a nonviolent resistant love to Japanese colonization serves as a hermeneutical point of departure in reimagining Mari's unconventional colonial love in "the Third Space."[21] *Sam-ae* Spirit entails love that is not defined by boundaries but sees a potential growth in acknowledging ambiguity without decentering difference as radical alterity. It reimagines the ethos of love by drawing attention to Christ' teaching that accommodates the weak, the marginalized, the oppressed, the downtrodden, the neighbour, the Other. Such reimagining of love beyond boundaries creates space for those that exist at the periphery of the sociopolitical structure.

Rev. Pai Min-Soo confronts the norms of Christianity, proving that defiance can positively reshape and emancipate distressed communities and societies. He addresses the inhumane struggles of the rural community/farmers in Korea following the post Japanese colonization and those under the Japanese occupation.[22] Rev. Pai's praxis establishes the connection of "the spiritual and practical life, the Kingdom of God on earth and the Kingdom of God in heaven, and the church and society."[23] The practical aspect of such theology incorporates the human struggle in terms of sociopolitical and economic turmoil. The *Sam-ae* Spirit saw that liberation/freedom must be experienced through the lens of the past, present, and the future of the subject to find relevance just as, "God is self-actualized in and

---

[20] See Chammah J. Kaunda and S. M. Kim, "'Samae Spirit' Assist toward 'Ubuntu Spirit' Model for Rural Adult Christian Education in Zambia," *Religious Education*, 117: 40.

[21] Bhabha, *Location of Culture*, 53.

[22] Albert L. Park, "Religion, 1876-1910," in *Routledge Handbook of Modern Korean History*, ed. Michael J. Seth (London: Routledge, 2016), 75. Albert L. Park, "Social Renewal through the Rural: Agricultural Cooperatives in South Korea as a Form of Critiquing Capitalism," *Global Environment* 9 (2016):82-107.

[23] Minsoo Pai, *Who Shall Enter the Kingdom of Heaven?*, 1st ed., trans. Nowon Park (Seoul: Yonsei University Press, 1952), 315.

through the historical process and historical events."[24] For those marginalized (the *minjung*), the presence of God is evidenced in Korean history. Rooted deeply in the socio-political and economic turmoil post Japanese colonization paints clearly the Korean history and Korean justice movement. Such act of repression and oppressive reality necessitate an interpretation of Christian faith, in order to make it relevant to those particularly of the suffering group. Rev. Pai contends, "Jesus taught and lived the life of love, but it seemed we got lost something somewhere."[25] Rev. Pai's love's multiplicity predominantly *Sam-ae* Spirit throws light and helps us to reimagine love outside the binaries and structural norms of society. He appropriately focuses on the rural community of Korea, which was one of the most poverty-stricken situations (at that time). In finding a space for the poor and suffering community drives his understanding of the Kingdom of God. Rev. Pai saw the importance of an appropriation of faith that addresses the issue of the needy, the oppressed, the ostracized, and the Other. According to him, the Kingdom of God and the love of Christ stand in solidarity and build on such communities and groups who find themselves in an unconventional space. He notes:

> Just as the gospel of God's kingdom was developed with a focus on rural, fishing, and mountain villages such as Galilee, Zebulun, Naphtali, and Samaria, Korean farmers are the poorest and unluckiest of all of the farmers in the world. As such, the rural regions of Korea are the most suitable site for dealing with issues of God's Kingdom…it is meaningful to save those who are faced with hardship through the practice of the love of Christ.[26]

Rev. Pai's *Sam-ae* Spirit or the love's multiplicity could benefit from Spivak's thought on "planetarity." To quote Spivak, "If we imagine ourselves as planetary creatures rather than global entities, alterity remains underived from us; it is not our dialectical negation, it contains us as much as it flings us away."[27] Spivak's imagination focuses on the move beyond the globe driven by its neocolonizing impulse, and so emphasizing on inclusivity but also on the alterity of human existence on earth. It engages imagining from

---

[24] Nam Dong Suh, *In Search of Minjung Theology* (Seoul: Hangilsa, 1983), 171; Yeong Mee Lee, "A Political Reception of the Bible: Korean Minjung Theological Interpretation of the Bible," *SBL Forum*, http://sbl-site.org/Article.aspx?ArticleID=457.

[25] Pai, *Who Shall Enter the Kingdom of Heaven?,* 315.

[26] Min-soo Pai, *The Kingdom of God and Rural Korea* (Seoul: Yonsei University Press, 2017), 118.

[27] Gayatri Spivak, *Death of a Discipline* (New York: Columbia University Press, 2003), 72-73.

afar and anticipates for a future that is yet to take shape. Imagining planetarity instead of globality is not to desert the concept of collectiveness, but to reimagine them from the precedents set forth by colonizers. *Sam-ae* Spirit allows us to rethink the compartmentalization of love that is too often categorized into likeness or unlikeness, conventional or unconventional, or insider or outsider. This compartmentalization becomes defaults and serves as logics for differentiating, dominating, and obliterating, particularly in the patriarchal postcolonial context. This raises the question whether the binaries of love have to be at odds or mutually exclusive? Instead of seeing love as an entity to be grouped or separated based on what is conventional or unconventional, the *Sam-ae* Spirit propels us to see beyond these binaries and contestations. Therefore, engaging Rev. Pai Min-Soo's '*Sam-ae* Spirit' doctrine offers a space to re-conceptualize unconventional love in Mari's colonial story – a love that transcends socio-political, cultural, and racial barriers. In so doing, the study enables me to draw implications for the postcolonial feminist love in the context of war and displacement.

SAM-AE SPIRIT & *MARI* – IMPLICATIONS FOR POSTCOLONIAL FEMINIST LOVE

Rev. Pai's teaching embodies love that stands in solidarity with all humanity, particularly the marginalized, oppressed, discriminated, the other and dares to see love beyond boundaries. His teaching of God's love incorporates loving the neighbor, a love that finds space along the horizontal and vertical axis. As he said:

> Now let us love God, and let us love others as He taught us to. He who loves God must also love other people and he who does not love other people who can be seen cannot love God who cannot be seen. Therefore, to love God is to obey and put into practice the law that God has commanded. Loving others at the center of God's principle and truth, which will open the path to your life."[28]

Pai's *Sam-ae* Spirit reimagines the Christian language of love and reorients Christ's teaching to love the neighbor even if that means seeing beyond the boundaries, hybridity, and polarity. He sought to develop an emancipatory love in all positive aspects, involving people from all walks of life. Such reconceptualization of love creates a profound space for narratives like Mari to find representation in their own existential history, which embodies different facets of love.

---

[28] Pai, *The Kingdom of God and Rural Korea*, 121.

Pai's critique of Christian teachings of love speaks to the context of women who do not fit the mold of the traditional perception of the so-called 'ideal woman.' Musa W. Dube reads the idea of inclusion as a form intended for legitimate control, which is achieved only in unequal relationships.[29] How love's plays out in the dichotomy between sociopolitical and racial power dynamics?

LOVE AND ITS POWER RELATIONS

Victor Turner writes, "the high could not be high unless the low existed, and he who is high must experience what it is like to be low."[30] Similarly, as members of society, "most of us see only what we expect to see, and what we expect to see is what we are conditioned to see when we have learned the definitions and classifications of our culture."[31] In the colonial context, power associates with domination and subjugation of the weaker/lesser/vulnerable population. Any effort to change the status of the marginalized/women begins with the question of the nature of power.[32] This entails that the power relations necessitate researching of its epistemological groundings. Mari's colonial love centers this radical love in a disoriented state primordially in search of freedom and dignity. As Mari narrates: "It was impossible for us girls to do anything adventurous, as our parents were very protective of us."[33] This echoes a patriarchal hierarchy that construes the participation of women, limiting them to exercise their humanity. Monalisa Changkija contends,

> Much as Naga scholars' acclaim Nagas' "purest form of democracy" in sovereign village-republic and compare it to the "democracy" of the Greek city-states, the fact is, this "democracy" is pertinent only to males – only males have the right to land ownership; only males can participate in the village parliament. It's patriarchy in its purest form, actually."[34]

---

[29] Musa W. Dube, "Reading for Decolonization," in *John and Postcolonialism*, ed. Musa W. Dube and Jeffrey I. Stanley (London and New York: Sheffield Academic Press, 2002), 70.

[30] Victor Turner, *The Ritual Process: Structure and Anti-Structure* (Ithaca, NY: Cornell University Press, 1969), 97.

[31] Turner, *The Forest of Symbols,* 95.

[32] Namsoon Kang, "Re-constructing *Asian* feminist theology: toward a *glocal* feminist theology in an era of neo-Empire(s)," in *Christian Theology in Asia*, ed. Sebastian C. H. Kim (Cambridge, UK: Cambridge University Press, 2008), 217.

[33] Kire, *Mari*, 36.

[34] Monalisa Changkija, "Equality's Time Has Come," *The Indian Express*, 7 Feb. 2017, https://indianexpress.com/article/opinion/columns/nagaland-violence-kohima-protest-against- women-reservation-4511227/.

Partly resulting from the imposition of patriarchal colonial state, women remain insignificant and are deprived of any power relations. This view is similar to Marilyn French's analysis of the patriarchal colonial context where the relationship of the colonizer to colonized when transposed to men and women fits the description of the precedent relationship almost at every point. From every aspect, patriarchal culture defines "women as different in kind from men" depriving women of the right to own property.[35] *Sam-ae* Spirit finds fault with such a mode of segregation, particularly in response to Japanese colonization. Rev. Pai identifies how in the midst of the power relations, humanity gets lost in the mix of the rich and poor, the urban and rural, the insider and the outsider. His focus remains on the love of God that redefines loves power relation and provides a motive, a space for the marginalized community (the minjung), the oppressed, the neighbour.[36] By extension, Rev. Pai's polyvalent love contends the subjugating power that defines love in the colonial context. His legacy firmly stood against such a trajectory of power relations of love and objectifying of the weak, the oppressed, the marginalized, the women, and so on. Similarly, Mari finds herself in the power relation of love that includes tradition and non-tradition, native and foreigner, colonized and colonizer. Mari's love language finds itself in a continuum of homogeneity and heterogeneity – the betweenness. How do we define this radical love that involves a native woman and a foreigner/colonizer in the context of war? Is it an invasion where the classic form of foreigners invading foreign land and women?[37] Could it entail a love that speaks beyond an invasion of love? Every aspect of love identified in Mari points to this so-called "double consciousness."[38] Women in patriarchal and colonial context must juggle this aspect of double consciousness.

DOUBLE CONSCIOUSNESS OF LOVE

As W. E. B. Du Bois defines "double consciousness" as the dichotomous state of finding oneself in the condition of in-betweenness. Du Bois writes:

> It is a peculiar sensation, this double-consciousness, this sense of always looking at one's self through the eyes of others, of measuring one's soul by the tape of a world that looks on in amused contempt and pity. One

---

35 Marilyn French, *Beyond Power: On Men, Women and Morals* (New York: Ballentine Books, 1985), 121-22.

36 Pai, *Who Shall Enter the Kingdom of Heaven?*, 347.

37 Musa W. Dube, "Reading for Decolonization," 70.

38 W. E. B. Du Bois, "The Negro and Imperialism," in *W. E. B. Du Bois Speaks, 1920-1963*, ed. Phillips S. Foner (New York: Pathfinder, 1970), 45.

> ever feels his twoness – an America, a Negro; two souls, two thoughts, two unreconciled strivings; two warring ideals in one dark body, whose dogged strength alone keeps it from being torn asunder."[39]

By extension, this shows that "[n]either race nor language can any longer define nationality[love]."[40] From the postcolonial feminist discourse of love, this "double consciousness" then represents the contestation of love on the account of native/foreigner, insider/outsider, or man/woman. For this "double consciousness" of 'in-betweenness' makes them 'daydream.' They dream of an alternative reality where domination and subjugation are overcome and all forms of alienation on the basis of a difference of ethnicity, race, sex, class, or religion disintegrates and peace prevails.[41] Mari finds herself in this "double consciousness" pertaining to the relationship with the white men, a colonizer(s). This raises the question of love defined by ethnic, racial, and socio-political boundaries. Should the binaries of love be at odds or mutually exclusive? Achille Mbembe explains: "What defines the postcolonised subject is the ability to engage in baroque practices fundamentally ambiguous, fluid, and modifiable even where there are clear, written, and precise rule."[42] The consciousness becomes an empowering tool in a context where contestation of love appears on the account of insider and outsider dichotomy. In Mari's postcolonial feminist love, refurbishing traditions and cultures are essential in the re-imagination of love. Rev. Pai's polyvalent love champions such re-imagination of love for those that find themselves at the peripheral edge of a love conundrum.

Traditionally, Mari's love could be ridiculed and mischaracterized, especially from the nationalist standpoint and religious tradition. The narrative speaks of a woman who, in the times of war, falls in love with a colonizer, a white man, who from every aspect is an outsider. She is also sandwiched between this consciousness of being a Naga woman and a Christian, the virtue of both that sets high moral standards. It is not a farfetched idea to see characters like Mari, who will often serve as examples of what traditional women or ideal women ought not to be. From the traditional context, there is no such thing as individual undertaking when it

---

[39] Du Bois, "The Negro and Imperialism," 45.

[40] C. Keller, M. Nausner and M. Rivera (eds.), *Postcolonial Theologies: Divinity and Empire* (St. Louis: Chalice Press, 2004), 1.

[41] See also Janer Wolff, *Resident Alien: Feminist Cultural Criticism* (New Haven and London: Yale University Press, 1995); Elisabeth Schüssler Fiorenza, *Discipleship of Equals: A Critical Feminist Ekklēsia-logy of Liberation* (New York: Crossroad, 1994), 335.

[42] Achille Mbembe, *On the Postcolony* (California: University of California Press, 2001), 129.

comes to love. This more or less speaks of the subjugating power that defines love in the patriarchal and postcolonial context. Women that find themselves in such context constantly have to defend their principles, love, or simply being as an identifiable entity within the existing structure.

Engaging love's multiplicity provides space to question any attempts of undiluted love. There can be potential growth in acknowledging ambiguity without decentering difference as radical alterity. From every aspect, Mari's story radicalizes the language of love, where unlikely characters find hope and purpose amidst war and displacement. There is such an aspect in Naga tradition where a foreigner could be nativized in marriage, like in the case of Mari and her family, who welcomed Vic as part of their family and community. This radicalizes the whole idea of love, acceptance, and accommodating a stranger, an outsider, even a colonizer. Such landscape is possible by engaging radical thinking of Pai's polyvalent love, which saw a nonviolent resistant love beyond traditions and boundaries arguably during one of the most turmoil phase of Korea post Japanese colonization. This conscious uprising became a powerful tool of empowerment of reasoning, particularly of Christian faith in the context of postcolonialism. Mari's story identifies this very praxis of loving, which serves a locus of freedom in itself.

LOVE AS THE LOCUS OF FREEDOM & LIBERATION

In a patriarchal Naga context, the emancipation of women has long been construed between tradition and cultural stereotypes. Mari's story adds another element to this existing structure, which is a colonial notion of love. From a postcolonial feminist perspective, Mari suffers from 'double colonization.' She experiences the oppression of colonialism and patriarchy as a colonized subject and as a woman. Her language presents itself in a conundrum because it narrates the love between a colonised and a colonizer. As a native, she must simultaneously navigate and negotiate her love for her family and community, and by extension, the love for the other. Anne McClintock observes that "Nationalism is . . . constituted from the very beginning as a gendered[love] discourse and cannot be understood without a theory of gender[love]power."[43] For a colonized subject, freedom is a restricted choice, in the context of extreme socio-political oppression. The question remains as to how one can inversely infuse love in such a scenario in a liberating sense? For Mari, her love for Vic becomes her locus of

[43] Anne McClintock, *Imperial Leather: Race, Gender and Sexuality in the Colonial Context* (London: Rutledge, 1995), 355.

freedom and exuberant meaning-giving hope in war times. However, Mari's love extends beyond Vic, because life did not stop for her after his death as she became a single parent. For Mari, love champions the differences and alterity in the context of war and displacement. This re-imagination of love echoes Pai's own legacy that seeks to find space and landscape which transcend colonial and patriarchal structure. His engagement of the love with God saw the need to pursue the vulnerable population for whom the Kingdom of God was wide open. How would Mari's language of love sit with the Naga church, which predominantly leans towards conservatism? Mari experienced a tabooed love through the turmoil of war and displacement.

Today, Naga women who find themselves under such pretext also experience displacement within the church. The church must begin to see theology of love beyond the binaries of conservative and liberal, or traditional and nontraditional. For this to materialize, the church must reengage love's multiplicity that could potentially become a space of empowerment and liberation. The realities of women who find themselves on the similar axis of Mari, and who are made invisible must be brought to visibility not to be condemned and serve as examples of the forgiving God but to exemplify the love of God that encapsulate those that are invisible. These women fill the back pews of the church, but what is needed today is to hear more lived experiences of those that identify and exist outside the norm/marginalized/the other and legitimate those narratives coming from the space of marginality.

Narratives like Mari can be a powerful mechanism to show the legitimate impact of love at war times. Fixating on the difference based on race, ethnicity, sex, culture, or socio-politics tends to disintegrate "the interactive mediations between differences, and obscure the overlapping and hybridizing that takes place in the contact space in between differences." [44] The infinite layers of differences and borders will continue to exist, but how we maneuver such layers will cradle a re-imagination of love and acceptance. Virgilio Elizondo suggests: "Borders will not disappear, differences will not fade away, but they need not divide and keep peoples apart… we can see borders as the privileged meeting places where different persons and peoples will come together to form a new and most inclusive

[44] Kang, "Re-Constructing Asian Feminist Theology," 215.

community"[45] Pai's polyvalent love fought to create such alternative landscape for the vulnerable population on the grounds of socio-politics, economic, ethnicity, race, age, gender, and class.

BRIDGING THE GAP WITH LOVE OF ONE'S NEIGHBOR

What does love of one's neighbor look like in the context of war and displacement? The words of the late African John Mbiti – "I am because we are; and since we are, therefore I am" – captures the foundational feature of the Naga notion of neighbour.[46] For Mari, neighbourly love and compassion extend beyond ethnic, racial, national, and socio-political boundaries. It subverts the default systemic order that determines who to show love and who not to. Similarly, Rev. Pai's polyvalent love was clear: to love and to empower those vulnerable without compartmentalization. In response to the segregation of the vulnerable community, Pai shows that love needs to play out in action, accepting those that are seemingly unacceptable. For the most part, neighbour love requires transcendence towards the Other. Mari could very well become the Other, the neighbour to whom love need to be shown. She became a widow and single parent at eighteen, she was abandoned by the man while she carried his child, all of these in the midst of war and displacement. Neighbour love ought to show in action and empower by standing in solidarity in such a disheartening context. As Mari narrates, "We have to grab life and love when we find it and hold fiercely on to it."[47] In any postcolonial and patriarchal context, the Other is everyone who is deprived of love on account of sociopolitical, ethnic, racial, cultural, and gender boundaries. Nevertheless, love's multiplicity/neighbour love transcend such binaries, as evidently discussed in Pai and Mari's notion of love.

The lived realities/narratives such as Mari require attention on the "ethical indignation"[48] which recognizes colonized/marginalized/vulnerable population as the subject, experiencing God's grace/love in the midst of oppression. It also requires the church to reassess its perception of normality.

---

45 Timothy Matovina, ed., *Beyond Borders: Writings of Virgilio Elizondo and Friends* (Maryknoll: Orbis, 2000), 183.

46 John S. Mbiti, *African Religions and Philosophy* (London: Heinemann, 1969), 141. *Cf.* Nitoli Sheqi and Chammah J. Kaunda, "Your Neighbour Is Yourself Reflected in the Mirror of Life: A Naga Reading of the Good Samaritan Narrative in the Context of Covid-19," *The Ecumenical Review* 72, no. 4 (2020): 614.

47 Kire, *Mari*, 143.

48 Jung Mo Sung, "The Human Being as Subject: Defending the Victims," in *Latin American Liberation Theology: The Next Generation,* ed. Ivan Petrella (Maryknoll, NY: Orbis Books, 2005), 9

Pai's *Sam-ae* Spirit identifies that Christ shares in the struggles of humanity, their sufferings, dignity, freedom, and liberation. For those that occupy the space of marginality, the love of God in the redemptive work of Christ conveys an important message.[49] K. C. Abraham writes:

> The primary objective of theological reflection… is to help people in their struggle for justice and freedom. It is not enough to understand and interpret God's act, that is, to give reason for their faith, but also to help change their situation in accordance with the utopia of the vision of the gospel.[50]

This reflects the shift in the epistemological approach to interpreting our normative theology. We must realize that God takes part in our struggle for freedom and dignity. Christian aptitude requires us to extend love's multiplicity both within and beyond the church in solidarity. *Sam-ae* Spirit validates that the threefold love spirit knows no boundary. This challenges the church to emulate such love by placing one foot in the church and one in the world. If the Naga church today continues to maintain the status quo of normalizing the hegemonic practices of love within the four walls and pews, it will fail its own proposition of liberation of the love of God.

CONCLUSION

This article attempted to engage with Rev. Pai's polyvalent concept of *Sam-ae* Spirit alongside the unconventional love of Mari, a protagonist in Easterine Kire's novel of the same name. It identifies how love's multiplicity created a space for the re-imagination of love in the context of war and displacement. The radical love lived out in Mari's narrative requires attention to elements of differences and boundaries like socio-politics, race, nationality, ethnicity, and gender. Pai's practical undertaking of threefold love, which requires love to play out in action, becomes vital for a Christian re-imagining of love. To accommodate and stand in solidarity with those that identify as an 'Other' in their own existential space, love of one's neighbour must take form. To bridge the gap, neighbourly love that knows no boundary must be emulated as it empowers. For Mari, love was the validation, the locus of freedom and dignity, and the ultimate hope amidst war, displacement, loss, and disheartening episodes.

---

[49] K. C. Abraham, "Third World Theology: Paradigm Shift and Emerging Concerns," in *Confronting Life: Theology out of Context*, ed. M. P. Joseph (Delhi: ISPCK, 1995), 207-8.

[50] Ibid., 207-8.

CHAPTER 11

SAM-AE SPIRIT AS DIALOGICAL LOVE: A RESPONSE TO VULNERABILITY AND UNEMPLOYMENT IN SOUTH AFRICA

BUHLE MPOFU

INTRODUCTION AND CONTEXT

Migration is not a new phenomenon and Dill has observed that "most national borders have become permeable"[1] and these fluid borders present new challenges in the context of competition for limited resources especially as most economies are recovering from the impact of the COVID-19 pandemic. In South Africa, some locals feel that their experiences have been ignored by the government this has led to frustrations and vigilantism as some disgruntled communities take the law into their own hands, targeting foreign nationals through xenophobic attacks. There is a need for the development of a theological framework for a Christian response to augment government efforts in strengthening social cohesion in local communities.[2]

One of the recent developments in South Africa is the situation of migration has come on spotlight following an increase in unemployment rate and a rise in criminal activities, particularly with regards to crimes committed by undocumented migrants. Understandably, undocumented people are often difficult to trace as they easily evade authorities when crime is committed and there is a need to balance these concerns with the protection of sustainable livelihoods for cross border traders, among them, children and women who are often vulnerable to exploitation. For example, Mpofu "highlights survival strategies for young migrants and demonstrates how the changing global socio-economic landscapes as a result of COVID-19 . . . [has] dire consequences . . . on poor communities . . . [and]

---

[1] J. S. Dill, "The Moral Education Of Global Citizens," *Global Society* 49 (2012): 541.

[2] In her first public commitments, the new elected Premier of Kwa-Zulu Natal, Nomsa Dube-Ncube met with faith-based organisations in the Msunduzi municipality on Sunday 14 October 2022. For details see: "Premier Dube-Ncube Meets with Faith-Based Organisations," eNCA News, 14 Aug. 2022, https://www.enca.com/news/kzn-premier-marks-100-days-office.

how some migrant women use situations of deprivation to promote socio-economic transformation through radical doctrines of resistance."[3] The vulnerability of women and children presents gender intersecting trajectories and highlights processes of socialisation which must be recognized as "socially constituted, fluid, wide ranging, and historically and geographically differentiated."[4] Theology has an important role to play in interrogating these processes and mitigating the impact of migration challenges on the livelihoods for displaced families through developing life affirming practices and values. In Southern Africa, migration studies have tended to be devoid of engagement with religious experiences of migrants and religion is often mentioned in passing in a context where political instability, wars, famine, and environmental crises create a range of socio-political and ethical challenges for governments, relief organization, and communities. Another example was during the time of the Covid 19 crisis, migrants were some of the most effected by lockdowns as restricted movement meant that their informal businesses had to close. Although these measures were intended to limit the spread of the virus, enforcing social distancing measures without considering the plight of the poor migrant communities tended to be inhuman. For example, Mpofu[5] lamented political "demagoguing" and the exploitation of poor families affected by the COVID-19 lockdown and observed how the mission of the Church shifted to the margins, and posited that; "[t]he post-COVID-19 church should emerge as a church whose mission is God's mission *(missio-Dei*) not merely the activities of the church where the poor are marginalised and exploited by the rich and powerful. Solidarity with the poor should be the essence of being church."[6] Expressing solidarity with the poor will require a closer analysis of our context. It is therefore important to highlight some these socio-economic conditions and

---

[3] For more details, see Buhle Mpofu, "Mission to Live: A Gendered Perspective on the Experience of Migration in Southern Africa," *HTS Teologiese Studies / Theological Studies* 77, no. 4 (2021), https://doi.org/10.4102/hts.v77i2.6513.

[4] Robert W. Connell, "Hegemonic Masculinity and Emphasized Femininity," in *Feminist Frontiers IV,* eds. L. Richardson, V. Taylor, and N. Whittier, 22-25 (New York: McGraw-Hill,1997).

[5] Buhle Mpofu, "Missio-Pastoral and Theological Implications for Migration and Increased Demagoguing in South Africa: A Call to Prophetic and Transformative Engagement with Migrants," *Missionalia* 50, (2022): 51–73.

[6] Buhle Mpofu, "Mission on the Margins: A Proposal for an Alternative Missional Paradigm in the Wake of COVID-19," *HTS Teologiese Studies/Theological Studies* 76, no. 1 (2020). https://doi.org/10.4102/hts.v76i1.6149.

their implications for migration before exploring the threefold aspects of love through the concept of *Sam-ae* Spirit.

SOCIO-ECONOMIC & POLITICAL IMPLICATIONS FOR MIGRATION

As one of the Church leaders Bishop Kizito has indicated "it is clear that it is not enough for the Christian community simply to know and proclaim the demands of the Gospel: it must bring them to bear on situations in daily life like the migrants and refugees. This theological framework can assist us to engage with those who are concerned like the department of Home Affairs, the Police, healthy, education and social workers."[7] This initiative is a timely response to the call made in the report by the Soweto Ministers' fraternal who have made a clarion call pointing that as ministers in Soweto:

> [they] are . . . ready to partner with other community organisations, ministries, or government programs, or by ourselves take on programs and initiatives in combatting this scourge. We further… recommend workshops to be run in churches . . . [and] that as the Church is diverse in terms of culture, age, gender and nationality, this is in itself a possible effective model that Church can emulate in their respective communities, as part of their pastoral role in society…The church desperately needs government in addressing support and empowerment especially when facing challenging issues that affect even our ordinary church members. Unemployment, inequality, poverty and rape are on the rise, with little to nothing at our disposal to resolve such challenges. The Church has not lost hope in the transformation of our beautiful country. It is time to defuse South Africa's Xenophobic time-bomb! [8]

Migration challenges are linked to current global economic architecture when the capitalist system relies on cheap labour. This has generated a tendency for exploitation of poor people and natural resources. South Africa has a history of migrant labour but this has taken a new turn as the government moves in to address rising unemployment, crime and violence. According to Mpofu, South Africa is one of the preferred destinations in the region and has received a lot of migrants and refugees,

> [those who seek] safety from poverty, wars and persecution and the World Migration Report (2010) estimated the number of international migrants in Africa in 2010 to be 19 million, while 10% of all African migrants were hosted by South Africa. . . . [M]ost migrants heading for South Africa originate from the Horn of Africa, particularly Ethiopia and Somalia, with

---

[7] M. Gololo and L. Mokgatlhe, *Observation of the Situation Regarding Foreign Nationals in Soweto by the Soweto Ministers' Fraternal,* Report to the SACC, 12 Aug. 2022.

[8] Ibid., 2.

> significant numbers also leaving from the Democratic Republic of Congo (DRC). . . . While the exact numbers of African migrants living in South Africa . . . the South African Department of Home Affairs (DHA) ranked the top 15 sending countries as follows: Zimbabwe, Ethiopia, Nigeria, DRC, Malawi, Somalia, Ghana, Burundi, Mozambique, Uganda, Congo-Brazzaville, Cameroon, Tanzania, Lesotho, and Senegal.[9]

Managing the complex socio-economic outlook culturally diverse communities presents a myriad of challenges for governments. The processes that shape the global society have been a result of many years of multi-directional international and regional movement of people most of whom their livelihoods and families are now spread across borders. This has a historical background and various academic disciplines have attempted to develop migration theories and frameworks such as transnationalism[10] and simultaneous embeddedness[11] to help us appreciate that migration has created families that are spread out across borders. Some scholars have looked at the remittances and financial implications for the poor, or examined companies and private entities that make profits from commercialization of migration through 'externalization' of border management.[12] There has been concerted efforts to develop theologically informed frameworks but little has been done in the African context.

SAM-AE SPIRIT – THE THREEFOLD ASPECTS OF LOVE

In this section I will employ the concept of '*Sam-ae Spirit'* to discuss the challenge of unemployment and migration in South Africa and highlight how human relations between local South Africans and foreign nationals need to be reconstructed to reflect the threefold aspects of love – as the love for God, love for humanity, and love for work.

---

[9] Mpofu, "Missio-Pastoral and Theological Implications," 51–73.

[10] For more details, see Steven Vertovec,"Trends and Impacts of Migrant Transnationalism," *COMPAS Working Papers,* no. 3 (2004): 1–78.

[11] Peggy Levitt and Nina Glick Schiller, "Conceptualizing Simultaneity: A Transnational Social Field Perspective on Society." *The International Migration Review* 38, no. 3 (2004): 1002–39.

[12] Eternalization is a concept used by scholars to describe how destination countries delegate responsibility of border management to institutions or countries outside of their territories in order to indirectly prevent 'unwanted migration.' Another concept, soft-externalization is used to describe activities that do not qualify as border control such as using NGOs to spread information that discourage 'undesired' migration. When there is no state sovereignty like the seas and in-between borders, it becomes easy for states to evade responsibility.

DIALOGUE NOT DEBATE – ON GOD'S LOVE AND JUSTICE

According to Sauca[13] "[t]he relationship between God's love, mercy or grace, and justice is not a new theme in theology and its relationship with philosophy." Therefore, the threefold aspects of love; the love for God, the love for humanity, and the love for work are the intersecting themes which reflect on love and justice. Overcoming evil through emphasis on Love and justice are important themes for our communities ravaged with injustices. God's love for the world as reflected in Christ's love, is one key theme that has always been central to Christianity and this theme need to be explored through dialogue with the concept of *Sam-ae* Spirit.

In my view, there has been very little dialogue and too much debate on a lot of pressing issues in our communities and most people have become more emotional than rational in addressing the challenges that confront us. Emotions and frustrations impede on mutual and transformative dialogue. In this regard, there is a need for creative dialogue between the intersecting trajectories of the threefold aspects of love; the love for God, the love for humanity, and the love for work to engage with the concept of 'love's multiplicity' as championed by Rev. Pai Min-Soo, a Korean Presbyterian minister in 'mobilizing discourse' for rural emancipation and transformation during the Japanese colonization of Korea. Although the South African context is different, the concept can be applicable to the South African situation to promote dialogue on migration challenges. According to Nash,

Dialogue is an interpersonal process of communication between two or more equal parties with strong commitments and divergent perspectives on given issues, for the purpose of mutual enlightenment and transformation. [14] Dialogue is "mutual enlightenment and transformation" and it is a way of discovery. Debate is about winning one's point. Debate has dominated public discourse on controversial matters such as migration and this rhetoric often distorts reality and for the most part debate has deepened our sense of division.[15]

> No one should expect or desire that everyone thinks alike in all our wondrous diversity; sustaining diversity of outlook (a principle of dialogue) is mutually enlightening and enriching, and, if we are to enjoy the values of community and justice, we need to be able to talk to each other without rancor. Dialogue should not be confused with the

---

[13] Ioan Sauca, "God Is Love—The Experience of the Just, Compassionate, and Merciful God," *The Ecumenical Review* 73, no. 3 (2021): 356.

[14] Nash qtd. in J. M. Childs, "Can We Talk?: The Church's Witness in the Ethics and Practice of Dialogue," *Currents in Theology and Mission* 49, no. 2 (2022): 19-22.

[15] Ibid., 20.

> process of negotiating a compromise or reaching an agreement though either of these may emerge in the process, depending on the sort of issue under discussion. Dialogue is its own reward when honestly and respectfully pursued.[16]

There is a lot of demagoguing and scapegoating.

> For dialogue to succeed it is necessary that all participants recognize one another as equals or peers, regardless of any differences that... might otherwise distinguish them from each other. Considering the other person or group as representative of a class or ethnic group with certain characteristics that automatically undermine their credibility is fatal. People will speak from their experience to be sure but as individuals not stereotypes. Only in this way can dialogue express love's quest for the egalitarian justice that is a promise of God's ultimate reign (Gal 3:28-29). A key to this mutual respect is careful listening to one another.[17]

THE LOVE FOR GOD

According to Matthew 22:36-40, a Pharisee lawyer inquired from Jesus: "which is the great commandment in the Law?" and Jesus commanded, "You shall love the Lord your God with all your heart and with all your soul and with all your mind. This is the great and first commandment." In his epistle, Paul also reminded us in Romans 13:8-13 that "love is the fulfillment of the Law. Love worketh no ill and would seek to do good to all..." Therefore, our Love for God would prompt us to do justice as a fulfillment of the law;

> Let no debt remain outstanding, except the continuing debt to love one another, for whoever loves others has fulfilled the law. The commandments, "You shall not commit adultery," "You shall not murder," "You shall not steal," "You shall not covet," and whatever other command there may be, are summed up in this one command: "Love your neighbour as yourself." Love does no harm to a neighbour. Therefore, love is the fulfilment of the law. (Rom. 13:8-10)

According to Sipayung, "Love is being vulnerable for the sake of others" and in fulfilling the law of love, we are required to be vulnerable for the sake of others.[18] Exploring the themes mentioned in "Without Vulnerability, There is No Love: Toward a Cosmo-Theological Beauty of Being Vulnerable," Sipayang observes:

---

16 Nash qtd. in Childs "*Can We Talk?*," 21.

17 Childs, "*Can We Talk?,"* 21.

18 Parulihan Sipayung, "Without Vulnerability, There Is No Love: Toward a Cosmo-Theological Beauty of Being Vulnerable," Insight, Council for World Mission, March 2022, https://www.cwmission.org/insight/.

> In the context of postmodern competition, there is an assumption that being an ideal person means being successful, advanced, strong, healthy, winning, and perfect. Vulnerability is often considered weaknesses and needs to be repaired, corrected, restored, and normalised. Vulnerability also refers to a social burden such as the elderly group, the children, the sick, the victims, and the poor.[19]

Therefore, our genuine love for God should be expressed in our love for one another as humanity.

THE LOVE FOR GOD AS EXPRESSED IN HUMANITY

Our love for God and for humanity can be expressed through the values of humility, trust and openness in our relationships. These values can be developed and framed theologically to guide communities in mutual dialogue regarding challenges which we face. As James Nash put it in his paper, those who suffer from certitude have reason to fear dialogue. Dialogue opens the possibility that one's views may be faulty and in need of change, that truth can be obscured by one's cherished opinions. Rigid certitude runs the risk of arrogance. de Hass summarises migration theories across five analytical dimensions as follows:[20]

- At different *levels of analysis*: macro-, meso- and micro-level explanations of migration may require different conceptual tools. For instance, forms of exploitative labour migration that seem to fit within the neo-Marxist paradigm can still be rational for migrants and their families.
- In different *(geographical, regional, national) contexts*. For instance, functionalist neo-classical theories may work better to explain relatively unconstrained migration in wealthier countries, while historical-structural approaches may be more useful to explain migration within and from poor or 'developing' countries or occurring under conditions of oppression and violence.
- Across *different social groups*: even at the same point in time and in the same geographical and national context, migration is a socially differentiated process; different theories are therefore likely to have varying degrees of applicability to different occupational, skill, income, class or ethnic groups. For instance, neo-classical assumptions may hold

[19] Sipayung, "Without Vulnerability," 1.

[20] Heine de Haas, "A Theory of Migration: The Aspirations-Capabilities Framework," *Comparative Migration Studies* 9, no. 8 (2021), https://doi.org/10.1186/s40878-020-00210-4.

relatively well in explaining the migration of higher-skilled migrants, whereas neo-Marxist theories may be more useful in understanding the migration of less-skilled and relatively poor manual workers.

- At *different points of time*. The drivers and internal dynamics of migration processes often change over time and over the various trajectories and successive stages of migration system formation and decline;[21] so too, do the social, cultural and economic mechanisms explaining such migration. For instance, Garip identified four distinct types of Mexico–US migrants over the 1970–2000 period and argued that these types gained prevalence during specific time periods depending on the changing conditions in the two countries.[22]
- From *different thematic or disciplinary perspectives*. We can look at the same manifestation of migration from various analytical perspectives. For instance, we can study how social transformation processes shape migration processes simultaneously from cultural, political, economic, technological and demographic perspectives as well as through the use of various methodologies and data. This provides different – and generally complementary – angles from which to study and explain the same social process.[23]

THE LOVE FOR GOD AS EXPRESSED IN OUR LOVE FOR WORK

The concept of *Sam-ae* Spirit can be helpful in addressing South African challenges related to migration, unemployment and competition for limited resources. The SOWETO ministers fraternal identified, among other challenges, that "the infrastructure for water and sanitation services has deteriorated badly over the years, leaving many communities with poor water quality, inadequate access to clean water and poor, to no sanitation services." They also note that "The impact of such government constraints in delivering basic housing manifest not only in tensions between South Africans and migrants, who are perceived 'to steal our houses,' but also creates further fissures within South African communities."[24]

---

[21] Ibid.

[22] Filiz Garip, "Discovering Diverse Mechanisms of Migration: The Mexico-US Stream 1970-2000," *Population and Development Review* 38, no. 3 (2012): 393–433.

[23] For more details see H. de Haas, S. Fransen, K. Natter, K. Schewel, S. Vezzoli, *Social Transformation* (Amsterdam: University of Amsterdam, 2020). https://www.migrationinstitute.org/publications/social-transformation.

[24] Gololo and Mokgatlhe, *Observation of Situation,* 3.

These observations provide a synoptic overview for the underlying circumstances which reflect circumstances that have created a fractured South African society and these can be summed up as follows:

- Challenge of undocumented migrants, porous borders and border security concerns.
- Socio-economic challenges such as rising unemployment, crime, violence, etc.
- Deteriorating infrastructure and challenges with basic service delivery especially with regards to water, sanitation, shelter/housing and health care services.
- Xenophobia, violence, competition for jobs and hostility towards foreigners.
- Politically motivated rhetoric – what Mpofu identified as "demagoguing."[25]
- Competition for limited resources and allegations of 'foreigners taking jobs of locals.'
- Human trafficking,[26] substance abuse, illegal mining, and other undesired activities – such as prostitution, rape, mugging, theft, environmental pollution, erection of informal/illegal structures, etc.

MISSIO-DEI AND RESPONSES TO MIGRATION CHALLENGES

The mission of the church with the migrants has been driven by ecumenism and the lived experiences of the people on the move should be at the centre of *missio-Dei*. According to Dill, "most national borders have become permeable" as the poor seek better living conditions in the face of wars, famine, drought and other climate induced disasters.[27] The ecumenical movement needs to be united in developing and implementing coordinated responses to these challenges. For example, Keum asserts that there are three vantage points in the role of mission and ecumenical movement. Of the three roles he identified, first one is relevant for this study:

---

[25] Mpofu, *"Missio-Pastoral and Theological Implications,"* 22.

[26] Sixty-four percent of people trafficked in Sub-Saharan Africa are children. See *Trafficking of Persons* Report, United Nations Office on Drugs and Crime Global Report on Trafficking of Persons, 11-12 (2016), https://www.state.gov/j/tip/rlstiprpt/2017 .

[27] Jeffrey S. Dill, "The Moral Education of Global Citizens," *Global Society* 49 (2012): 541.

> [M]ission can play a prophetic role in bringing together unity and justice discourses in the ecumenical movement. Mission provides a holistic approach that helps to affirm the integrity of the ecumenical movement because of the way in which it connects people and contexts.[28]

Bosch has a more comprehensive, ecumenical definition of mission as it encompasses almost everything at the heart of the mission of the World Council of Churches (WCC). For him, having an ecumenical perspective refers to a perspective that emphasizes the active role of missions and communicates with the world. Mission is a multifaceted ministry, in respect of witness, service, justice, healing, reconciliation, liberation, peace, evangelism, fellowship, church planting, contextualization, and more.[29] Indeed, this ecumenical perspective needs to be indigenous or contextualized. This is undergirded by the concept of the missional church which is now a common approach.

According to Rhee,[30] it was possible to establish the concept of the Missional Church because of the contributions of scholars such as Karl Barth, Lesslie Newbigin, and David Bosch.[31] At the International Missionary Council (IMC) meeting in 1952, the concept of 'm*issio Dei*' was explored after it was first used by Karl Barth in 1932,[32] and was later adopted as a specific church methodology, by Stransky,[33] and Ross.[34] According to

---

[28] Jooseop Keum, "Prospects for Ecumenical Missiology," in *Ecumenical Missiology: Changing Landscapes and New Conceptions of Mission,* eds, Kenneth R. Ross, Jooseop Keum, et al (Oxford: World Council of Churches, 2016), 573-75.

[29] David J. Bosch, *Transforming Mission: Paradigm Shifts in Theology of Mission* (Maryknoll, NY: Orbis Books, 2011).

[30] H. K. Rhee, *The Evangelism of the 18-19th Century and the Three Streams of the Ecumenical Movement of the Twentieth Century* (Seoul: Presbyterian Church of Korea, 1999).

[31]David Bosch harshly criticized the situation facing a mission in his book *Transforming mission; Paradigm Shifts in Theology of Mission*, which is regarded as a textbook of mission theology. The author diagnosed the problems facing the Western church after postmodernism as follows. Faith has weakened amid secularisation caused by the development of science and technology, and as a result of the rapid de-Christianization of Western society and the imperialist missions of the past, Western missionaries are facing their limits. In order to overcome this crisis, the author insisted on abandoning the mission of unilaterally spreading individualism and Western values.

[32] Michael Kinnamon and Brian E. Cope, eds., *The Ecumenical Movement: An Anthology of Key Texts and Voices*. (Geneva: WCC Publications, 1997), 339-342.

[33] *Dictionary of the Ecumenical Movement*, 2nd ed., s.v. "Missio Dei," ed. Nicholas Lossky (Geneva: WCC publication, 2002), 780-781.

[34] Kenneth R. Ross et al., eds., *Ecumenical Missiology: Changing Landscapes and New Conceptions of Mission*. vol. 35, (Oxford: Regnum, Edinburgh Centenary Series, 2016), 62-68.

Guder,[35] the concept of *missio Dei* can only be understood by connecting between ecclesiology and missiology.[36] Being a church in mission also means participating in the creation of the Triune God.[37]

KEY THEMES FOR A THEOLOGICAL FRAMEWORK BASED ON *SAM-AE* SPIRIT

In addressing the socio -economic challenges related to all forms of movement of people in the context of competition for limited resources, it is important that we listen to the stories of migrants and local South Africans on how they wish to address the challenges they face in their local communities. *Sam-ae* Spirit is a concept that could help us address selfish political leadership and poor governance, so that we address crime, violence and security concerns without undermining the love for God and humanity. Promoting human dignity (*imago-Dei),* is at the heart of the mission of God (*missio-Dei).* Such an approach leads to transformative models of providing support to migrants. Below is a summary of some practical activities that could be developed through the notion of the *Sam-ae* Spirit – such as developing sermons and Bible studies on migration themes and stories in the Bible as follows:

- Mary and Joseph flee to Egypt with Jesus as a baby (Matt. 2:13–23).
- Joseph is sent into slavery in a strange land (Gen. 37-46).
- Moses flees to Midian and finds shelter in the house of a Priest (Exod. 2:15-22).
- Ruth and Naomi in a foreign land and she finds favour in the eyes of Boaz (Ruth 2).

We also need to conduct more reflections on what the Bible says about migration, foreigners and strangers through the following examples:

- "When a stranger resides with you in your land, you shall not wrong him. The stranger who resides with you shall be to you as one of your citizens; you shall love him as yourself, for you were strangers in the land of Egypt" (Lev. 19:33-34)

---

[35] Darrell L. Guder and George R. Hunsberger, *Missional Church: A Vision for the Sending of the Church in North America* (Grand Rapids, MI: W. B. Eerdmans, 1998).

[36] See also Craig Van Gelder and Dwight J Zscheile, *The Missional Church in Perspective: Mapping Trends and Shaping the Conversation* (Grand Rapids, MI: Baker Academic, 2011).

[37] Tormod Engelsviken, "Missio Dei: The Understanding and Misunderstanding of a Theological Concept in European Churches and Missiology," *International Review of Mission* 92, no. 367 (2003): 482.

- "Cursed is anyone who withholds justice from the foreigner, the fatherless or the widow." Then all the people shall say, "Amen!" (Deut. 27:19).
- Then you shall declare before the LORD your God: "My father was a wandering Aramean, and he went down into Egypt with a few people and lived there and became a great nation, powerful and numerous (Deut. 26:5).
- The same law applies both to the native-born and to the foreigner residing among *you."* (Exod. 12:19).

As part of the concluding section, the contribution will also highlight the centrality of God's empathy and demonstrate how God is empathic and stands on the side of the weak and vulnerable. This section will identify challenges which require dialogue in the South African context and will argue that vulnerability experienced by economically marginalized youth in South Africa opens up new alternatives for human relations in the context of competition and limited resources. The section will also propose pointers towards a theological framework which can be employed to address migration challenges in South Africa.

CHURCH ACTIVITIES FOR THEOLOGICALLY SOUND RESPONSES

- Listening to the stories of migrants and local South Africans on how they wish to address the challenges they face in their local communities (narrative therapy).
- Getting to grips with original sin – need for compassion and empathy
- Addressing the socio-economic challenges related to all form of movement.
- Socio-economic realities? – economic exclusion, competition for resources, etc.
- Selfish Political Leadership, poor governance, border control, Home Affairs.
- Addressing crime, violence and security concerns to ensure peace and security.
- Addressing poor Governance, corruption and divisive political rhetoric
- Business (especially mining) being owned and protected by powerful conglomerates and employing local militia and or private security

companies, responsible for atrocities and human rights abuses. Militarisation of the capitalist system?

- Autocracy vs Democracy (Moses vs Aaron styles of leadership).
- Promoting human dignity as the image of God (*imago Dei*).
- The social reality of the lived experiences of migrants should be a starting point for all mission and theological practice and reflection.
- The Church should draw on tradition for mission practices that focus on caring for strangers and advocate the preferential option for care with strangers.
- Transformative models of providing support to migrants should value and acknowledge their role in contributing to the development of host communities.
- Attending to undocumented movement of people needs a humanly dignified approach centred on values such as care, compassion, love, tolerance, etc.
- Practical activities such as cultural awareness Sundays to celebrate cultural diversity and the presence of different nationalities in South African communities as part of '*rainbowism*.'
- Promotion of human dignity in the affirmation that all people are created in the image of God – *imago Dei.*
- Using religious premises as safety nets and a place of comfort for the community's marginalised and vulnerable people such as the foreign migrants.
- Move from providing temporary shelter, and develop missional programmes *with long-term sustainable interventions which foster community integration and cohesion.*
- Faith based community leaders should speak out against demagogues who exploit declining socio-economic conditions for political gain to counter vigilantism.

CONCLUDING REMARKS

There is a need for the development of a framework that will promote dialogue on a number of issues which have been identified in this study. South African communities are currently dealing with a wide range of issues related to the challenge of migration and the study has noted that there is a tendency to debate in ways that polarise communities instead of engaging through constructive dialogue. Drawing on the Korean concept of *Sam-ae* Spirit which refers to a threefold aspect of love – the love for God, the love for humanity, and the love for work – migration challenges can be engaged with from the perspective of 'love's multiplicity'; this underscores the importance of dialogue for the unemployment challenges facing South Africa and highlights how human relations need to be realigned to incorporate this threefold aspect of love. We conclude by emphasizing the need for a theologically sound framework based on *Sam-ae* Spirit that is reinforced through practical activities that can be undertaken by churches, while also listening to the stories of migrants and local South Africans to foster mutual dialogue in addressing the challenges facing local communities.